Mind Match Soccer

Daniel Memmert · Bernd Strauss ·
Daniel Theweleit

Mind Match Soccer

The Final Step to Become a Champion

Daniel Memmert
Institut für Trainingswissenschaft
Deutsche Sporthochschule Köln
Köln, Nordrhein-Westfalen, Germany

Bernd Strauss
Münster, Germany

Daniel Theweleit
Köln, Germany

ISBN 978-3-662-68034-6   ISBN 978-3-662-68035-3 (eBook)
https://doi.org/10.1007/978-3-662-68035-3

Translation from the German language edition: "Mind Match Fußball" by Daniel Memmert et al., © Der/die Herausgeber bzw. der/die Autor(en), exklusiv lizenziert an Springer-Verlag GmbH, DE, ein Teil von Springer Nature 2022. Published by Springer Berlin Heidelberg. All Rights Reserved.

© The Editor(s) (if applicable) and The Author(s), under exclusive license to Springer-Verlag GmbH, DE, part of Springer Nature 2023

This work is subject to copyright. All rights are solely and exclusively licensed by the Publisher, whether the whole or part of the material is concerned, specifically the rights of reprinting, reuse of illustrations, recitation, broadcasting, reproduction on microfilms or in any other physical way, and transmission or information storage and retrieval, electronic adaptation, computer software, or by similar or dissimilar methodology now known or hereafter developed.
The use of general descriptive names, registered names, trademarks, service marks, etc. in this publication does not imply, even in the absence of a specific statement, that such names are exempt from the relevant protective laws and regulations and therefore free for general use.
The publisher, the authors, and the editors are safe to assume that the advice and information in this book are believed to be true and accurate at the date of publication. Neither the publisher nor the authors or the editors give a warranty, expressed or implied, with respect to the material contained herein or for any errors or omissions that may have been made. The publisher remains neutral with regard to jurisdictional claims in published maps and institutional affiliations.

Einbandabbildung: © gopixa / stock.adobe.com

This Springer imprint is published by the registered company Springer-Verlag GmbH, DE, part of Springer Nature.
The registered company address is: Heidelberger Platz 3, 14197 Berlin, Germany

Paper in this product is recyclable.

Preface

International soccer tournaments have been globally perceived as major events for many years now, linked to all kinds of issues and interests. The 2006 World Cup shaped a new image of the Germans; four years later in South Africa, the self-esteem of an entire continent was boosted. In 2018, Russian warmonger Vladimir Putin was able to use the 2018 World Cup in Russia for his fatal self-promotional lies, and the 2022 World Cup in Qatar has the explicit purpose of cementing the desert state's status in the Middle East's difficult power structure. Focusing on soccer in this context of tension is becoming increasingly difficult, for the players as well as for spectators and observers.

When the 2014 World Cup in Brazil became charged with a large-scale mission accompanied by intra-societal conflicts, the Selecaó collapsed in the madness of a semifinal overloaded with hopes and expectations. The Brazilians' defeat by Germany, 7-1—"sätschi—um" in Portuguese—has passed into common parlance as a frequently used metaphor for resounding defeats. It is hard to imagine the influences that soccer players often have to cope with when their competitions are politically exaggerated when nations suffer along with them when life's dreams are threatened with bursting and half of the earth's population is watching.

In the decisive moments, this is especially true at the end of most major tournaments: Psychological, social, and mental factors are even more important than differences in soccer quality. One of the eternal truths of the game is that close games are always decided in the mind. However, the ideas of what exactly might be meant by this statement remain rather vague for most people involved in the sport. Terms such as "double six," "counter-pressing" or "switching play" have long been part of the standard repertoire of stadium language; soccer has become a sport that is increasingly well understood in its tactical-strategic dimensions and has thus gained an intellectual component. But why is Germany victorious in almost all penalty shootouts, while England fails miserably time and again?

In this book, such questions are answered on the basis of findings from science, although even these are never incontestable and irrefutable. Some things have been clarified or even revised since a first edition of this book was published in 2013 under the title "Der Fußball. Die Wahrheit" (Soccer-The Truth) was published by the Munich Süddeutscher Verlag, to whom we would like to express our sincere thanks, as well as to Springer Nature for their cooperation during the creation of this revised new edition, first in German language and published as "Mind Match Fußball" in the beginning of 2023. Due to the success of this edition the Springer Nature asked us for an English translation of this new German 2023 edition, what you have now in your hands.

Since 2013, many new answers to the big questions of the game have been found and many new puzzles have arisen. For example, the development of the Video Assistant Referee (VAR) led to fundamental changes in refereeing, which were scientifically accompanied from the beginning. The years of the pandemic, with many games played in empty stadiums, provided a unique environment for research on the influence of the audience on the players and on the phenomenon of home field advantage. While soccer will never reveal some of its secrets, the following ten chapters provide well-founded, often surprising, and sometimes contentious answers to the question of which psychological and mental processes determine victory and defeat.

And the focus is by no means only on the players. Of great importance are also referees, coaches, managers, and spectators. The findings in this book apply equally to both female and male people in the world of soccer. In any case, like knowledge of tactics and strategy, psychological soccer knowledge can make the engagement with this most beautiful game in the world a bit more enjoyable for both women and men.

July 2023

Daniel Memmert
Bernd Strauß
Daniel Theweleit

Contents

1	**Faith and Knowledge**	1
1.1	"Home Advantage is Nowadays no Longer as Significant as it Once Was"	2
1.2	"Self-Confidence"	8
1.3	First Match Away? No Matter!	12
1.4	Voodoo, Sorcerers, Urinals	14
1.5	"Sports Psychology Work is Background Work"	16
2	**Art and Intelligence**	21
2.1	Reading The Game	22
2.2	Head Thing	25
2.3	From Street Soccer to Creativity	27
2.4	Doers and Thinkers	31
2.5	"Mentality Monsters": A Mystery	33
2.6	The Clueless Experts	36
2.7	Computers Decrypting the Game	39
2.8	The Scouting Approach Must Never Override the Development Approach	42
3	**Friends and Enemies**	47
3.1	The Myth of the 11 Friends	48
3.2	Free Speech, Control and Communication	51
3.3	Fans, Hate, Violence	55
3.4	When Citizens Freak Out	59

4 Power and Powerlessness   63
- 4.1 Cold Love—Pressure, Exhaustion and Depression   64
- 4.2 From the Turnvater Jahn Principle to a Flat Hierarchy   67
- 4.3 Who Kicks the Penalty?   70
- 4.4 The Coach, the Multi-Talent   72
- 4.5 Lord Over Time   75
- 4.6 "Dominant Body Language is Critical in These Scenes"   77
- 4.7 "Where There is Cooperation Based on Trust, There is the Greatest Likelihood of Success"   78

5 Illusion and Reality   81
- 5.1 Is It a Good Idea, that the Fouled Player Takes the Penalty Shot?   82
- 5.2 The Run that Does not Exist   83
- 5.3 Chance, Fate, Luck, and Bad Luck   86
- 5.4 New Coach, New Luck?   89
- 5.5 Does Money Score the Goals?   93
- 5.6 Basking in Reflecting in the Glory of Others   96
- 5.7 Winning is Not Everything   100
- 5.8 Need for Explanation, Evasion, Self-Deception   102
- 5.9 "There Are Phases When It's Absolutely Clear that You, of All People, Score that Decisive Goal."   105

6 Red Light and Yellow Fever   107
- 6.1 The Audience Shows Yellow: The Impact of Spectators on Referee Decisions   108
- 6.2 When the Referee Gives Yellow   110
- 6.3 Sex Training Session   113
- 6.4 The Winner Wears Red?   116
- 6.5 "A Soccer Match is like a Painting."   118

7 Perception and Deception   123
- 7.1 How to Make the Goalkeeper a Penalty Killer   124
- 7.2 The Blind Spot   126
- 7.3 Referee Offside   129
- 7.4 The VAR—Cursed Be Justice   132
- 7.5 The Big Disadvantage   135

8 Pressure and Failure   139
- 8.1 Penalty Shootout is not a Lottery Game   140
- 8.2 The Fear of the Englishman at the Penalty Kick   143
- 8.3 "Haste Increases the Likelihood of a Miss-Kick."   145

8.4	The Zinédine Zidane Enigma	147
8.5	When the Nerves Fail	150
8.6	Social Loafing	154
8.7	Tired Bodies, Tired Minds	156
8.8	Clap Your Own Team to Defeat	159
8.9	"For the Very Greatest Successes, It's Important for a Team to Breathe, to Be Able to Operate Independently."	164
9	**Harmony and Drama**	**171**
9.1	The Pleasure of Conflict	172
9.2	The Magic of the Wave	174
9.3	You'll Never Walk Alone	177
9.4	Trapped in the History of the Game	180
9.5	Goals with Handwriting	183
10	**Risk and Side Effects**	**185**
10.1	Capricorn and Aquarius Prevail	186
10.2	First Play, Then Practice	189
10.3	Loyal, More Loyal, *Die Hard*	191
10.4	Palpitations	196
10.5	Real Interest in Teammates Helps to Play Better Football	198

Source graphics 203

References 207

1

Faith and Knowledge

© Rauch/nordphoto/picture alliance

There are millions of people who accumulate vast amounts of rather useless soccer knowledge, memorized lineups from the deepest past, for example, or years of construction of stadiums. Some people can even explain in detail how the patterns get into the stadium turf. And of course, many soccer fans think they know the answer when asked why it's an advantage to play away first in a European Cup duel with a home and away game. Or why it is particularly difficult for visiting teams to take points from tight, noisy arenas like the Westfalen Stadion in Dortmund. But are these observations actually true? Or are they based, like so much else in soccer, on a kind of historically grown belief? Or why this phenomenon is disappearing at a similarly rapid pace as the polar ice caps.

This chapter begins with questions like these, but it will focus on the often still unused knowledge in soccer about how soccer players can become better if they train their heads. How does self-confidence develop? What is the term self-efficacy all about? How can athletes learn to successfully manage the key moments of their careers? How are functioning groups formed? Answers based on knowledge and not on faith are provided by Hans-Dieter Hermann. Probably Germany's best-known sports psychologist, who was appointed to the staff of the national team in 2004 under the aegis of then national coach Jürgen Klinsmann, tells us where he can help make the dream of winning a major tournament a little more likely.

1.1 "Home Advantage is Nowadays no Longer as Significant as it Once Was"

"There is no place like home," says Judy Garland as Dorothy Gale in the famous 1939 film version of the Wizard of Oz, as she returns home chastened by her adventures in the magic land of Oz. It was the English jurist Edward Coke (1552–1634) who first used the phrase "the home is my castle, describing one's home as a castle that may and must be specially protected, and which thus also acquires special powers. Many people associate positive feelings with their own home. It is seen as a place to which people like to return, a place that needs to be protected. In a very sad way, this sentiment became visible in 2022 at the beginning of the terrible war in the Ukraine, in which people were fighting with all their power and at the risk of their lives for their freedom and their homeland.

In a peaceful, playful variant, such forces are also important in sports, for example, when it comes to the phenomenon of a home advantage. In competitions, where details often determine victory and defeat, positive feelings associated with the own home could be crucial. In fact, the phenomenon of home field advantage exists in all team sports, whether in basketball, rugby, handball, ice hockey, even baseball and, of course, soccer. Scientifically, in all these sports, more than 50 percent of all decisive games (not counting draws) are won by the home team. But contrary to the subjective impression of many fans and observers, not even in many hundreds of games without spectators during the COVID pandemic could it be proven that this home advantage was related to the presence of spectators, at least not in the main, as will be shown below.

Also knowing this, UEFA President Aleksander Čeferin stated on 27 June 2021: "It is fair to say that home advantage is nowadays no longer as significant as it once was. (…) Taking into consideration the consistency across Europe in terms of styles of play and many different factors which have led to a decline in home advantage…". The influential official's statement was by no means referring to the particular COVID-19 situation facing the world from 2020 onwards, but to the abolition of the away goals rule in first and second games in European cup competitions (see also Sect. 1.3). Since the 2021/2022 season, away goals no longer count double in the event of a goal tie after first and second game. This rule change is based on the need for more spectacle, as it increases the likelihood of extra time and penalty shoot-outs, which in turn makes soccer more attractive. But home-field advantage, which has been scientifically observed over many years, also seems to have played a role in the decision, as Čeferin's words suggest.

A large study conducted by the research group around Bernd Strauss from the University of Münster in 2014 analyzed 305,217 matches in the first men's league from 194 FIFA countries (208 in total at the time) between the 2000/01 and 2011/12 seasons. And indeed, 61.9 percent (the so-called relative home advantage) of the matches decided worldwide during the study period (not counting draws, but only decided games) were won by the home team. However the fluctuation is enormous: In San Marino there is no home advantage at all (48.6 percent), in the soccer country Uruguay only a very small one (53.5 percent), while the host first division teams in Indonesia (79.7 percent) or in Nigeria (92.3 percent) win particularly frequently. In the German Bundesliga, there is a (relative) home advantage of 62.6 percent for this period. Germany is thus roughly in line with the global average (similar to England and Spain).

If we now consider all matches and the absolute home advantage, i.e. including draws, an average of 47.5 percent of all duels in Germany's top division in the first decade of this century were won by the home team; in the 2009/10 season, the figure was as low as 40.8 percent. In the nine years before Corona, from 2010/11 to 2018/19, the average was even lower, at 45.8 percent (see Sect. 8.3). Only three times, in 2000/01 (52.3 percent), 2001/02 (52.3 percent) and 2003/4 (52.3 percent), the 50 percent mark was exceeded in a season of this millennium, meaning that a so-called absolute home advantage did not exist in the recent past in the men's first Bundesliga in Germany. Fifty years ago, this was quite different: In the 1960s and 1970s, 60 percent of all games were won in front of a home crowd.

This gradual disappearance of home field advantage in men's soccer can be observed worldwide, as was also shown by the Münster study, which analyzed 694,478 matches since 1888 in a further analysis. The results clearly show that the host team's chances of winning have been steadily declining for the last 30 years. An even more detailed analysis by the Münster team also showed that this decline is particularly noticeable in Europe (Fig. 1.1).

The reasons for the slow decline in home advantage have not yet been adequately investigated; it is possible that much more professional preparation plays a major role here. Travelling is becoming more and more comfortable (a recent study can show for the Bundesliga that travel distance may have

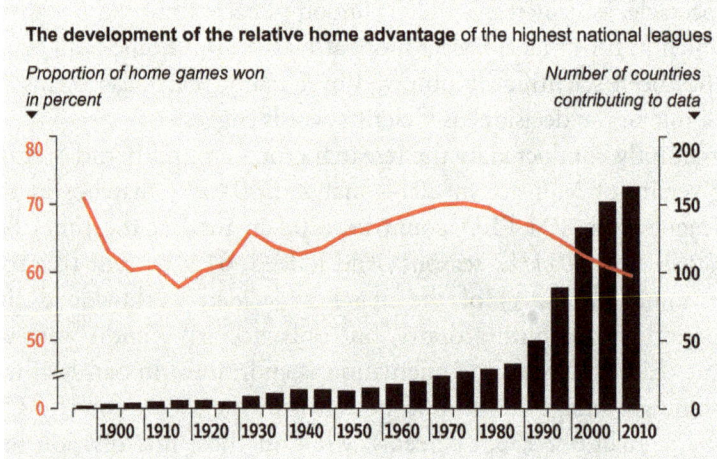

Fig. 1.1 The worldwide (relative) home advantage (draws were not taken into account) of the highest national leagues between 1888 and 2010 (red line). From 1900 onward, the plot is in a five-year interval. The black bars show the number of countries included in the data. The more countries that could be included, the more precise the result (the so-called standard deviations—the intervals around the measured mean values become smaller and smaller) (from Riedl, Staufenbiel, Heuer & Strauss, 2014)

played a role in the past, but not anymore), arenas are becoming more and more similar, referees are better trained, most teams spend the night before a matchday in a luxury hotel, no matter if it is played at home or elsewhere in the world. There is simply less and less difference between the home and away situations, especially in European soccer. And yet, teams that have a reputation for being particularly strong at home keep popping up.

Sometimes, the impression even arises that a club can no longer win away from home at all, while the same players appear almost unbeatable in their own stadium. Like the German premier league team Borussia Mönchengladbach in the 2002/2003 season, when the club achieved a goal difference of plus 20 at home, while at the end of the season this figure was minus 22 in the away table. The team lost only twice at home, while twelve games away from home ended without a point. Or another example from the 2016/17 season: Hertha BSC managed to finish sixth in the season, mainly because the club won twelve games at home, but only three away from home. But there also seems to be the opposite phenomenon: VfL Wolfsburg lost eight games away from home in the same season, while nine games were lost in front of their home crowd. That's unusual, because more games are usually still won at home than lost.

Andreas Heuer, a physics professor from Münster, has addressed this question of supposed home strength and also home weakness in his book "Der perfekte Tipp".(english: the perfect bet). To do this, he looked at all the games in the first division from 1995/96 to 2010/11. Heuer wanted to know whether certain teams are particularly conspicuous in terms of their home strength, or whether there are only the statistically expected fluctuations to which no particular significance should be attached. His findings are quite sobering: although there is the general home advantage already mentioned above (at least still), it applies equally to all. Statistically, over a longer period of time, neither a club that is particularly strong at home has stood out, nor a club that does particularly badly away from home.

But, many readers will now ask, didn't the Corona pandemic also produce the realization that home field advantage has disappeared without the many spectators and that this is evidence that spectators are so important after all that a significant home field advantage is created? Let's take a striking example: between August 2015 and March 2020, The BVB, this is the German Premier league team of Borussia Dortmund lost only five German Premier league games at its home stadium in more than four and a half years. Then, when no spectators were allowed to attend due to the Corona pandemic, six teams managed the previously rare away win at BVB within a few months

(Fig. 1.2). Doesn't this support the thesis that the power of the crowd is effective, especially in Germany's biggest stadium?

It's worth taking a closer look here, even beyond Germany's borders. There are now numerous studies around the world that have looked at the odds of winning home games in the 2019/20 season before and after the outbreak of the pandemic, in which referee behavior (for example, in the allocation of tickets) was also examined before and during the pandemic. As a reminder; In March 2020, ongoing competitions were suspended almost everywhere due to the COVID-19 outbreak. Some leagues did not finish the season at all (like the French one), many others resumed play from May 2020, but in empty stadiums, in front of very few spectators or else with many other changes. There were unusual infection-related regulations, think of the five substitutions instead of three. Several times games had to be postponed because of infections of the players and infections in the environment of the players. It was often impossible to think of an orderly and long-term preparation.

In the German Bundesliga, which started playing again as the first soccer league after the first hard lockdown in May 2020, the home win rate

Fig. 1.2 Dortmund's fallacy: Lost home strength as an exception. (© firo Sportphoto/Ralf Ibing/dpa/picture alliance)

dropped dramatically from 43 to 33 percent. Teams actually earned more away wins than home wins during the COVID period in the 19/20 season. Many commentators, as well as early studies, concluded that the lack of spectators had been the deciding factor and seemed to have found "proof" that spectators were the major factor in creating the home advantage. However, they overlooked the fact that home field advantage is diminishing in the Bundesliga, throughout Europe and even worldwide, and that, given the large influence of coincidences, a very large number of matches need to be studied in order to obtain solid results pattern.

The 83 Bundesliga matches played under COVID conditions are simply not enough to make reliable statements. Moreover, there was a very different picture in the second Bundesliga, as the home win rate increased a little, but it remained unchanged in the third league. When looking at a single league, the picture is distorted: In Serie A in Italy and in England, there was an increase in the home win rate during the period with matches without a crowd, but not in Spain, and so on (see Table 1.1). In short, there were very heterogeneous results in soccer worldwide, also because the number and selection of leagues included varied widely and the periods of comparison (only the same season, or numerous seasons before) differed. Studies that included many countries either concluded that home field advantage did not change at all within the 2019/20 season after the exclusion of the public, or only to a very small extent of two to three percent. And since home field advantage remained worldwide even during the pandemic ghost matches, it can be concluded that the presence and behavior of spectators is rather not the decisive factor for the occurrence of home field advantage.

What the scientific studies largely agreed on is that the elimination of the crowd led to a change in the way referees awarded cards. Away teams received significantly fewer yellow cards (about 30 percent) in games without an audience, which appears to have been the case in numerous leagues. In this respect, the results suggest that spectators provide decision guidance to referees (we described this in more detail in the Sect. 6.1).

Soccer spectators are only too willing to (hastily) deduce general causes from snapshots. This may also be true for some scientists—but many of them are also soccer fans. In the thicket of information, they search for confirmation of their own impressions, which can hardly be upheld on closer and longer examination. But myths are what make soccer interesting, whether UEFA and its president are right: "Home advantage is nowadays no longer as significant as it once was," with or without Corona.

Tab. 1.1 Home wins in the respective league in the 2019/20 season before and after Covid-19 outbreak; examples

League/Country	Percent home wins before Covid-19	Percent home wins by COVID	Difference Percent
Albania	47	46	−1
Australia	47	40	−7
Austria	36	30	−6
Costa Rica	35	37	2
Denmark	49	39	−10
England I	45	47	2
England II	43	38	−7
Germany I	43	33	−10
Germany II	42	43	1
Germany III	41	42	−1
Greece	48	33	−15
Hungary	41	48	7
Italy I	40	44	4
Italy II	46	42	−4
Poland	50	34	−16
Portugal	40	44	4
Romania	46	46	0
Russia	37	34	−3
Serbia	51	52	1
Slovenia	45	31	−14
Spain I	48	41	−7
Spain II	39	44	5
Switzerland	42	42	0
Turkey	43	46	3
Ukraine	45	45	0

1.2 "Self-Confidence"

First and foremost, it must have been a nice marketing stunt when the shirt designers at Germany's leading sporting goods manufacturer decided to incorporate FC Bayern's motto into the record champion's shirts in the spring of 2011. "Mia san mia" (not actual German language, it is a Bavarian phrase: translated: "We are us") has been printed in small letters on the shirt collar ever since. It's possible that this idea is actually boosting merchandising sales. And perhaps the club credo on the back of the neck is even conducive to sporting performance, because "Mia san mia" describes the conviction of not being dependent on anyone, the identity and togetherness, the untouchability and the great self-confidence of this club. After all, it can't hurt to be constantly reminded of one's own strengths. Those who believe in themselves and their own qualities ultimately benefit in sporting competition (Fig. 1.3).

Fig. 1.3 Self-confidence as a recipe for success: FC Bayern and its "Mia san mia" mentality. (© Ulrich Wagner/Wagner/picture alliance)

To describe this effect, the recently deceased re-owned American social psychologist Albert Bandura, one of the greats in his field, created the term "self-efficacy" in the 1990s, which still has a firm place in the psychology of competitive sports. A player has a high level of self-efficacy if he is firmly convinced that his skills, his special and hard training, his knowledge of the opponent, his experience and other qualities will enable him to put in a good performance, to take advantage of the next scoring opportunity or to combat a striker so skilfully for 90 min that he cannot create any danger. While the more general term self-confidence tends to describe a fundamental belief in one's own ability to successfully accomplish a wide variety of tasks, the term self-efficacy describes the belief that one can develop very specific potential. For example, there are soccer players who have the most incredible confidence in themselves on the pitch, they have a high level of self-efficacy, while in the TV interview afterwards they appear shy and insecure—their general self-confidence is less pronounced.

In the meantime, numerous studies have shown that a high level of self-efficacy makes a significant contribution to successfully completing upcoming tasks. And in soccer, of course, there is also the team, in which a kind of collective self-efficacy can develop: the common belief, shared by everyone, that the team has realistic possibilities of being successful. The decisive factor here is that the players are convinced that they can function as a unit, and that they believe that strength emerges from the totality of their abilities that holds out the prospect of very good chances of success.

Before this state is reached, however, considerably more complex processes are required than simply spouting optimism. And even general self-confidence alone is not enough. A very precisely conducted study with American wrestlers from the 1990s made the mechanisms behind strong self-efficacy visible.

During most of the matches that were analyzed in a first step, training condition or fundamental differences that were already apparent in earlier matches were much more useful for predicting tournament results than the self-efficacy of the individual wrestler. Applied to soccer, this means that if Manchester City plays Fulham FC, Manchester is most likely to win because of fundamental differences in quality. In that case, it helps if the underdog's players build up a great deal of self-efficacy, but that will at best be enough to make an unlikely sensation a bit more likely.

The situation is different when similarly strong teams or even wrestlers fight each other. The authors of the study therefore explicitly looked at the matches with overtime, i.e. "wrestling stoppage time", in the course of which a decision must be reached. In these duels, the wrestlers were roughly equal in strength, otherwise there would have been a winner already at the end of regular fighting time. And in exactly these fights between two equal teams—or wrestlers in this case—the head played a decisive role. The winners are likely to be those athletes who ascribe to themselves a high degree of self-efficacy, who are firmly convinced that they have the means and opportunities to decide the match in their favor. The question of how such self-efficacy can be generated is now exciting, and there are many well-founded findings on this as well.

The most important factor is a repertoire of authentic experiences and adventures that have shown very concretely that one's own resources and ability have contributed to victory. Based on this knowledge, Matthias Sammer, during his time as sports director at the German Football Association, always took the stance—which was sometimes controversial—that youth selection teams should win titles at all costs so that later, as adults, they could draw on these experiences in the decisive moments in the semifinals of a World Cup or in a major Champions League match. Previously, people shied away from burdening teenagers with overly high expectations, saying: Success is not so important, after all, it's about training.

To this day, the coaches of the junior selection teams sometimes have to fight against resistance to be allowed to nominate the best players for tournaments. This was the case at the 2021 Olympic Games in Tokyo, where many clubs did not give their talents the go-ahead to take part in the tournament. For them, it was more important that the players took part in the preparation for the league season. German U21 coach Stefan Kuntz had to deal with a particularly depleted squad, and his team had no chance. At clubs, U19 players are often brought up to the pros to fill the back of the squad instead of seeing final games in the Youth League, Junior Bundesliga or Cup with their peers. Even in the senior national team, there have been groups of players who could have participated in tournaments with the U21s as leaders, but instead sat on the bench in the senior national team and were thus deprived of valuable title experience.

But there is a second source of great self-efficacy: physiological, physical states that give athletes a sense of superiority. It is possible that one secret of home field advantage is that teams secrete increased doses of the sex hormone testosterone in front of their own crowd, in response to the feeling of having to defend their own territory. Testosterone increases aggressiveness and the desire to dominate, thus increasing the willingness to exert effort and, in the end, the belief in one's own superiority. The many people in the soccer business who claim that doping in soccer is not really helpful must realize, at the latest against the background of this finding, that the seductive power of banned substances in this sport must be enormous.

However, comparable self-efficacy effects can also be achieved through challenging training, through exercises that are not just about improving one's own physical condition, but also about experiencing previously unknown personal physical strengths. The training methods of legendary coach Felix Magath, who won the German championship a total of three times with FC Bayern Munich and VfL Wolfsburg, could be an example of this effect. The controversial soccer teacher always brought his teams into excellent physical condition, the players felt this physically and developed a special confidence in their own strengths. However, in order to create quite sustainable positive effects lasting for several months, it requires the team's willingness to surrender to such methods, otherwise resistance to the coach may be built up quite soon. In this case, the positive effect of self-efficacy threatens to fizzle out quickly because the energy generated is used to work against the trainer's measures.

The experience that one's own abilities are superior to those of the opponent and the knowledge of one's own physical condition are thus important sources for the development of self-efficacy, but group cohesion can also generate such effects. However, this factor is difficult to control and often only really comes to fruition under the influence of the irresistible force of success. A convincing trainer's work and approach or, at times, vicarious experiences, such as examples from other teams in the same situation ("Others also prevented relegation in this situation.") can also promote belief in one's own strength. However, the most important source of self-efficacy is previous experience and the knowledge of having the necessary means for success.

Now, it stands to reason to assume that teams with a high level of self-efficacy have the best prerequisites for entering what is known as a "positive run", an upward spiral. After all, previous positive experiences are available here, which should have a favorable influence on self-efficacy. But as you can read in Sect. 5.2, this form of statistical series does not exist, as physics professor, Andreas Heuer from Münster in Germany has found out. Although we can assume that self-efficacy is quite certainly increased when one hits or wins several times in a row, this does not necessarily lead to a series of exclusively winning games. The only thing that can be proven is the downward spiral, the so-called negative run, as Heuer has shown us. At this point, a particular problem with self-efficacy usually comes into play: once teams are caught in such a vortex, it is very difficult for them to break free again. The probability of losing the next time after a series of defeats is actually higher than if they had won before.

It is easy to understand that soccer players suffer from self-doubt after many defeats, but in most cases, such crisis-like crashes are based on earlier mistakes in the club. Often, the team failed to build strong group cohesion or to establish solid trust in the coach and his methods. These are fundamentals that can stand up in defeat. When the downward spiral begins, it is usually already too late.

However, a high level of self-efficacy on the part of the players and belief in one's own work, provided it is realistic, offer a thoroughly high level of protection against crashes—even if there are, of course, no guarantees. At least as long as the team does not lose its most important forces due to other reasons, such as extraordinary bad luck with injuries.

1.3 First Match Away? No Matter!

For years, the same phrases were trotted out when the traveling club representatives commented on the results of the European Cup draws at UEFA's noble headquarters in Nyon, Switzerland. "Of course we would have liked to play away first," said BVB Dortmunds official Lars Ricken in the spring of 2013 after Borussia Dortmund was drawn to face Real Madrid in the Champions League semifinals. The belief that it is an advantage to first play away from home in order to then be able to turn around a possible first-game defeat in front of a home crowd is widespread. Even the regulations take this assumption into account: The group winners of the Champions League preliminary round are rewarded by being "allowed" to play away first in the round of 16. Added to this was the rule, introduced in 1965 but abolished in 2021, that in the event of draws in the first and second game, away goals counted double. During this period, teams could gain a particularly favorable starting position by scoring one or two goals in an away game played first, or so the belief went.

The course of the above-mentioned duel, however, then told a completely different story. The BVB won its home match 4:1 and traveled to Madrid so confidently after this success that the team ended up entering the final quite confidently. And in the other semifinal, Bayern Munich dismantled FC Barcelona first at home and then a week later away, while Schalke 04, the third German Champions League participant that year, was knocked out of the competition by a 3–2 loss at home to Galatasaray Istanbul after what was actually a respectable 1–1 draw in the round of 16 first game. Were these games really just a strange twist of fate? Or is the supposed advantage of playing away first actually overestimated?

At first glance, the statistics seem to confirm Lars Ricken and all the others who prefer to play at home in the second game The study examined a total of 152 round of 16, quarterfinal and semifinal pairings in the Champions League from the 1994/95 season to the summer of 2010. And indeed, 85 winners of these 152 duels had home rights in the second game, meaning that 56 percent of those teams that first made the away trip reached the next round. So the advantage seems to be demonstrable.

But these calculations do not take into account the fact that in the round of 16 first games, the clubs that finished the group stage top of the table automatically play away first. As a rule, these are the teams with the strongest quality in the respective Champions League season. As soon as the statistics are cleared of these games, there is no longer any discernible advantage and the probability of advancing one round drop to exactly 50 percent for the team that plays away first. If only the quarterfinals and semifinals are compared, where the draw alone decides the location of the first game, there are no longer any differences, so it is statistically irrelevant whether the first match is played at home or away.

1.4 Voodoo, Sorcerers, Urinals

Most Western Europeans feel very entertained when they hear bizarre stories of superstition in African soccer. Particularly around the 2010 World Cup in South Africa, there were extravagant reports about voodoo masters and Zulu sorcerers (Fig. 1.4), and a year after the world tournament, the stadium at the Polokwane venue actually had to be partly equipped with artificial turf because traditional doctors had spread a magic salt mixture on the pitch before the matches of the home professional teams Black Leopards and Baroka, causing irreparable damage.

"Almost every African club employs a witch doctor, just as there is a masseur at every professional club in Germany," former Ghanaian international

Fig. 1.4 Magic on the sidelines: South Africa lost 1–0 to Egypt in 1996 despite magical support. (© Empics Matthew Ashton/dpaweb/dpa/picture alliance)

Anthony Baffoe once recounted many years ago in an interview with the soccer magazine "11Freunde." There were the wildest reports of slaughtered cows in front of the stadium, orgies with chicken blood and animal bones, or bonfires in the rooms of five-star hotels—whether this is still the case, we do not know. In Europe, cow slaughtering might be unusual anyway, but superstition is also widespread among European players and coaches. Just in a slightly different form.

The kisses of French defender Laurent Blanc on goalkeeper Fabien Barthez's bald head during the 1998 World Cup are unforgotten, and in the players' minds, they aroused the sympathies of the gods of fortune for what was later to become the world champions. John Terry, the long-time captain of Chelsea FC, always wanted to sit in the same seat on the bus, he always listened to the same songs by Usher on the way to the stadium, he always parked the car in the same spot, he wore the same shin guards for ten years of his career. He even introduced a ritual that the English Football Association (FA) complained about because it resulted in games starting late. There are three urinals in the Stamford Bridge dressing room, and at one point Terry and Frank Lampard began urinating in the same basin before games. Because the team was winning, more and more players joined in, so the queue for the loo got bigger and bigger, and the time until kickoff got shorter and shorter.

In almost every team there are players who wear lucky underpants, who perform certain rituals when putting on work clothes, coaches who believe that choosing a certain sweater increases the chance of success and so on. All just nonsense? Undecided. In fact, conflicting research exists to suggest that superstitions have a positive impact on motor and cognitive performance. For example, there is circumstantial evidence that routines contribute to strong competitive performance.

From a psychological point of view, all cognitive, motivational and emotional determinants of athletic performance are addressed by performing the same sequences over and over again. This makes it easier for athletes to optimally adapt their actions to the current course of play and their own playing ability. This already shows that a good routine consists of different elements that optimize the individual determinants of athletic performance with regard to the current game situation and the intended goal achievement. It is therefore not enough to (simply) say before a competition that you want to win. More success can be achieved by precisely coordinating all the cognitive, motivational and emotional processes that accompany the action in order to achieve the sporting performance exactly when it matters.

In this context, many studies show that successful athletes think comparatively positively, are able to concentrate well on their tasks, and strive to obtain important information about their actions in the analysis of their competitions, both after a success and after a failure. This optimizes mental processes. Furthermore, they are characterized by a strong intrinsic motivation, a high self-efficacy expectation and a realistic goal setting. This is particularly conducive to their own motivation.

A plausible explanation for the importance of routines and rituals in sports could thus sound something like this: People believe in the power of ritual, thus feel empowered and approach the task more courageously and with greater inner conviction. It would only be logical if this resulted in better performance. The fact that soccer players are often superstitious should therefore be beneficial to performance, because players who have performed their ritual probably face their challenges with increased self-confidence. However, the rite must be credible to them and linked to success, which is considered in more detail in Sect. 1.2 on self-confidence and self-efficacy.

1.5 "Sports Psychology Work is Background Work"

Hans-Dieter Hermann is a well-known man; after all, the glamour of the German national team radiates off everyone who plays an important role in it. However, the psychology graduate, who was brought in by former German coach Jürgen Klinsmann in 2004, likes to stay in the background. It is probably also because of this reserved manner, which is rather rare in the soccer business, that he has become an important interlocutor for some national players, even beyond the international match dates. And as a team psychologist, he is something of a pioneer in soccer (Fig. 1.5).

Fig. 1.5 Dr. Hans-Dieter Hermann, the sports psychologist of the German national team. (© Gladys Chai von der Laage/picture alliance)

Mr. Hermann, at the beginning of your work with the national team, there was a photo showing you talking to the then national goalkeeper Oliver Kahn. A major newspaper then ran the headline, "Kahn to the psycho-doc." Has your presence now become so normal that something like that no longer happens?

Hans-Dieter Hermann: This headline didn't even have a question mark. As a result of this and similar experiences, I am still very cautious and, for example, no longer get off the bus together with players when media representatives are there. I also don't go into the stadium together with the team through the players' tunnel. I try to avoid situations in which such photos can arise.

You like to Stay Hidden at All, is This Behavior Part of Your Job?
I'm not hiding, but you're right: sports psychology work is background work.

And What Exactly is Your Job?
In short, the task is training in the head and for the head. In terms of match or tournament preparation, it's about optimizing processes and improving cognitive skills. For example, we work on the ability to concentrate or the stability of new techniques and tactics. The content of such units with the team is put together in close consultation with the coaches, especially to match current training priorities.

But You also Work Individually with the Players, don't You?
Yes, of course. It's about their individual challenges, desires, or also about development steps that are necessary from a sporting perspective. In addition, there are personal situations, phases, and sometimes even real crises, in which players actively seek psychological support. Ideally, we can even work preventively to avoid personal crises or a threat to mental health under the demanding conditions of professional sports.

Do the Players also Know Such Offers from Their Clubs?
To my knowledge, half of all Bundesliga clubs now also work consistently with sports psychologists. There are also other clubs that use sports psychologists on an irregular basis. Only a few teams in the first and second Bundesliga completely dispense with any form of psychological support. In the youth performance centers, however, psychologists are mandatory in all clubs.

Is It Really First and Foremost About Teaching Certain Techniques that Basically Anyone Can Learn? or is It also About Getting to the Personality of Players?
The techniques are often just the entry point. But you can't just go to players and say, "Think this! Do that! And then you'll succeed!" It is important to see the whole person, to recognize and develop their perspective, concerns, but also their strengths. Only then athletes can put themselves in a position to sort out and optimize their thoughts and emotions under the most difficult circumstances so that they can call up their potential to the letter.

To what extent do things like visiting a climbing park or taking part in a rafting tour help? Aren't such team-building activities primarily about brightening up the exhausting daily routine of a training camp?
Climbing or rafting were typical team-building activities years ago; they are somewhat less in demand in competitive sports today. They have been replaced by more complex activities in which teams have to organize themselves even more and work out solutions. No matter what is done, such events within a training camp also try to provide lightness and variety. But is only the superficial part.

And What Are the Underlying Intentions?
The main intentions of such measures are to promote communication, strengthen mutual trust, and develop so-called transformational structures. To ensure that the experience is not just an exciting afternoon, but also has lasting effects, it is important to follow up the action with measures for transfer and anchoring in everyday training.

What Do You Mean by 'Transformational Structures'?
The idea is that a team learns to draw motivation from the community and from what they experience together, as well as to solve upcoming problems on their own. Soccer is often very hierarchical, and many teams are ultimately guided by their leaders, who makes the decisions. Nevertheless, you have to see eye-to-eye, because everyone in the team is needed for medium- and long-term success, and almost everyone has to take on responsibility over the course of a season. That won't succeed if only a few always make decisions.

Is It Difficult to Bring Together the Blocks from the Clubs that Compete in the Bundesliga in the National Team?
From the outside, you might think so, but when you experience the national team in everyday training and tournaments, it quickly becomes clear that

this is not a problem. At least they respect each other as colleagues, many are friends and already know each other from youth national teams. The days of players disliking each other personally just because they wear different jerseys in the league seem to me to be very long gone.

After Your years of Experience in Soccer, Do You Actually Have an Explanation for Why Many More Teams don't Work Closely with a Psychologist?
A lot has happened in this regard in recent years, and the trend is still rising. Where there is no continuous cooperation with sports psychologists in German professional soccer, there are two main reasons. The first is that the coach in that club does not attach importance to it or is worried that a psychological specialist will rather hinder him and his work. The second reason relates primarily to 1:1 discussions: In the case of individual, often very private problem situations, some players prefer to have access to someone who is not directly from the club. Due to the obligation to maintain confidentiality, this should not play a role, but the desire is understandable. For this reason, some clubs have a double-track approach and have a team psychologist who is part of the extended coaching staff, so to speak, and also have external psychological experts on hand who are available to the players if necessary.

2

Art and Intelligence

© Sammy Minkoff/Sammy Minkoff/picture alliance

A central feature of modern soccer is the intellectualization of the game, which is evident in completely different areas. Professionals have long since received all-around care from highly equipped medical departments. Computers are used to measure training effects and match performances. The data collected by the tracking systems installed in all Bundesliga stadiums also play a role in the margins of this chapter. But the focus is on the question of what cognitive abilities can make good players to very good players. In today's high-speed soccer, which is characterized by ubiquitous time pressure, perceptual and information-processing processes are of elementary importance. However, the recognition and interpretation of game situations are only slowly being understood as a skill that can be specifically practiced and improved.

This process was forced by the successful years of FC Barcelona and the Spanish national team between 2005 and 2015, when rather filigree players like Andres Iniesta or Lionel Messi dominated world soccer. In a next phase, more and more emphasis was placed on physical aspects and the term mentality became the focus of many discussions. But what exactly is meant when coaches, players, and reporters distinguish between bad and good mentality?

2.1 Reading The Game

One of the most famous neologisms that Germany's soccer has produced is the image of the "depth of space" from which former German national player Günter Netzer, as the artistic center of the legendary 1972 national team, is said to have directed the game. Karl-Heinz Bohrer, then literary editor of the daily German newspaper *Frankfurter Allgemeine Zeitung*, created this unforgotten term after a German team had won against England at Wembley for the first time. France's L'Equipe celebrated the team's 3–1 win in the quarter-finals of the European Championship as "dream soccer from the year 2000," and to this day Bohrer's term fires the imagination of many soccer aesthetes. What fascinated the journalist about Netzer's performance was the all-seeing general's attitude and the midfield strategist's amazing feel for spaces and running routes, based on which he repeatedly steered the game into those areas of the pitch where the opponent was vulnerable. That's where Netzer played his balls in, that's where he moved himself with the ball at his foot.

From today's perspective, Netzer's game naturally seems ponderous and slow, but players with a particularly fine eye and an unusually pronounced sense of space will probably be admired for all eternity. The more precisely and quickly a soccer player recognizes gaps and anticipates the running paths of others, the more subtly he identifies playable spaces, and the greater the likelihood of finding good solutions on the pitch. Terms like "creativity" or even "art" often come up in this context, but basically, this aspect of soccer is about gathering and processing information.

Thus, skilled soccer players are considerably better able to "read the game" because they simply know more precisely where to find the crucial information. Professional players, in contrast to beginners, focus their gaze on far fewer areas, even ignoring certain zones altogether, while their eyes rest longer on the important places. This type of information gathering can be observed both when in possession of the ball and when playing against it. Defenders who want to stop a dribbling opponent, for example, look particularly intensively at the opponent's hip, because that's where the next movement can be detected earliest. It is astonishing that many professionals are not even aware of where they find the most valuable information; in the course of many training sessions and games, they have accumulated unconscious knowledge that is automatically applied. With this knowledge, they manage to predict, i.e. anticipate, the opponent's actions (Fig. 2.1).

But this knowledge can also be used consciously, from which goalkeepers in particular can benefit. Most scientists have used penalty kick situations as a study situation to determine how which information can increase the chance of holding a ball. In these studies, the regions identified as relevant (for the goalkeeper) for anticipation in the shooter were the head, the upper body, the hip area, the standing leg, and the shooting leg. In addition, experienced goalkeepers increasingly look at the player's supporting leg to optimize their anticipation performance.

Very similar mechanisms run in the process of tactical-strategic decision-making. Here, it's all about information that can be found in very specific regions of the pitch. Soccer beginners are hardly able to identify the right gaps, and the hidden spaces into which Kevin de Bruyne, German national players Joshua Kimmich or Toni Kross play their amazing passes are often not even recognized by opposing defenses and practiced connoisseurs in the privileged perspective of the TV viewer. This type of creativity is mainly developed in the first years of life (cf. chapter 2.8), but existing potentials can be exploited more thoroughly through certain exercises.

Especially in the field of junior soccer, there are possibilities to improve the anticipation and the anticipatory action of the players (see chapter 2.2). Today, it is known that this skill can be practiced and progressed quickly with special sport-specific video programs. Video clips are played to the soccer players that stop in the middle of an action, and the respondent then have to decide how they would continue the situation (Fig. 2.2).

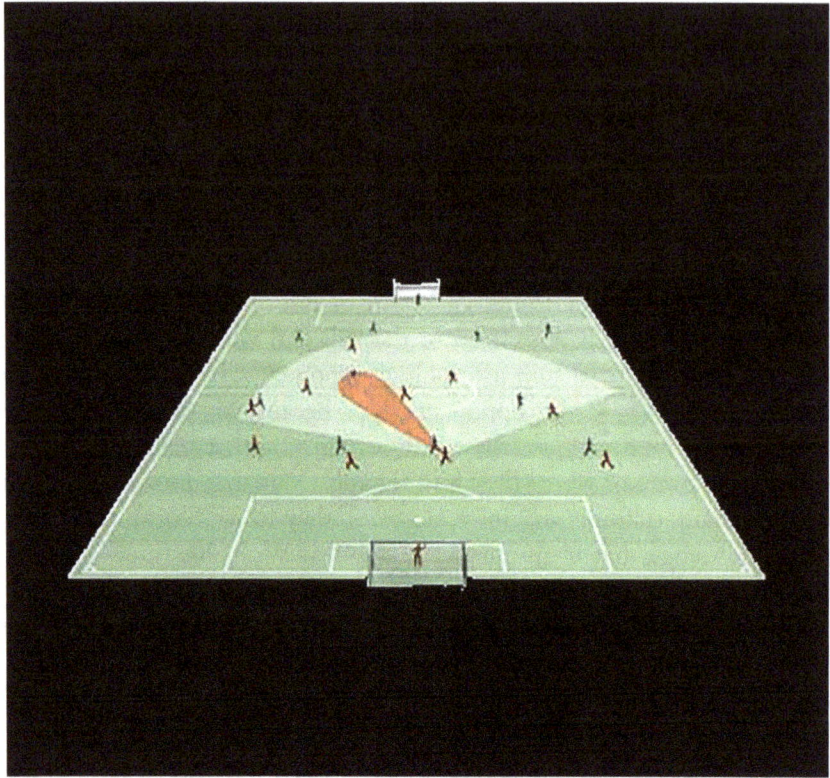

Fig. 2.1 Experienced soccer experts concentrate their gaze on those areas where they can find the appropriate information they need to make good decisions (black field of view). Novice soccer players, on the other hand, look everywhere and easily overlook the important teammates, opponents, gaps, and spaces (gray field of view)

With this type of video anticipation training, it is not even necessary to integrate motor solutions; the exercises can be done on a laptop or with a tablet. Such measures are also interesting because training times are often scarce, especially at the youth level, or because talents are overloaded during additional physical sessions. However, when traveling in hotel rooms, on the many bus rides, or even in phases of rehabilitation, players often have free capacity to work on their ability to read the game.

However, even more important for the training of the so-called pre-orientation, which is the result of the anticipation process, remains the work on the training field, as recent work of the Cologne working group led by Daniel Memmert shows. Higher-ranking coaches, as well as coaches with more experience, incorporate a greater number of exercises into their

Fig. 2.2 This is what a video training to improve anticipation in soccer can look like. The players see a situation on the screen and have to decide quickly when to tackle. Sensors on the three boxes at the bottom of the screen tell the computer which solution the trainee has chosen

program in which players are asked to repeatedly "scan" as much information as possible from their surroundings by turning their heads and incorporating it into their plan of action. In addition, these coaches provide more and better quality pre-orientation feedback to their players, who may eventually come out of the depths of the room at Wembley like Günter Netzer once did.

2.2 Head Thing

In very complex situations, players like the well-known Kevin de Bruyne, Ilkay Gündogan, or Jamal Musiala manage to "conjure up" unusual but also technical-tactical best solutions on the pitch seemingly effortlessly. With such exceptional players, successful coaches, players and scientists like to talk about the speed of thought. These players are said to be "very quick in the head" or "intelligent". The term "speed of action" also crops up time and again. "Football is played with the head. Your feet are just the tools", says former Italian world-class player Andrea Pirlo. From all these statements it is clear that the head and thus so-called executive cognitions play a fundamental role in soccer and other sports, experts from the sport also see it that way. In science, there are now numerous models describing executive functions that regulate goal-directed, future-oriented behavior, i.e. processes such as decision-making.

"In terms of physical presence, soccer has its limits. In the cognitive area, on the other hand, there is infinite scope. A chess player thinks ten to twenty moves ahead; the soccer player must be able to do the same in the future. Some can. Özil, Kroos, and Pirlo play balls into the depth because they know someone is going to run in, and they think ahead. There is potential to think ahead. That's why I still see great resources in cognitive training. Running data or statistics on possession are not decisive in my view," former German national coach Joachim Löw said in 2017, elaborating: "You can't beat the Spanish players with aggressiveness, with tackling strength and with toughness, because you can't hit them with that. They are too fast mentally. And that will be an important task and development for all footballers. It's about always being faster mentally. The speed of thought is perhaps still to be placed above the physical speed. If a player has good technique and good basic speed but is slow in his mind, that can reduce his value to the team."

More complex cognitive abilities have been discussed in sports science for many years. In meta-analyses of the Cologne working group, in which various individual studies were summarized, small to medium effects of basic cognitive performance could be demonstrated in experts, which seems to indicate superior (basal) cognitive abilities of elite athletes. Individual research groups have also found that professional soccer players in particular appear to have outstanding basal cognitive abilities. Another cross-sectional study of highly talented junior soccer players conducted by the Cologne scientists nourishes the hypothesis that, for example, a large attention window can be advantageous for more complex motor skills such as dribbling. In addition, better working memory has implications for more precise ball control and dribbling skills. These findings need to be replicated in the near future, especially in larger samples.

However, it must be critically pointed out that the number of studies on executive cognitive functions in competitive sports is still quite small, the methodological quality is manageable, and there are published and unpublished studies that have not demonstrated any correlations. As also shown by a systematic review of commercial cognitive training programs and their effects on use in sport, many questions are still open and need to be clarified in follow-up studies.

In the meantime, various models have been developed for this purpose. A process model of the sequence of human decision actions from the Cologne

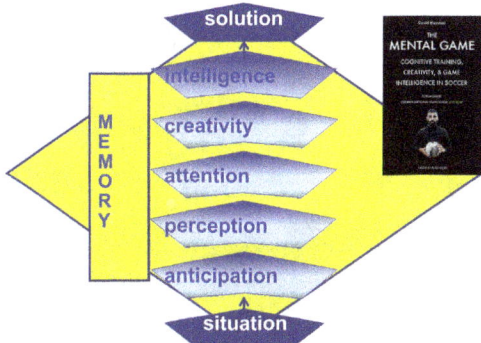

Fig. 2.3 Different cognitive processes that generate solutions for specific situations in soccer.

researchers contains the cognitive abilities of anticipation, perception, attention, creativity, game intelligence, and memory (Fig. 2.3). This model was developed primarily for sports games. In swimming or athletics, creativity and attention do not play as central a role as in soccer, for example, because: In sports games, many different solution possibilities are needed to reach the goal.

Specifically, for soccer, this means: Because soccer players want and need to anticipate a situation based on their previous experiences, which are stored in memory, individual environmental factors are perceived unconsciously or consciously, and attention is paid to them by the players. After the often unconscious mental development of some solution variants, the best solution or a creative idea is finally selected.

In addition, new findings are also linked to coaching practice. With a single word, coaches can vary players' attention. In situations where variability and creativity are required, players need the broadest possible focus of attention. If, on the other hand, movements and actions have to be anticipated or attention has to be paid to specific events, then a narrow focus of attention helps (Fig. 2.4).

2.3 From Street Soccer to Creativity

In addition to the moment of a successful shot on goal or the cozy excitement that a great chance generates, there are also a few variations of rapture among soccer spectators that have only secondarily to do with the phenomenon of scoring. A mixture of willpower, energy, and technique that leads to winning a duel can excite a soccer stadium just as much as a flash of

Fig. 2.4 Andrea Pirlo's brain working. (© Actionplus/picture alliance)

inspiration from a player who turns an action with the ball into a small work of art.

In African soccer, this sometimes goes so far that the public cheers completely pointless dribbles through its own half more exuberantly than a shot against the post. Artistic moments that amaze teammates, coaches, experts, and fans alike contribute a great deal to the game's fascination.

In the 1970s, this effect drew Germany's upper class to the stadiums. The era in which the German players Günter Netzer and Franz Beckenbauer hit their fabulous passes and when Holland's national team around Johan Cruyff played their "total soccer" contributed to this sport getting rid of its proletarian taint. However, no one has yet been able to provide a definitive answer to the fascinating question of where these highly gifted players got their universally admired skills.

For a long time, the theory of the street soccer player circulated, whose learning environment was particularly conducive to the development of creative potential. Various studies conducted by the Cologne and other working groups now actually prove that unguided and, as far as possible, free experimentation in game-like and unstructured situations promotes creativity in childhood. In the meantime, in most youth departments of clubs, stubbornly prescribed passing sequences and agreed-upon running routes are a discontinued model among the forms of exercise.

In adult soccer players, the production of original decisions can be stimulated primarily by so-called *hope instructions*. For this purpose, motivating formulations can be used in training that increase the generation of unusual solutions. Thus, "Try to play a lot of surprising passes today." rather than "You have to play a lot of surprising passes today."

Such simple approaches, however, have long since ceased to be sufficient for many coaches in highly equipped professional soccer to promote the precious commodity of creativity. The German premier league team Leipzig has the *SoccerBot360* (Fig. 2.5), and Borussia Dortmund and Hoffenheim have installed a training device called *Footbonaut*, a closed box in which eight ball machines play at a trainee. The player has to process the ball and pass it on

Fig. 2.5 The *SoccerBot360* (Umbrella Software Development GmbH, Leipzig).

to an illuminated box. This is supposed to optimize basic skills such as speed of action and perceptual ability, thus enhancing creativity. However, the benefits of such a machine have not been scientifically researched, nor has the idea that soccer simulations on game consoles could increase creativity.

This idea is quite exciting, though, because console soccer is one of the favorite pastimes of young soccer players who travel a lot and spend dozens of evenings in hotel rooms in front of the screen. In his exciting book The *Soccer Matrix*, renowned German soccer author Christoph Biermann reports on his attempt to confront Lionel Messi with this thesis. In a personal interview, the world's best soccer player for many years revealed that he not only regularly played soccer on the console but also his own virtual replica in his own team, FC Barcelona. "You see certain things and try to imitate them on the pitch," Messi told us about this kind of pastime, "but some of it is impossible." So, Messi was even better at the console than in reality (Fig. 2.6).

The idea that the joystick could promote the feeling of space and inspire the invention of new tricks has not been proven, but there is certainly scientific evidence for the correctness of this theory. Experiments have shown that people who regularly play action computer games are 16 times more likely to detect the surprisingly appearing gorilla in the filmed basketball game

Fig. 2.6 Quick thinking and exclusive ideas: Creative player Lionel Messi. (© David Blunsden/Action Plus/picture alliance)

(see chapter 7.2). Accordingly, daddling at the console seems to promote the ability to detect unexpected objects. And this in turn, as we know, increases the probability of finding unexpected solutions on the soccer field.

2.4 Doers and Thinkers

1990 was Lothar Matthäus' big year. The record-breaking German national player became World Player of the Year, and he was allowed to kiss the golden World Cup trophy as Germany's captain. But there has always been a flaw in this moment of greatest personal triumph for today's TV pundit. In the 85th minute of the final against Argentina, Matthäus discreetly strayed into the center circle, because there was a penalty kick for Germany, with the score at 0–0. "When it came down to it, Lothar had already turned tail more often," in truth the World Cup hero was "a real pisser," writes German national player Stefan Effenberg in his book *Ich hab's allen gezeigt*Matthäus' longtime teammate is alluding to the historic events of that summer night, among other things, and many people still think like Effenberg today. After all, Matthäus was the national team's best penalty taker until Michael Ballack surpassed him in that ranking in 2005. However, the most significant penalty kick in German soccer history was converted by Andreas Brehme.

Matthäus later explained his withdrawal by saying that the sole of his shoe had been broken, but Karl-Heinz Rummenigge, who at the time was assisting the legendary German journalist and reporter Gerd Rubenbauer with the commentary on the live broadcast, had told the TV nation even before the winning goal that the captain had also left the important penalty kicks to his colleague Brehme at his then club Inter Milan. At that moment, this was above all interesting information for the feverish TV nation. Later, Rummenigge's words contributed to the legend of the coward, which Effenberg summed up in his book with a hefty dose of perfidy. With a little knowledge of the theory of action control, however, this story can be analyzed quite differently.

The renowned German psychologist Julius Kuhl differentiates the more action-oriented from the situation-orientedtype. The first group essentially focuses on solving a problem or a task. Situation-oriented people, on the other hand, pursue similar intentions but are more often blocked in their actions because their attention is primarily focused on the current state rather than on the task and the search for adequate solutions. With the help of questionnaires, it is easy to find out whether an athlete is more situation-oriented or action-oriented.

There is evidence that certain demands of an athletic task influence expected performance. Playing positions and the tasks associated with them may favor, to varying degrees, players with an action orientation or a position orientation. For example, center players in basketball are more likely to indicate that they are action-oriented types. This means that they have the ability to quickly and efficiently transform an actual state (basketball throw, ball must go into the basket) into a target state (basket/score). In soccer, many strikers who put the ball in the goal intuitively rather than on the basis of a well-considered plan belong to this category (Fig. 2.7). Their inner voice says, "I must do everything necessary right now to get to the goal as quickly as possible." Reflection is rarely one of their greatest strengths. In contrast, situation-oriented players tend to prefer the role of the strategist. They first want to conscientiously analyze the current situation (We're down 0:2, how can we realign?) before taking action. They develop strategies that go beyond a single situation; these are usually players who are particularly receptive to coaches' instructions during the 90 min.

In athletic performances, therefore, the match between the personality of male and female athletes and the current situational environmental

Fig. 2.7 Forgetting the scope of one's own actions: Penalty-taker Andreas Brehme at work. (© Frank Leonhardt/dpa/picture alliance)

requirements always play a decisive role. This knowledge opens up an interesting approach to performance enhancement based on psychological diagnostics and individualized motivational targeting. In soccer, an analysis of personality in youth can prevent players from being trained in unsuitable positions. And later, an analysis of personality can help, for example, in choosing the right penalty taker, who should be more action-oriented.

In the final phase of the World Cup final mentioned at the beginning, Lothar Matthäus may simply have known that he himself is a situation-oriented type who reflects. A person who could recognize the overwhelming importance of the moment. One might not even imagine what happens in a soccer player when, before a decisive penalty kick in the World Cup final, he realizes what significance this moment can have for the lives of millions of people and an entire nation. As a more action-oriented player, Brehme is probably the more suitable shooter at such particularly important moments. At the time, he was able to concentrate fully on the execution of his task, and Matthäus knew that. What Effenberg sells as a weakness was actually a strength: the ability for realistic self-assessment.

2.5 "Mentality Monsters": A Mystery

A creature from the world of childhood nightmares has crept into soccer, or at least into the language used to communicate about the game: the monster. Defenders fire up the crowd with "monster straddles," teams chasing the ball particularly aggressively are celebrated as "pressing monsters," and coach Jürgen Klopp celebrated his legendary Liverpool pros, who won the Champions League in 2019 and the Premier League title in 2021, as "mentality monsters." This term captures "Liverpool's relentlessness" in words, wrote the "Independent" after the two major titles of the traditional club and tried to trace the mystery mentality. "It takes time to build it, but it can evaporate in a moment. If there's anyone who can manufacture it, it's Jürgen Klopp."

The fact that this special ability is attributed to a German is quite fitting because in no other country such a persistent and controversial debate about the so-called "mentality" as there is here exists—a term, incidentally, that does not exist in this form in scientific psychology – just as little as the "mentality monster" (Fig. 2.8). In essence, this is a very soccer-specific debate that, just like considerations of tactical developments, is shaped by the best teams at the given moment. When FC Barcelona and the Spanish national team enchanted the world with virtuosic possession soccer between

Fig. 2.8 Sometimes becomes a monster: mentality specialist Jürgen Klopp. (© SVEN SIMON/FrankHoermann/picture alliance)

2008 and 2014, it was more about intelligence and artistic beauty than physical power and mental strength, whereupon many friends of martial arts remarked that something was missing in the soccer of these teams.

Particularly in Germany, people still like to reminisce about times when header monsters like German player Horst Hrubesch and dogged fighters like Lothar Matthäus, Matthias Sammer, or Guido Buchwald forced major titles for the national team. Admittedly, some of these successes were surrounded by a whiff of bad conscience, because of course it was always clear that Brazilians, Argentines, Dutch, or Spaniards could play more beautifully and artfully. But the ability to pack a winning punch was the source of enormous self-confidence. At least until the collapse of the old soccer Germany in 2000, when the entire training structures were renewed after the disastrous European Championship. As a result, brilliant technicians, as well as fleet-footed dribblers, were trained and a honed playing culture was developed around the erratic 2010 World Cup, which, enriched with a little maturity, ultimately led to the 2014 World Cup victory. With the then immature captain Philipp Lahm, the skinny Thomas Müller and the lanky Mesut Özil in key positions.

Compared with previous generations, some footballers in the twenty-first century have appeared almost androgynous. In psychology, a distinction is made between more masculine, androgynous, and feminine people, and there is also a debate outside of soccer about which type masters which tasks most successfully. It has been shown that masculine and feminine people are particularly effective in clearly defined situations that clearly correspond to their type. But: These people tend to depend on the situation actually being suitable for them. They have a harder time adjusting. Androgyny means being able to react more flexibly and assert oneself over the longer term in situations with very complex requirements. Androgynous types are more versatile in finding solutions. This shows an important form of intelligence that can be very beneficial to the game on the field.

This mix of male and female elements is also evident at the bodies of professional players. There are extremely powerful and aggressive types, but some of the world's best players are rather slender, not lugging around thick muscle packs. Often they are hairless all over their bodies, and their game is at some moments of dancing beauty. But to say that these players are not mental monsters because they would rather play a beautiful pass than make their mark in energetic duels is wrong, says former German national player Christoph Kramer, one of the 2014 world champions.

For him, mentality doesn't mean "eating grass!", says the midfielder, rather there are different manifestations of mentality: "Courage, for example, is a mental characteristic that is very rare. Players who always want to have the ball are courageous," even in very tight spaces where pressing opponents lurked for mistakes. This form of courage is "a much more blatant mental trait than someone straddling an opponent in midfield," Kramer says. So a particularly strong, promising mentality is not only fleeting and in danger of evaporating, it's also multifaceted.

A paper published by the *German Football Association* (DFB) states that a combination of physical strength, initiative, and the will to perform, as well as openness to feedback from others, helps players develop a strong mentality. Whereas the aspect of physicality has become more important again after the years of dominance of FC Barcelona and the Spanish national team after 2015. France became world champions in 2018 in no small part due to the imposing physical energy of players like Paul Pogba, Kilian Mbappé, and N'Golo Kanté. The Premier League is also exceptional because of the physical intensity of its games, and Klopp's mental monsters from Liverpool suddenly weren't so unyielding as bodies grew tired of playing 50 or more games a year.

2.6 The Clueless Experts

Matthew Benham is one of the most enigmatic club owners in professional soccer, because the physics graduate is not just an investor, he has acquired the club he has loved since childhood (Fig. 2.9). And indeed, under Benham's leadership, Brentford FC achieved promotion to the English Premier League in 2021-an astonishing success with a remarkable

Fig. 2.9 Betting without gut feeling: Matthew Benham. (© Mike Egerton/empics/picture alliance)

backstory. After studying and working for a few years in London's financial district, Benham moved into the betting industry in 2001, betting on the outcome of soccer matches under professional conditions. His company, "Smartodds", employs IT experts, match analysts, and mathematicians who try to predict outcomes using state-of-the-art software. But a gambler Benham is by no means, quite the opposite. "I've never bet for fun or to pass the time," he says in an interview with soccer magazine *11Freunde*. "We're all about probability calculations using mathematical models," says the entrepreneur, explaining his business model that made him a multimillionaire.

Benham and his staff try to "find and exploit market weaknesses," says the boss, "Numbers are the holy grail for me." Computers use complicated formulas to determine the probability of certain teams winning and put the results in relation to the odds. Professional betting obviously works in such a rationalized way. If, on the other hand, the millions of soccer connoisseurs from the stadiums and the regulars' tables bet their money, the betting providers have almost won. The betting behavior of supposed experts who regularly bet on the outcome of soccer matches is no different from that of bettors who know next to nothing about the game.

Even people who invest time in betting, who regularly put money on the outcome of soccer matches and take into account all sorts of aspects such as the sickness levels of teams, current form, recent winning or losing streaks, and the like, are by and large no more successful than the unsuspecting layman who is not actually interested in soccer at all. After all, we know from studies conducted by the Cologne working group that typing according to the FIFA soccer world rankings is one of the best ways to optimize one's results. Surprisingly, however, experienced soccer tipsters do not know them much better than people with no special soccer knowledge.

However, there is a difference between soccer experts and people without specialized knowledge about the sport. People who know their stuff are considerably more convinced that their predictions will come true than the clueless. This reveals a general phenomenon: people generally tend to overestimate themselves, and this finding obviously applies to experts in particular. Precisely this finding is one of the guiding ideas of the professional better Behnham. In the Englishman's favorite book called "Fast Thinking—Slow Thinking," written by Nobel Prize winner Daniel Kahneman, there is a chapter on cognitive bias: "The Illusion of Validity." There, it explains in great detail "how ridiculously over-optimistic people are about their predictive ability," Benham says. "Even in the face of highly specious evidence, we draw our conclusions with conviction."

For these reasons, at the moment people are no longer asked, but rather computers, more precisely simulations. Several scientific studies confirm that the betting market is an excellent way to predict the results of sports events. This applies in many different sports and especially soccer.

There are several reasons for this: First, bookmakers thrive on their accurate assessments of future sporting events, so they have a huge financial incentive and the expertise to forecast them accurately. Secondly, the betting market brings together a wide variety of players (bookmakers, professional sports bettors, and a huge amount of recreational sports bettors). So the final betting odds can be assumed to be a joint assessment of many savvy observers, and these (keyword "crowd wisdom") are usually much better than the assessment of individual experts. Third, the betting market can take into account all relevant information, unlike other sources of forecasts such as rankings or past results. In particular the home advantage, the tournament draw, or the current squad composition and absences of injured players. Another important aspect is the consideration of the time dependency of the team strength, which can fluctuate around a team-specific value in the course of a season or a tournament. This shows that the offensive team strength is more important for the final success than the defensive team strength.

Various probabilities can thus be derived from the betting market data, based on different factors in a World Cup tournament, for example:

- The overall tournament forecast, i.e. the probability of each national team winning the tournament, which is always adjusted during the tournament and in response to the results.
- The forecast for each match, that is, the probability of the outcome of each match: win team A, draw, win team B.
- For knockout matches, the additional probability of advancing, i.e. a prediction of who will qualify for the next round, considering possible extra time and the possibility of a penalty shootout.

In the run-up to the next big soccer tournament, many people will nevertheless again enter match results into the lists of betting syndicates organized by friends or colleagues on the basis of their supposed soccer knowledge. But if you really want to increase your chances of success, it's best to follow a simple piece of advice: "Get the betting odds, stick to them when you're betting, and you'll very likely do pretty well."

2.7 Computers Decrypting the Game

Video analyses of soccer matches have long been part of everyday life in professional soccer. Coaches and their staff even work through their own mistakes during halftime using current images from the first half of the game or visualize the strengths and weaknesses of opposing teams. This is already being done at the higher level of youth soccer. In addition, certain performance values are collected in real-time, especially running distances and running intensities, which often appear in current reporting. But all these tools represent only a fraction of the insights that a comprehensive study of the games produces. To completely cover a soccer match, analysts need six to eight hours, during which a video recording of the 90 min is combed through for different categories. For example, a team's play structure is screened: Is there more action with lots of short passes over one to two meters, with the two outside defenders playing to their respective offensive wingers? Or are the two central defenders looking for the two strikers with long balls over more than 25 m?

Elaborate technical installations are used to record the position of all players and the ball for entire games; analysts can thus access the coordinates of 22 players and the ball at any time during a match. At a sampling frequency of 25 frames per second, this results in 135,000 data for each player; if the ball is added as the 23rd object of investigation, the impressive amount of 3,105,000 data is then available (Fig. 2.10).

However, a meaningful interpretation of such a huge amount of data was a great challenge for a long time. The problem was only solved with the use of so-called neural networks. In common parlance, a neural network refers to certain structures, such as those found in the human brain. Nerve cells are connected to each other via synapses to form a network. An artificial neural network, as modeled in computer science, is a mathematical model of a biological neural network (Fig. 2.11).

The goal is to replicate the function of both neurons and synapses in the human brain. These computational structures can identify higher-level correlations between game scenes to determine which constellations on the court lead to which results. In this way, very large amounts of data can be classified according to differences and commonalities within a few minutes. In seconds, an unmanageable number of game situations are classified according to success and failure. This makes it possible to analyze the formation of Team A's back four in relation to the offensive behavior of Team B's

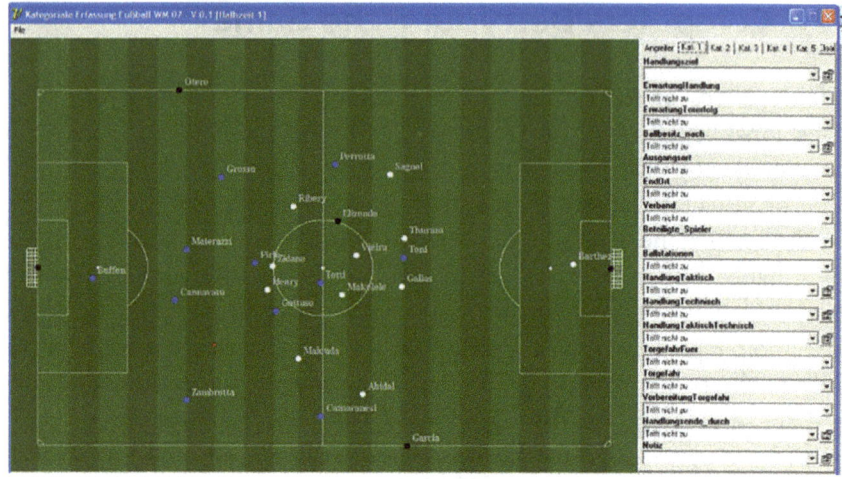

Fig. 2.10 Each point on the playing field represents a player. The soccer players move across the field like a swarm. The computer stores the corresponding position data at every poin time, so that complex relationships behind tactical behavior and possible strategies for success can be analyzed in addition to running distances and speeds

strikers and midfielders. In this way, it is possible to calculate in which constellation the probability of preventing a goal threat for Team A and creating a goal threat for Team B is greatest.

In addition, the network-based approach helps to identify standard game sequences, but also rare and surprising moments, and to evaluate them in terms of their success and functioning in the situational context. Often, extraordinary actions or rare types of scoring are dismissed as coincidence, before closer analysis reveals spontaneous creative processes and perhaps even hidden abilities of a player.

New advanced Key Performance Indicators (KPI) have been developed and tested for several years now. In the first Big Data field study, a total of 50 matches from the 2014/15 season were analyzed and eventually, 11,160 performance values were generated and examined. The focus was on the analysis tool *SOCCER* (© Perl, 2011), which combines conventional data analysis, dynamic state-event modeling, and artificial neural networks. All calculations are based on positional data, events like winning or losing the ball are reconstructed from player and ball positions. If we now draw comparisons between winning and losing teams, we first see that winning teams in the vast majority of cases overplay more opponents in the build-up

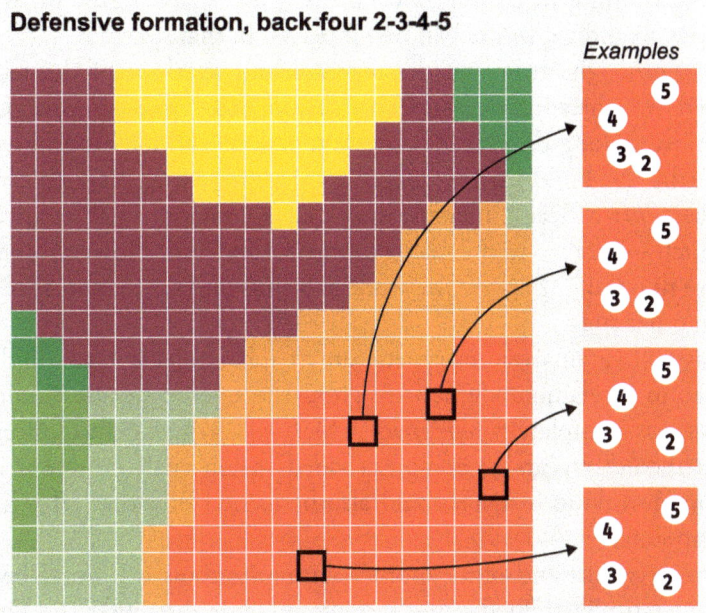

Fig. 2.11 This is a typical neural network. The different colors of the net illustrate the different arrangements of a team's back four. This is not the case in a specific game situation, but rather the most frequently occurring constellations are shown here. For example, in the four-man backfield shown here, the left back tends to play a little closer to the left center back, while the gaps on the right side are a little wider. Information like this can be of great value when analyzing opponents in top-level soccer. The Fig. is taken from Memmert, Strauss, & Theweleit (2013, p 0.44)

of the game. In addition, the winners face fewer opponents on average in possession than the losers—even in the case of vertical passes in the offensive area.

It is also interesting to note that a greater number of switching actions and consequently higher pressing values tend to characterize the performances of inferior teams. Here, pressing is defined as determining the distances to the ball of all players "chasing" the ball and then adding them up across the entire team. Meanwhile, in clear victories, that is, in matches decided by a margin of at least two goals, the space control indicator is the predominant difference between the two teams. The winning teams convince with significantly higher space control shares and with greater space gain in their own build-up of play. In front of the opponent's goal, the winning teams' space gains are also significantly greater. Controlling space means determining which player occupies which space on the pitch in each second, i.e. would get to the ball first if played in that space.

Furthermore, the teams in the top and bottom third of the table were compared over the course of the entire season. Here, space control proved to be the most striking difference between top clubs and relegation candidates. Whether in the build-up to the game or in attacking play: In almost all areas, there was a clear difference in spatial dominance in the critical zones of the pitch—in favor of the teams from the top third. However, these findings have not really changed the work of scouts and coaches in soccer—different in other sports.

In baseball, a smarter interpretation of the available data in the early 1990s led to fundamentally new insights. The significance of certain player strengths was completely redefined, which was a minor revolution at the time. In the early years of computer-aided match analysis, it was believed that groundbreaking insights could also be gained in soccer. This hope has since evaporated.

Neural networks and other sports informatics tools will never be able to replace analytically trained game interpreters, but they offer the possibility of providing coaches with targeted data and information at high speed and thus in interactive communication, which they can then interpret and classify with their expertise.

2.8 The Scouting Approach Must Never Override the Development Approach

Ernst Tanner, who is now sports director of Major League Soccer club Philadelphia Union in the USA, was previously head of the youth academies at Austrian RB Salzburg and German TSG Hoffenheim. He is considered one of the most innovative minds in the use of match analysis data in scouting and team development (Fig. 2.12).

Mr. Tanner, the search for suitable players for your own team is being conducted with increasing effort. When you look back: Where do you see the most serious changes in the work of a scout?
The development in recent years has clearly gone from live to data scouting! More and more data are also being included in the talent search. First and foremost, this are event data, i.e., from tackling rates to passes to ball

Fig. 2.12 Specialist for innovative scouting: Ernst Tanner

conquests, but also simply goals scored. This now extends to the youth level. But now positional data are increasingly being added to round off the picture of a player. This started with the running data of the players but is also increasingly used for tactical analyses.

How do you process this data?
There are three main areas of scouting: First, data scouting, through which we pre-select a group of players. Next, we take a closer look at interesting players in videos, but the final decision is still made on the field in live scouting. These three areas are becoming more and more coordinated at many clubs. Whereas I myself am a fan of also looking at the player's background, his family and social situation, his motivational situation, and his education.

Can it happen that you overlook players in your pre-selection based on data, who in the end turn out to be exactly the type you were looking for at another club?
You can't rule that out. But there is no other way. We now have data from over 100 leagues, and we need filters. Otherwise, we'll be swimming in a huge sea of data and will only randomly find someone who fits the bill. That's exactly what we want to avoid with the data.

How exactly do you set the filter function that you want to use to minimize the random factor?
That is always the crucial question. We look for certain indicators that are most likely to be used to evaluate players in the way we see them in the club.

We have certain indicators that we focus on, and I'll give you an example: We look more at the cognitive area, and for that, we focus on interceptions (balls intercepted). And because we try to attack as close to the opponent's goal as possible, we also look at where the interceptions took place. We also look at recoveries (ball recoveries in one-on-one situations). The idea behind this is that players who make a lot of interceptions and recoveries in interesting spaces usually anticipate well. They perceive situations correctly and usually still have the courage to move out of their position and defend forward. That's what we want to see.

How reliably do these findings describe the players?
This way we get a ranking of interesting players, but we still have to check how someone really behaves in the game. It's not uncommon that the interceptions from the database are based more on coincidence than good anticipation, for example, because a pass was deflected somehow.

For more and more clubs, scouting is part of a business model: just as important as the question of whether a player will strengthen one's own team is his expected value development. For many clubs, it is clear that a player who plays five good games is a candidate for a lucrative resale. Can functioning teams emerge under these circumstances?
I'm very critical of this business model. During my time at RB Salzburg, we dealt intensively with precisely this question, and my resolution was always: the scouting approach must never override the development approach. In other words, the development of the players must be evident throughout; only in this way, real teams with the corresponding social ties can be created. If I scout first and foremost with the intention of finding people who can soon be sold on at a profit and then put them in front of the players I have trained myself, then I will always be more likely to cause frustration at all levels than to generate a financial return.

Does this observation also apply to junior soccer?
Yes, I often see that many players have already had three or more clubs by the time they reach U19. Many youth development centers define themselves far too much by the quality of the players they bring in. This is detrimental to the entire system because it inhibits development. As a rule, a player is not trained over two or three years, but over eight or ten years. If a player is bought at 18 and sold on for 20 million at 20, that's a clever deal, but it has little to do with the development of a team or a player.

How can the resolution to train seriously be filled with life with all the pressure that the clubs and their coaches usually have from the first to the last match day?
That is precisely the problem. The greater the pressure, the less work is done on aspects that need to be developed over a long time. The daily routine of competition forgives far too few mistakes, and the people acting are immediately attacked—usually by the media. That is the flaw in the system. But there are niches: SC Freiburg, for example, allows itself the luxury of saying: We're happy to be in the first league, and if we're relegated at some point, that's not the end of the world either, and we'll just get back up again. That's how sustainability can be developed.

3

Friends and Enemies

© Sebastian El-Saqqa/augenklick/picture alliance

Of course, soccer is not an affair that could credibly be described as peaceful. Two teams fight each other on the pitch, competing factions of fans meet in the stands, and there are authorities such as the referees, the security, or the football associations that also make a wonderful bogeyman. Without the others, who are mocked, defeated, blamed, and insulted, the love for one's own team and the communal experience with the many like-minded people in the stands would only be half as enjoyable. There is usually a uniqueness that is lacking in other areas of life: Us versus them—a primal principle that is undoubtedly one of the most important reasons for the incredible success of the game.

The good thing is that conflicts and disputes are regulated; within clearly defined limits, aggression and disputes are permitted or even desired. But what processes are conducive to the social fabric of teams? At best, do eleven friends walk up? Or is friction desirable, as experienced coaches say again and again?

In any case, soccer provides an environment for all kinds of boundary transgressions. Players use their power and popularity for their own interests and thus harm their clubs. There is a minority in the audience that looks for opportunities to use violence. Even normal family men develop behaviors in the stadium that they would be ashamed of in any other environment. Mostly, it's just nice to fight the opponent with your friends. And to defeat them, of course.

3.1 The Myth of the 11 Friends

There are plenty of significant and almost as many trivial soccer truths with which German legendary national coach Sepp Herberger enriched the world, so it's no wonder that the authorship of the famous phrase "You must be eleven friends to win" is also attributed to the former national coach. Presumably, this has something to do with the legendary "Spirit of Spiez". This little village on Lake Thun in Switzerland was the training camp of the German national team during the 1954 World Cup, and it was here that the cohesion that carried the team to the World Cup title was formed (Fig. 3.1). In fact, Herberger often and gladly recited his "Elf-Freunde" phrase. ("11 friends"). But the great coach by no means invented the slogan.

Apparently, it already adorned the base of the Victoria, the trophy presented to the German soccer champion from 1903 to 1944. In the 1920 textbook *Football. Theorie, Technik, Taktik (Football Theory, Technique, Tactics)* by the Berlin teacher Richard Girulatis of the "Deutsche Hochschule für Leibesübungen" (German Physical Education College). Herberger used the phrase only for his own purposes, and it had many imitators. German Sammy Drechsel, a Munich sports reporter and cabaret artist who died in 1986, published a book in 1955 with a similar title now a classic of German youth literature. And which soccer fan doesn't know the very popular German monthly released magazine *11Freunde*, which pays tribute to the immortal quote in a

Fig. 3.1 Inspired by the spirit of Spiez: Happy world champions after winning the 1954 final. (© dpa/picture-alliance)

purist short form? Obviously, the image of the eleven friends conveys one of the great emotions of soccer. But is the statement behind it actually true? Do eleven friends have to be on the pitch for a team to be successful?

There is no question that the relationships between group members and cohesion, as it is called, are of great importance. Well-being grows in a harmonious group characterized by mutual affection and a willingness to work together constructively. And fundamental well-being is conducive to performance. Let's take a look at a back training group of a health insurance company: People are much less likely to leave such groups if they feel accepted if there is a positive atmosphere within the group and if a sense of belonging develops. The saying about the eleven friends seems to apply here, at least in a figurative sense. But soccer is not Halma, and a professional team is not a back school group.

The now deceased, world-renowned Canadian group researcher Professor Albert (Bert) Carron distinguishes between social-related and task-related cohesion for teams from top-level sports. This differentiation is important for finding out whether the cohesion of a team leads to greater success and better performance.

In social cohesion, the focus is on shared experience and friendly relations, not on the effectiveness of the group. A high level of task-related cohesion, on the other hand, is expressed by the fact that the group members are prepared to make every effort to pursue the same goal, to develop common mental models (the term *shared mental models* has become established in English) about their actions on the pitch, and to put personal interests aside for a certain period of time. At least as far as they do not correspond to the team goal. In soccer, for example, this is about resisting the temptation to play oneself to the fore. There are strikers who take their own goal quota too seriously, players who reveal internal details to journalists so that they can be graded better at the weekend, and many other scenarios that can damage team cohesion. And that quickly becomes a big problem. Because when it comes to group cohesion, task-based cohesion is the most important driver of success on the field. At least in interactive sports like soccer, where communication and joint action are key.

The fact that task-related communication (i.e., what is important for successful task performance) on the pitch is a decisive factor for success was made clear in a study a few years ago: This type of communication and its extent were examined in a very detailed network analysis of all players from two soccer teams playing against each other in a match. The result was that the players from the winning team communicated with each other much more frequently on the pitch in a task-related manner and exchanged information.

So, it is of utmost importance that the players communicate with each other, about what is important for the task. That they pursue a common goal and develop common so-called mental models and that everyone puts their ego aside. And it's important that soccer players internalize that they themselves benefit when the team succeeds. Whether the professionals in this interpersonal structure are actually friends or not, on the other hand, plays a subordinate role in success. However, good social cohesion is a promising starting condition for pursuing common goals and often makes things easier.

However, too much harmony can also have a paralyzing effect, especially if everyone has become accustomed to a good mood and this slows down change processes. In such a case, it is better if there are also disputes and controversies from time to time. These conflicts or, as German Borussia Mönchengladbach's long-time sports director Max Eberl says, "friction points" (cf. Sect. 4.1), are inevitable and necessary in such a tough, competitive and performance-oriented system as professional soccer. It is only important that conflicts are dealt with openly and that they do not lead to personal injuries. Task-related cohesion should always be the priority.

Only when these conditions are met, conflicts can make a productive contribution to success. And Sepp Herberger, was he wrong? A close look at Jürgen Leinemann's biography of Herberger reveals that the former national coach was very competitive and did not shy away from conflict at all. He used the image of the eleven friends as a vehicle to work out a common goal with his team: to become world champions.

3.2 Free Speech, Control and Communication

Most clubs engage in an astonishing contradiction with their expectations of players. Sports directors, club presidents, and coaches agree as a matter of course and without any hesitation when asked if they want mature professionals for their teams. In the 1980s and 1990s, when it became clear that teams improve when soccer players think for themselves, when they don't just soldier on following orders but develop their own ideas, the "mature professional" was a central feature of soccer progress. However, they were not supposed to go too far with their own views.

Because being of age often does not at automatically mean that free expression of opinion is desired, at least not publicly. It has long been stipulated in the employment contracts of professionals that no interviews may be given to print publications without the press departments combing through what is said for sensitive statements. Relevant passages—often perfectly innocuous remarks—are rigorously deleted. And players who publicly criticize their coaches, teammates, or club management face harsh punishments.

Like German player Philipp Lahm, when he gave an interview to the German daily newspaper *Süddeutsche Zeitung* in the fall of 2009 which the club knew nothing about. At the time, the captain of the record champion defended the controversial Dutch coach Louis van Gaal and soberly analyzed the reasons why things were not going well at FC Bayern in sporting terms. Basically, as team captain, he had put himself in front of his coach and his team and pointed out that the club lacked a long-term strategy.

Hardly anyone doubted the relevance of the content of the statements, but Lahm was severely sanctioned. He had to pay 50,000 euros because it was not proper to criticize his own club management. And because he had the audacity not to have the interview proofread by his employer's press department. He knew, of course, that all the important passages would have been deleted there. In the summer of 2013, when Bayern had just won its historic triple, Lahm then stated in another interview that he believed his

2009 push had made "a small contribution" to the subsequent successes. After all, Lahm's criticism had been punished, but it had also contributed to a change in thinking.

The man who helped Lahm with his spectacular action is player advisor Roman Grill. He considers this form of breach of contract to be a sensible remedy in some situations. "The player must be aware of his responsibility, and he must reflect on the effects of his statements," says the former soccer player. In addition, a critical professional should "express himself in such a way that it helps the team," Grill says. "The team should be able to work together better afterwards or achieve a better result." In Lahm's case, that worked out brilliantly, but the consequences of such criticism are usually hard to predict.

This is because an environment of journalists, consultants, confidants, and secretaries of various kinds has formed around the large teams, the entirety of which is often not even transparent to insiders. Everyone involved has to face constraints and pressures, and interests are highly heterogeneous. It is not surprising that the players take a very active role in shaping their jobs and their environment, and often it is not at all about improving the club's medium-term prospects. Instead, the holders of relevant information try to place their own interests with the coach, sports director, president, or the public, and cooperation with media plays an important role in this.

Most forms of this cooperation remain invisible. Players and advisors, but also coaches and officials, give background information to journalists, for which they then receive good marks or are praised with benevolent interjections in the stories. In almost every long interview, there is a part of the conversation before in which it is explicitly agreed that it is not intended for publication. This conspiratorial exchange is often enough to create a feeling of familiarity among the reporters, which then leads to a less critical attitude in another situation (possibly also unconsciously) (Fig. 3.2).

Former German Bundesliga coach Hans-Dieter Tippenhauer, who died in 2021, found the topic so interesting that he explored the matter scientifically in his doctoral dissertation in Münster in 2010—making him probably the only head coach in the German premier league to receive a PhD (Fig. 3.3). In 1979, Tippenhauer (who also coached BVB Dortmund and Bielefeld, among others) took Fortuna Düsseldorf to the final of the European Cup Winners' Cup, where the Rhinelanders lost to FC Barcelona. As part of his research, he conducted extensive interviews in the Bundesliga and spoke with players from the first teams of 1. FC Köln, Borussia Dortmund, Arminia Bielefeld and Werder Bremen, among others. In addition, there

Fig. 3.2 Between cooperation and mistrust: protagonists of the game (like German Thomas Tuchel) and their relationship with the medie. (© Erwin Scheriau/dpa/picture alliance)

were the respective coaches, sports directors, and numerous media representatives. No one has ever examined the environment so thoroughly from the inside.

Tippenhauer came to the conclusion that there are usually three to four leaders on teams who, along with the coach and support staff, provide athletic leadership. The influence of these leaders is enormous. Their opinions and actions are of the utmost importance for teammates, cohesion, and especially for the coach's position on the team, in the club, and in the public eye. And the media serves as an important tool for leaders. According to Tippenhauer, passing on insider information to reporters is part of everyday life, and it often reaches the public only in hints or as background to journalistic expressions of opinion.

In recent years, however, this mechanism has probably become less important. *Facebook, Instagram, TikTok, Twitter*, and so on make it possible for players, coaches, and clubs to communicate media content directly to a broad audience without intermediary journalists. Many professionals and clubs have a great penchant for self-presentation online, for certainly different motives, ranging from their own ego interests to their own sales interests. Having as many subscribers to one's own channels as possible

Fig. 3.3 Germany's probably only German Bundesliga coach to date with a PhD: Hans-Dieter Tippenhauer. (© firo Sportphoto/augenklick/picture alliance)

helps enormously. FC Bayern München now has more than 30 million followers on Instagram alone and is far ahead of Borussia Dortmund on all social media channels. So, it's no surprise that Bayern players also lead the way with their personal accounts—Robert Lewandowski, who moved to FC Barcelona in 2022, reaches over 25 million followers. That's an enormous reach into their own fan base and into the business and opens up many opportunities for public influence. In this respect, players can now use these channels to represent their own positions and interests in public without the need for critical journalists who might want to know the background or have their say on opposing positions.

This was exemplified by Floyd Landis, a cyclist, suspected (and then convicted) of doping after the 2006 Tour de France, who tried to convince his fan base via numerous tweets that he had been wrongly accused. Landis tried to re-present himself in a positive way during this crisis and repair his image. The very well-known political scientist Professor American William Benoit has been working on such repair mechanisms since the 1990s and has worked out in his image repair theory which strategies are promising and which are not (from blaming to apologizing and taking responsibility). In the meantime, there are several individual scientific case studies from the world of sports, for example on doping cases, such as that of Michael Phelps, or on the drama surrounding Lance Armstrong. However, other crisis cases such as the fate of figure skater Tonya Harding or the interim crash of golfer Tiger Woods have also been examined in order to analyze and work out the communication structure in tweets, Facebook entries, press releases, or even all other media down to the smallest detail. But not only individuals and their statements are analyzed, but also associations and organizations, such as FIFA's crisis communication on the corruption scandal in 2015, when Sepp Blatter was still president and attempts were made to repair or polish up the bad image. Whether this then always succeeded, we do not want to evaluate here.

One thing seems clear, however: not only in the past (one or two decades ago) but also in times of social media, which can be easily and quickly operated by anyone with potentially worldwide resonance, internal consulting is necessary, otherwise you will end up like the Norwegian head coach a few years ago, who became the focus of a crisis himself through some very clumsy statements in the press after bad games of his team. Trine Andersen and colleagues have worked up this case meticulously and, in the end, have had to conclude: there are two different logics that have to be brought together: that of the media and that of the sport and the active players, and this does not happen automatically. Control and punishment, as was the case with Philipp Lahm, is rather the wrong form, but advice can certainly help.

3.3 Fans, Hate, Violence

The derby between the two rivalists Borussia Dortmund and Schalke 04 in October 2012 had just kicked off when suddenly wild scenes took place in the press box. A group of seven or eight young men sprinted up the stairs, wearing sneakers, sweatpants, and thin jackets. In a state of extreme excitement, they rushed along in front of the journalists' work tables and disappeared through a mouth hole in the east stand. Pursued by a small police unit, they managed to catch one of the troublemakers, three meters away from the well-known TV journalist Marcel Reif, who was commentating on the game for television. Immediately the prisoner was in a tight grip, he could not move, his breath was rapid, and his eyes were wide open. And they were shining. The violent excitement was visible on the man's face, it almost seemed as if there was a smile on his lips. In any case, he was intoxicated by all kinds of beguiling substances that his body had secreted. He looked as if he had gotten exactly what he wanted: a first-rate kick. Then the man was taken away.

Due to massively increased security precautions, such scenes have become a rarity in Bundesliga stadiums; however, the various groupings among soccer spectators seeking violent confrontations still exist (Fig. 3.4). There had already been quite violent riots in the run-up to the above-mentioned match in Dortmund, Dortmund's police director Michael Stein said at the time: "Both Schalke and Dortmund supporters displayed a high potential for aggression and violence like they have not done in a long time." There were eleven injured and 180 provisional arrests. There were no fatalities, which fortunately is a very rare occurrence in Germany around soccer matches.

Gunter Pilz, a fan researcher from the German University in Hanover, was certainly one of the most important experts on this scene for decades

Fig. 3.4 Escalation at the Euro 2016: An English fan after a street fight against Russian violent fans. (© Daniel Dal Zennaro/dpa/picture alliance)

until his retirement. Pilz makes it clear that rioters seek out the environment of soccer matches because a stage is provided here. Their defining characteristic is violence. And this is obviously highly interesting for many men, regardless of their profession and social status. On the one hand, the motivation lies in escaping the boredom of everyday life; on the other hand, it is about testing oneself in self-assertion against others. The acts of violence generate an emotionally relevant group experience in addition to the release of endogenous drugs. *Hooligans* and parts of the *Ultras*, the two groups that are repeatedly involved in confrontations, make it clear through their actions that they rightly belong to a particular group.

The publicly displayed exclusion of opposing factions increases self-esteem and status within scenes that have defined violence and discrimination as an important element of their association. This characterization is particularly true of *hooligans*, who sometimes appear in the vicinity of soccer matches solely because of their interest in tangible conflict.

On the one hand, confrontations with other *hooligans* are sought, but also law enforcement officers, and, more rarely, non-involved persons can be attractive opponents or victims. An important characteristic is that it was planned from the outset to instigate violent confrontations and that it is no longer even a question of affiliation with a specific club. *Hooligans* cannot be seriously categorized as fans, they do not come for soccer. Instead of feelings for one of the teams, they bring weapons or objects that can be used as weapons.

Now the assumption is obvious that these people are modernization losers, and there are definitely discussions in science about this. Many years ago, however, Gunter Pilz differentiated between the *yuppie-hool,* who has two identities (as an integral part of a middle-class environment and as a *hooligan*) and wants to appear as cool, self-confident and in control as possible, almost like a young manager, and the *chav-hool*. The *chav-hool* comes from a less upmarket class. This view would suggest that *hooligans* can belong to all sections of society.

Incidentally, where the term *hooligan* originally comes from is disputed. It is sometimes reported that in the late nineteenth century, a pair of Irish brothers called hooligans roamed London drunk, brawling, and rioting. Other sources emphasize that the origins of hooliganism can be found in the English working class of the nineteenth century. Whatever the case, in the twentieth century the word *hooligan* was often used synonymously with violent soccer fans.

But for some years now, there has also been the *ultra-movement,* whose members also repeatedly take part in violent confrontations, but whose motivation is completely different. Unlike most *hooligans, ultras* have a clear connection to their club. Although they like to wear expensive clothing from well-known brands, they also demonstrate their deep attachment through fan paraphernalia such as scarves and jerseys.

In Germany, however, the vast majority of *Ultras* are still primarily soccer supporters. Not all *die-hard fans* are *Ultras* (actually only very few, cf. Sect. 10.3), but *Ultras* are *die-hard fans* who are characterized by a high level of loyalty to the club and who also position themselves ideologically. For example, they oppose the commercialization of soccer with their actions. Above all, however, they use the stage of the big arenas for impressive productions. The choreographies in the arenas, for example, are usually developed and organized by the *Ultras,* and the impetus for the chants also often comes from these groups, whose leaders intone the songs via megaphones before the whole crowd joins in.

The *Ultras* want to portray themselves as genuine, fighting fans vis-à-vis rival groups, in some cases with forms of expression that glorify violence. Another area where boundaries are crossed is the forbidden burning of bengalos and other pyrotechnics as part of the staging. The sociologist Pilz has repeatedly made it clear that there are fluid transitions between the various groups, especially from *ultra* to *hooligan*. These people, whom Pilz calls *hooltras,* are moving further and further away from the fan scene, making violence a meaningful feature of their soccer affinity, but still assigning themselves firmly to a club.

Social media, with their very own dynamics, are now playing an increasingly important role in the scenes. Here, shitstorms ignite, containing not only verbal tasteless gaffes, but also hate speech and calls for violence. Dietmar Hopp, who earned many billions of euros with his software company SAP and supported the German team TSG Hoffenheim with his money to such an extent that the club was promoted from the ninth-class "Kreisliga A" to the Bundesliga, was attacked particularly hard in Germany over many years. Hoffenheim does not really have an established fan culture like other traditional clubs and regularly struggles to fill its small stadium. Critics believe that TSG is taking a place in professional soccer away from the big traditional clubs with their much more passionate supporters. Supporters of Dietmar Hopp and his financial commitment—which, by the way, is not limited to professional soccer—argue that Hopp's support for soccer is much more sustainable than the commitment of other patrons and sponsors.

Nevertheless, Hopp is regularly called a "son of a bitch" on social media but also in the stadiums. The entrepreneur's face in the crosshairs on a repeatedly displayed banner can be understood as a call to violence. To this day, fans, officials, and lawyers debate whether Hopp must endure this in the harsh climate of soccer, or whether individuals should be punished by courts for their postings, their placards, and disparaging chants, and whether clear boundaries must be drawn. This is a discussion that, in principle, cannot only be related to Dietmar Hopp but is already occupying the judiciary in the context of the digital public sphere as well. For example, when it comes to insults, name-calling, or hate comments against politicians and others.

In any case, the tendency of *Ultras* to transgress boundaries is now a major problem for clubs. Many officials find it extremely difficult to strike a balance between restriction and a willingness to communicate. After all, clubs in the professional leagues employ fan officers and operate fan projects that deal intensively with supporters, although there is criticism that such successful measures are not sufficiently appreciated and receive too little financial support. At the same time, the considerable police and legislative efforts inside and outside the stadium also involve high costs for the taxpayer. It may be that further investment in prevention measures would be worthwhile. Especially since youth work is being done here quite fundamentally.

Solving problems with fans who are on the borderline of legality in an exclusively restrictive manner only works in highly commercial professional soccer. "In an emergency", those who are prepared to use violence and "friends of pyrotechnics" simply migrate to other areas of society or to lower leagues. A look at the injury statistics from the 2020/21 season, which STATISTA recently published, shows that there were 15 injured spectators in the first division, while 21 people were injured in the second division and 237 in the third division. The risk of injury as a spectator in the third league is therefore much greater, compared to the first or second league.

3.4 When Citizens Freak Out

The stadium experience, this merging of the individual with a group of like-minded people, exerts a great attraction on many people. Soccer fans often perceive the excitement of others in the arena and the vibrations around them as a medium that can be used to increase the intensity of their own emotions. They sense that they are not alone in their joy, and in the event of failure, there are like-minded people who share the grief. Other people with whom they can immediately synchronize.

Part of the appeal is that on the stands of the arenas, it is possible to give up a piece of one's own individuality and emotionally merge with the masses. That can be beautiful, but it can also be dangerous. As early as 1895, the French sociologist Gustave Le Bon formulated the thesis in his widely published work *Psychology of the Masses* that "the individual in the crowd acquires a feeling of insurmountable power through the very fact of the crowd, which allows him to indulge in drives that he would necessarily have restrained for himself alone. He will give way to them all the more readily because, through the namelessness and consequently also irresponsibility of the mass, the sense of responsibility which always restrains the individual completely disappears." (retranslated from the German volume).

The fact that people in groups and crowds sometimes act out behaviors that they keep under control in everyday life is therefore nothing new. In soccer stadiums, this can be observed in every block, in every row of seats, and guests in the expensive seats hardly behave any better than fans in the standing room. But the vast majority of people leave it at that, insulting the referee, players, or opposing fans, which in the context of the stadium is not yet a border crossing. In some cases, this behavior is forced by alcohol consumption or by external factors such as cramped conditions or high noise level. Such conditions increase the likelihood of a wide variety of forms of aggression. However, there are other components that contribute to turning the friendly faces of well-behaved family men into unrestrained rabble-rousing grimaces.

The Californian social psychologist Philip Zimbardo meticulously worked out these conditions in 1969 when he conducted the famous Stanford Prison Experiment. Zimbardo divided a group of subjects into guards and prisoners, who were housed in a fictional prison in the basement of California's Stanford University. Over time, the guards became increasingly violent toward their inmates, so Zimbardo stopped the experiment after five days because the situation was getting out of control. The subjects could no longer distinguish between the experimental instructions and reality. Forms of impulsive aggression and violence occurred that the participants never thought they would ever use. It should also be added, however, that the experiment has been the subject of much criticism in the scientific community for a number of years, partly because after the archives were opened it was questioned whether the experiment had been conducted in exactly the same way. However, the opening and this information have also led to reinterpretations of leadership roles in such a context chosen by Zimbardo.

In any case, Zimbardo explains the excesses in the subjects' behavior with the process of loss of individuality that can occur in a group or a crowd.

This condition is characterized by a low level of control over one's own behavior; inhibitions and social norms are reduced, and a frequent consequence is aggressive behavior reinforced by a sense of anonymity and loss of responsibility. Very similar dynamics can arise in the stadium; the fan clothing, the jersey of the favorite club, and the actually very nice unison of the crowd lead to many spectators no longer perceiving themselves as individuals, whereupon the sense of responsibility for one's own actions can be lost (Fig. 3.5).

In mass demonstrations, where violent confrontations occur, and sometimes even in sport itself similar anonymization processes can be observed. Especially in sports where players have to protect themselves with helmets, face masks, and special clothing, such as in ice hockey or American football, this anonymization of players can lead to an increase in aggressive behavior. Of course, a stadium is not a prison, and a mass demonstration is different to a Bundesliga match, but there are certainly parallels.

Thus, in the stadium as in demonstrations and also in the prison experiment, groups pursue different interests: Supporters of rival clubs, prison guards and prisoners, or demonstrators and the police. They all see themselves as members of a particular community with which they usually identify. This own social group is called an *ingroup,* and where there is an

Fig. 3.5 Often people from the middle of society: fans who cross borders in the stadium. (© terovesalainen/stock.adobe.com)

ingroup, there must of course be an *outgroup*; in soccer these are the opposing fans or, in the case of clashes between supporters and the police, possibly also the uniformed officers. The mere separation between one's own group and the other is sometimes sufficient as a minimal condition to allow discrimination, devaluation, aggression, and sometimes even violence to develop.

In soccer, however, there are several other conditions that can encourage aggression and violence toward the supporters of a particular club: a particularly painful defeat in the previous season, a player who has moved from one club to the other, a historically grown enmity between two clubs, provocative statements in the run-up to a match, or simply too much alcohol. And since the stadium is a place where individual inhibitions fall in the process of merging with the masses, everyone is in danger of becoming a victim of discrimination, abuse or aggression at some point. And, of course, no one can rule out becoming a perpetrator themselves, even if it's just by shouting mean songs.

The freedom to break out of conventions may be a desired part of the emotional experience in the stadium and contribute to the magic of soccer—conflicts arouse interest (cf. Sect. 9.1), and even for a peace-loving and conformist member of society it can be appealing to shout a few very nasty swear words. However, in such moments of emotional charge, boundaries are unfortunately crossed far too often, for example by racist or homophobic remarks, which still too rarely results in social demarcation and ostracism by other viewers.

The spectators and referees at the German third-division match between Duisburg and Osnabrück shortly before Christmas 2021 behaved in an exemplary manner. The game was stopped after Osnabrück player Aaron Opoku was racially insulted by the stands, this seem to be the case at that moment (even if the prosecution later came to a different assessment after video analysis of the spectator behavior). Such an abandonment was the first of its kind in German soccer after the DFB opened up this possibility in its rulebook. However, it is even better to prevent such incidents preventively, e.g. through the work of fan projects, but also through very good planning by the police.

4

Power and Powerlessness

© Stefan Matzke/sampics/picture alliance

"Champion coaches" are what soccer coaches are called full of admiration when they have won the premier league title with their team. "In soccer, people are quick to build you a monument, but just as quick to pee on it,"

German coaching legend Hans Meyer once said, and most coaches know both extremes all too well. Life as a coach is an eternal interplay between power and powerlessness. When things are going well, the coach is an influential impresario; when the storm of criticism rages, he usually has to surrender to his fate.

Failure is even part of the system, because coaches have to meet a variety of demands that are almost impossible to manage, admits longtime Bundesliga head coach Ralf Rangnick. In the end, coaches tend to stand powerless on the sidelines and contemplate the results of their work. Whereby coaches still leave opportunities to exert influence unused, as studies on the choice of penalty takers and the interview with coach legend Ottmar Hitzfeld reveal.

In addition, coaches have to constantly reinvent themselves. The former German national coach Joachim Löw was fired in Stuttgart in 1998 on the grounds that many players couldn't cope with his interactive and participative management style. In 2014, he became a world champion with precisely this approach. Flat hierarchies are now the hallmark of a modern group structure. It's true that conservative experts still argue that such anti-authoritarian approaches are unsuitable for a men's sport like soccer. But are there any viable alternatives to this type of group leadership? Frank Wormuth, the long-time chief instructor of the German Football Association DFB, provides answers.

4.1 Cold Love—Pressure, Exhaustion and Depression

With increasing frequency, a spotlight is shining for brief moments on the darker side of careers in top-level soccer, where many stars actually like to stage themselves with images of wealth, fame, and fulfilled dreams. For example, former German national player Per Mertesacker reported at the end of his career in 2018 that he rarely felt like a great hero when he competed in the world's famous stadiums. Rather, the 2014 world champion, said he had diarrhea and struggled with nausea from the pressure and tension before each of his more than 500 games as a professional. The permanent assessments of the public, the constraints of the game schedules, and the high expectations were a heavy burden during all his years at Hannover 96, Werder Bremen, and FC Arsenal London. "From bed, I have to go to the toilet immediately, from breakfast to the toilet, from lunch to the toilet again, in the stadium to the toilet again," he described the usual course of his playing days to the German weekly magazine *Der Spiegel*. All food went through immediately, in the meantime, he could only eat pasta with olive oil. It was particularly bad in the minutes before kickoff, he said: "My stomach turns as if I have to throw up. I then have to retch so violently until my eyes water," the former defender recounted (Fig. 4.1).

He did not want to complain, Mertesacker assured because he appreciated the feeling of success and the money. But he never had a professional life full of joy and ease. Just like André Schürrle, who retired from professional life at the age of 29 and subsequently said, "All the money I've earned is an enormous relief," but this permanent stress to which he was subjected as a professional, he had hardly been able to bear: "I was completely at the end. It was as if everything inside me was on fire," he also told *Der Spiegel*. "Only

Fig. 4.1 Without anticipation of the game: Per Mertesacker. (© Joe Giddens/empics/picture alliance)

the performance on the pitch counts, vulnerability, and weakness must not exist at any time."

Such reports about the harshness of the professional game are always followed by the same reaction: some media start to investigate, publish big stories about the abysses of top-level soccer, interview psychologists and remind people that not much has changed since the suicide of the German national goalkeeper Robert Enke, who suffered from depression, in 2009. And after a few days, it's business as usual. Such was the case after the moving appearance of the well-known highly experiences German Max Eberl in 2022, after a decade as very successful sports director of Borussia Mönchengladbach (now with RB Leipzig), exhausted in the midst of a performance crisis of the team, asked to be allowed to leave. Eberl's farewell was touching because he had the courage to face the public in a state of acute despair to explain his retreat. He was "tired" and "exhausted" because he felt that his work was making him increasingly "ill," he told the audience in tears and formulated a few sentences that had to get under the skin of every listener.

"I just want to get out, I just want nothing to do with soccer, I want nothing to do with you," he said to the faces of the journalists. "I want to see the world, have no responsibility, just be Max Eberl. That's why I made this incredibly difficult decision at an incredibly inopportune time." There was sincere desperation in his words as he announced, "I'm ending something that was my life. I'm ending something that has given me a lot of joy and fun because soccer is my life because soccer is my joy." A joy that can drag some people down.

More detailed research is still insufficient on the effects of a professional day's work in the special industry of public and media professional sports on mental health and on various mental illnesses. But at least there are increasing studies exploring causes and more and more prevention and intervention programs. It is important to note that there are a variety of mental illnesses, some of which are caused differently, but some of which are treated differently. Burnout, for example, can have considerably more manifestations (and also causes) than bipolar depression.

A 2018 data collection by the University of Leipzig from 323 players in the Swedish and Danish premier leagues, as well as among U19 players, showed that 17 percent of participants had developed symptoms of depression. "What distinguishes many competitive athletes is perfectionism," said study leader Anne-Marie Elbe. "That has a positive, motivating effect at first, but it can also create anxiety, namely the fear of not being perfect. And that drives many professional soccer players, paired with the fear of being judged by others, so-called social anxiety. Our study clearly showed these connections."

Although mental illnesses are not more common in competitive sports than in the general population, the causes of the pressure to perform, constant stress, and physical phenomena such as eating disorders are particularly widespread among athletes. An Australian research team that evaluated 60 studies on the mental state of competitive athletes had already come to similar conclusions in 2016, concluding that top athletes have a risk of developing common disorders such as anxiety disorders and depression that hardly differs from the rest of the population. However, eating disorders are particularly prevalent among athletes, for whom a particularly slim body is advantageous, they said. In addition, athletes drink an above-average amount of alcohol outside of competition phases, and physical injuries, the end of a career, pressure to perform, or constant stress increase the risk of developing depression.

Furthermore, it is becoming increasingly clear that concussions suffered during sports can be among the causes of depression. Especially in sports with frequent head-to-head, head-ball, or head-impact incidents, concussions can sometimes have other serious consequences, such as early dementia. Anyone who has seen the movie "Concussions" *with* Will Smith will get a very good idea of this. While it is a work of fiction from 2015, it is based on the groundbreaking discoveries of real-life pathologist and neuroscientist Dr. Bennet Omalu. Omalu had studied the brains of deceased NFL football players and was able to establish a clear link between brain damage and the athletes' careers. The film describes this, but also the hurdles Dr. Omalu had to overcome in order for these results to be noticed by the NFL and the public.

4.2 From the Turnvater Jahn Principle to a Flat Hierarchy

The organizational structure behind the term "flat hierarchy" relies "increasingly on individual initiative and responsibility," according to Wikipedia, and actually many modern coaches would like to see precisely such a model of democratic cooperation, they emphasize consistently. But in the context of Joachim Löw's work as head coach with the German national team, the term had become heavily contaminated in the meantime. After the German team's elimination from the 2012 European Championship, the image of a "flat hierarchy" suddenly fueled suspicions that the DFB team lacked leadership. Probably more for peace of mind than out of genuine conviction, Löw said at one point: "We don't have a flat hierarchy within the team, but a clear structure. We have leaders who are clearly in charge." Although a clear structure is not contradictory to a flat hierarchy, conservative circles summarily declared the idea a failure.

Even Uli Hoeneß, then president of FC Bayern Munich, announced in an interview with the German weekly published newspaper *Der Spiegel*: "Löw has to say goodbye to his ideas of flat hierarchies. He has to put more pressure on." Presumably, many people at the regulars' tables agreed with this statement, although many people still didn't really understand what a flat hierarchy was actually about. Jürgen Klopp once said he preferred the term "responsibility for all," but meant the same thing. The coach, who won the Champions League with Liverpool FC in 2019, tries to create a climate in his teams where no one is prevented by any structures from contributing their skills. "It's really very important that you are empathetic, that you try to understand the people around you, and that you really support the people around you. Then everyone can take action," Klopp says.

This group structure forms a counter-model to the autocratic management style of the past millennium, explains Frank Wormuth. For years he headed the Hennes Weisweiler Academy, where the German Football Association DFB educates its coaches, who are admired around the world like former Bayern and Leipzig head coach Julian Nagelsmann or former Chelsea and new Bayern Munich coach Thomas Tuchel. Wormuth talks a lot, explains, and substantiated, he is deeply convinced of the model. "First of all, it must be clarified that 'flat hierarchy' does not mean that there is no hierarchy, of course," he emphasizes. "It's just not that hierarchy of the past, where the person at the bottom looks up and thinks, 'Oh my God, it's a long way to get there.

At the heart of this form of togetherness is "a different communication structure that is much more fruitful," says Wormuth. "In the past, there were a lot of ideas and information that didn't reach the top at all because there was too much distance to cover, including interests and vanity getting in the way. The new communication structure is significantly more effective." It's about information exchange in all directions, and also about making everyone feel important and taken seriously—just as Klopp intended. The players have changed, they have their own opinions, "you can't say do it anymore," Wormuth says. "You have to convince the players today. That's a general social development that has created two new parties that deal with each other in a different way." Highly paid soccer stars no longer take orders; they want to work out solutions and help create them.

This does not mean, however, that a soccer team does not need leadership with a clear distribution of roles. On the one hand, this applies to the roles within a team, in which there are leaders, so called spokesmen, Wormuth says "spokespersons". And on the other hand, of course, the coaching team with a head coach and his many assistants. Good leaders, however, do not understand their position as a position of power that they use for their own interests, but as the assumption of responsibility for the common interests of the group.

The old concept of leadership, which is becoming authoritarian in its extreme form, is being practiced by fewer and fewer coaches, which is a huge upheaval compared to the conditions of the previous century. In those days, unknown newcomers to the team sometimes had to shine the shoes of the leading players, and coaches also celebrated their power: Something is only going on here because I want it that way. I'm the boss, no one will dare question my decisions. At least until an even more powerful president or club owner fired them.

Today, such an approach can certainly be successful, especially in unclear situations, but the coach must be given great trust and competence. Because as soon as the team is no longer convinced in terms of content, the process of failure begins. If they tend to give orders and explain less, rarely ask for the opinions of others, and work in a less integrative manner, autocratic coaches in the classic sense quickly become the enemy of the players (at least in Central Europe).

This is because such figures are often rather self-centered, can only deal with situations that they have defined in advance, and have problems adjusting their behavior so that they can take on board objections and suggestions from players, staff, and superiors without losing authority. Wormuth calls this way of dealing with athletes the "Turnvater Jahn principle," (and refer here to a German pedagogist Jahn from the 19. Century who proclaimed gymnastics and a clear hierarchy as major educational principle) and in the long run, such steep hierarchies disrupt the all-important group dynamic processes of cohesion. Wormuth notes that there are players who have been socialized in a different culture and "want to be led according to the old principle. The Chinese, Japanese, and Koreans in particular like to hear: That's the way!".

Most Central European players, on the other hand, want responsibility and a voice. It's no wonder that the classic "lead wolf" is dying out. The

Fig. 4.2 Slap in the face for the authoritarian captain: Lukas Podolski against Michael Ballack. (© DB SWR/dpa/picture alliance)

commander on the pitch, whose instructions the others have to follow blindly, is only rarely well-liked in modern teams. The conflict-ridden Good Bye of Michael Ballack, the last great national team leader, from the DFB squad also had to do with different ideas of a modern leadership style. After the autocratic era, a group led by Bastian Schweinsteiger, Philipp Lahm, Per Mertesacker, and Miroslav Klose took over the leadership role and became world champions in 2014. Since then, the hierarchies have been flat (Fig. 4.2).

The changes are by no means about abolishing the leading player; there are still people in the squad who have a prominent role due to particularly convincing performances, experience, successes, or because of their ability to take on responsibility. But there should be a working atmosphere in which everyone involved, from the head coach to the captain to the third goalkeeper and the kit attendant, feels important and is motivated to contribute.

4.3 Who Kicks the Penalty?

There are quite complex processes that take place within a team before a penalty taker is found. Hierarchies are often involved, with the best or most powerful player claiming the privilege of taking the penalty. There is also the myth that the fouled player should not take the shot—which is just a myth and not well grounded—but that is worth a separate chapter. Another legend says that the player who feels best should kick off, and sometimes you can even observe a conflict between candidates who fight over execution and the prospect of scoring a personal goal. Yet coaches can actually determine relatively reliably which players are actually more comfortable dueling from the chalk point than others.

For this purpose, it is useful to distinguish two types of motivation: There are athletes for whom it is more appropriate to motivate themselves with the goal of avoiding mistakes; their preparation for the shot focuses on aspects such as safety and duty. Other soccer players perform better when they focus on achieving a goal. Players in this second category, who have a hope-oriented approach, are not particularly good shooters. While candidates who are more likely to avoid missing score more often.

Also important is the way a player was prepared for the penalty kick, Cologne scientists proved. When a person is confronted with a situation that corresponds to his or her own preferred approach, a performance advantage results that is referred to in science as "motivational fit." A distinction is made between so-called duty types and hope types. The hit rate is thus higher when coaches instruct their players in a way that fits their motivational type.

The very best penalty kicks were converted when dutiful players were given mandatory requirements. Apparently, the fit between the personality of male and female athletes and the current situational environmental demands plays a crucial role in the success of penalty shootings. Accordingly, coaches increase the probability that their shooter will score if they select players who have a pronounced duty attitude and communicate to them once again clearly that it is their duty to convert the penalty kick.

This leads to the question of whether entire teams also benefit when duty and hope types are used in the right positions. To investigate this, both types were tried out on the offensive and defensive positions in an experiment conducted by the Cologne working group. It was shown, consistent with the theory (goals must be prevented, goals can be scored) and consistent with the data (most defenders are duty-oriented and most attackers are hope-oriented), that a team fit occurs when duty types are used on defense and hope types are used on offense. These results extend the concept of individual motivational fit, as in penalty kicks, from individual to team performance and suggest collective fit as a possible important predictor of team success.

4.4 The Coach, the Multi-Talent

It was a fearless Irishman with plenty of black humor who summed up the grim fate of the soccer coaching guild more pointedly than any of his colleagues. "There are only two certainties in life. People die, and coaches get fired," Eoin Hand, who was in charge of Ireland's national team in the 1970s, once observed. Whereas many a coach would be happy if the threat of dismissal was the only annoyance he faced on a daily basis.

Because many coaches would prefer to work 40 h a day, their job has become incredibly demanding. Together with their assistants, they manage the training, they are usually involved in the medium-term personnel planning of the sporting management, maintain the social fabric in the team, act as entertainers in the media, coddle sponsors, and so on. (Fig. 4.3).

The requirements profile is so complex that a good soccer teacher is far from being a good Bundesliga coach. Especially since completely different skills are needed depending on the location. At a club like the German SC Freiburg, with its comparatively quiet media environment and its firm intention to introduce many home-grown players to professional soccer, a different type of coach is needed than at a media-saturated German club like Schalke 04, where the task is to tame vain stars and sensation-seeking reporters. But even the best coach in the world is not immune to dynamics developing in his club that can only be stopped by a change of coach.

Many of the necessary coaching skills are not tangible, and certain strengths or weaknesses only become apparent in moments of crisis: in conflicts with individual players, in phases of public criticism, or when player advisors turn the heads of the biggest talents in the team. And in the end, whether games are won often depends on things that the coach can't influence at all.

Coincidences such as a striker having trouble with his girlfriend and hitting the crossbar instead of the goal in two or three decisive moments out of distraction can lead to a spiral of failure that the club's management will eventually stop by firing the coach. For example, one of former German national player and later manager Matthias Sammer's core guidelines during his time as sports director of the German Football Association DFB was: "Performance can be planned, but whether success comes out of it depends on other things."

Soccer is probably the only game sport in which a team can be better than the opponent for a whole game and sometimes even for many games in a row without winning. This is due to the random element in soccer, which is much greater than in other sports. Soccer is thus particularly complicated

Fig. 4.3 Sometimes overwhelmed: Diego Simeone. (© Franz Waelischmiller/SVEN SIMON/picture alliance)

for its coaches. And coaches, for their part, are a difficult subject for research; sports scientists have defined four core competencies that professional soccer coaches must master, regardless of location.

First, a coach represents his interests and ideas in the selection of players to be signed. In contemporary managed clubs, the coach is intensively involved in the process of transfer business by the sports director. However, the managers always have the final say, and they also sit at the higher lever in the event of disagreements.

Once he has his team together, the coach must devote himself to the complex task of forming a collective that functions in terms of soccer. This is not just about physique, technique, and tactics, but also about developing group structures that promote performance. A hierarchy must emerge, and the squad should develop a sense of togetherness so that a climate is created in which each individual can deliver optimum performance.

The third central task of the coach is to optimize individual and soccer-specific playing ability. At its core, this performance potential relates to appropriate training planning, training diagnosis, and interventions, which are based both on the complex structure of individual performance and on load and requirement profiles. In particular, the ability to make young players better and thus increase the market value of these talents is becoming increasingly important, as the development and profitable resale of professionals is a key pillar in the business model (Fig. 4.4).

And fourthly, the coach takes care of competition planning, including game control: his goal is to influence the performance of his team and its individual players through strategic-tactical interventions in such a way that his own team functions as optimally as possible in its interaction with the game behavior of the respective opponent.

In the eyes of the sport directors who usually hire and fire their coaches, expertise, staff development, experience, communication skills, presence, charisma, and credibility are the most important competencies a head coach should possess. However, professional competence is still the primary recruiting criterion for coaches, claim those responsible for club management, who, however, by no means follow this motive for every new appointment to a vacant position in the Premier League. Often, it's about the name, old contacts, or past successes, with more and more professionals coming into

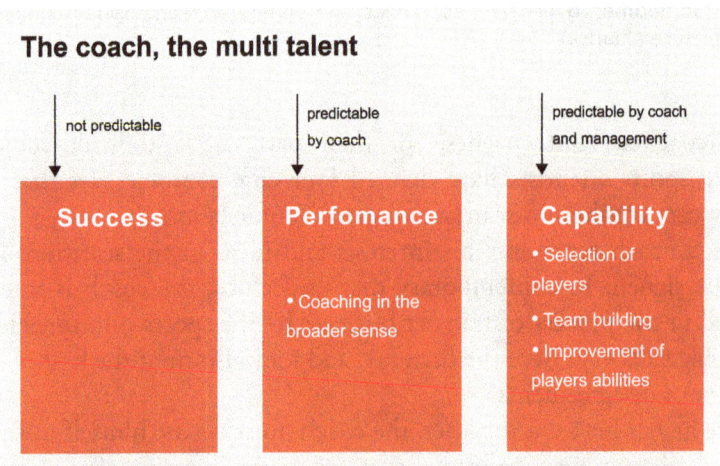

Fig. 4.4 Performance can be planned, but not success! What possibilities do coaches and managers in soccer have to influence performance in a targeted way?

positions of responsibility who don't carry big names but are trained to the most modern standards. Incidentally, the coaches themselves consider their social skills to be very important, especially in dealing with the team.

4.5 Lord Over Time

The 2012/13 Champions League season has been a monumental adventure for the German Borussia Dortmund. BVB supporters experienced a furious journey across the continent that only ended in the final at Wembley, but the wildest minutes of this European Cup drama took place in the quarterfinals. At 10:33 p.m. on that memorable April 10, 2013, the *BVB* was down 2–1 to Malaga FC, needing a miracle after a 0–0 first leg draw. The live ticker of the soccer magazine *11Freunde* posted: "Two goals in added time? Sorry, BVB, that's not going to happen. Not with this opposing goalkeeper, not with this chance exploitation, not with this defensive behavior."

Defender Mats Hummels felt very similarly: "When injury time started, you clearly had to say, it was actually over," said the BVB center-back after the final whistle. But the signals from the referees pulverized the paralyzing feeling of resignation. "When the fourth official indicated four minutes of added time, hope sprouted once again," Hummels recalled. "And with the 2:2, there was also the final belief that we would still get a chance, and we put it in." (Fig. 4.5).

Certainly, the special willpower of this Dortmund team, charged with energy by its coach Jürgen Klopp, the turbulent atmosphere in the stadium and the magic of the moment played a role in the course of this evening, which was described in the newspapers the next day with the term "miracle". However, if the referees had decided on three minutes of added time, which certainly no one would have complained about, the miracle would probably not have happened. So let's take a closer look at this game from the referee's point of view.

Basically, added *injury time* should always be given when there has been a prolonged stoppage in play, for example, due to injury. This duration is at the discretion of the referee (the introduction of VAR, by the way, seems to have led to a slight increase in stoppage time, at least in the Spanish league). A study in the Turkish *Süper Lig*, which looked more closely at 893 injury-related stoppages, just found that only 17.4 percent of stoppages ended with the player being unable to finish the game. And: injury-related stoppages were more common when players from the leading team were involved as injured players.

Fig. 4.5 Victory by two goals in injury time: Dortmund's ecstasy in 2013 against Malaga FC. (© firo Sportphoto/augenklick/picture alliance)

But let's get back to the memorable evening. Other research suggests that the referee would not have allowed so much stoppage time if the BVB had been in the lead and Malaga FC still needed a goal to reach the semifinals. In fact, analysis of many matches and the course of the play shows that referees on average allow more stoppage time when the home team is trailing by a goal at the end than when the host team is leading by a goal. This effect has already been confirmed several times for the Bundesliga.

According to a Münster research group around Bernd Strauss and physics professor Andreas Heuer who included all games between the 2000/01 and 2012/13 match years, the difference was 18 s on average: When the home team was behind and needed a goal, it was given an average of 18 s more to equalize than the away teams that were down a goal and threw everything forward to try to earn a point after all. Of course, these are only a few seconds, but the difference is more or less stable over this period. This can be proven in all years of play. And it can be seen from Mats Hummels' statement that the belief in one's own goal can also be spurred on when the fourth official's board shows four minutes, for example, instead of the perhaps more appropriate three. So it's not just about the time gained, but also about the psychological effect.

The reasons for this surprising behavior on the part of the referees are unclear, but scientists are fairly certain that unconscious processes underlie the differences in determining injury time. It is conceivable that the referees are influenced by the atmosphere in the stadium and the crowd, which is hoping for many more minutes of play. The spectators at least don't want to see the home team lose. But there are also much simpler explanations for the longer stoppage time: for example, the away team was more obviously trying to play for time in order to hold on to its lead.

Beyond the impressive example from Dortmund's Champions League history, however, the crucial question is whether these 18 s more playing time on average lead to a benefit for the home team that can be measured in goals. Here, the answer is no. This is what the same Münster study found. Home advantage is not affected by longer added time, firstly because the number of goals scored in injury time is very, very small, and secondly because it is quickly forgotten (even by researchers) that the away team can also score goals in injury time.

4.6 "Dominant Body Language is Critical in These Scenes"

Ottmar Hitzfeld is one of Germany's greatest coaches, winning the Champions League with Borussia Dortmund in 1997 and with FC Bayern in 2001, in addition to seven German championships and various other titles (Fig. 4.6). After a period of recuperation, he took over the Swiss

Fig. 4.6 Ottmar Hitzfeld, who won the Champions League with Bayern Munich and Borussia Dortmund. (© Hans-Jürgen Schmidt/HJS-Sportfotos/picture alliance)

national team in 2008, and during these many years as a coach, he has, of course, studied the fine art of penalty kicks, which is often considered a game of chance. Not by Hitzfeld, however.

Mr. Hitzfeld, are there any players who are particularly good at winning the psychological duel with the goalkeeper?
Ottmar Hitzfeld: Yes, of course. One of the best I've seen is Stefan Effenberg. He was totally confident in his demeanor, and exuded self-assurance, self-confidence as well, and great conviction. None of that guarantees a goal, but a player's dominant body language is crucial in these scenes.

What role does shooting technique play in the selection of penalty shooters?
Every coach can expect every player to have the technique to kick a penalty into the goal. More decisive are the nerves.

You are one of the coaches who have occasionally had penalty kicks practiced. How important are the impressions from practice to you when selecting shooters? It's always said that you can't simulate the penalty situation in a competition.
You can't simulate it, but you can practice it. In training, you can also see how a player tackles his own goalkeeper. Is he cold-blooded enough? What is the body language like in this duel? That already provides indications for the real thing.

Are there certain things, for example motivational or reassuring, that you say to players before a penalty kick?
The most important thing is that a player goes to the ball with conviction, which also includes not disturbing his concentration or even unsettling him as much as possible. In such situations, every player knows what is at stake, what needs to be done.

4.7 "Where There is Cooperation Based on Trust, There is the Greatest Likelihood of Success"

Ralf Rangnick is considered one of the first modern coaches in Germany. Earlier than others, the Swabian practiced modern playing systems, he stands for a contemporary style of leadership, and at Hoffenheim, Leipzig, and Manchester United, he repeatedly switched between the job of coach and the position of manager or sports director (Fig. 4.7).

Mr. Rangnick, originally Bundesliga coaches were soccer teacher whose first job was to shape a team and equip it with a suitable strategy. Is this work still the focus of everyday life in the profession at all?
Ralf Rangnick: Physically, you're really only involved in the actual coaching work around 50 percent of the time. There are simply an enormous number of developments and commitments. However, I've always devoted about 90 percent of my mental capacity to working with the team.

What other tasks are included in this mandatory program?
Talks with the team coach, the medical department and, if available, the sports psychologist and the scouting department staff. And then there are the media appointments, which suit some coaches, others less so. Good coaches focus on what is most conducive to the team's success at any given stage of a season. But that's not always easy.

Are there moments when aspects of the actual trainer's work come up short?
No area should suffer at all; at most, it should temporarily take up less time, as long as this does not affect the team's success. The key is to set the right priorities. And as a rule, those priorities lie in working with the team.

Fig. 4.7 Sometimes coach, sometimes manager, sometimes inventor: Ralf Rangnick. (© Darren Staples/ZUMAPRESS.com/picture alliance)

How important is a constructive working relationship with the sports director?
Very important. Basically, however, a trainer should have a constructive and trusting working relationship with every employee, colleague and supervisor. This aspect is often underestimated, but where there is trusting cooperation, the probability of success is greatest.

Is the English model of the manager who is also the head coach still in keeping up with time? Or a relic whose attempts at imitation in Hoffenheim and Wolfsburg were not progressive but rather anachronistic?
It certainly depends on the experience, talent and competence of a manager, on whom much higher demands are placed in the English model. In this case, it is crucial to have a competent team with trustworthy employees.

How important are player advisors for coaches, not in contract negotiations, but in everyday life when it comes to personnel decisions, expressing opinions in the media, negotiating positions with players or officials?
A good consultant, like a good coach, always has the player's best interests in mind. However, both sometimes have different access to information about the player and his interests. So they can support each other and, through an exchange, try to find the best for the player together. That would be the ideal case.

5

Illusion and Reality

© Wolfgang Zink/Sportfoto Zink/picture alliance

All people who are somewhat intensively involved with soccer are familiar with the beautiful phenomenon of so-called *runs, winning in a row*. Undoubtedly, there are long winning streaks in which strikers seem to succeed at practically everything. The phrase "they're on a roll" is part and parcel of the jargon, and former German national striker Fredi Bobic explains in great detail on the following pages what such runs feel like, how they can be prolonged, and how they end. Whereby physicist Professor Andreas Heuer was able to show with the help of statistics that these runs don't exist.

The question of to what extent perceived truths can be empirically proven arises more frequently in this chapter. Do around half of all goals in soccer really fall by chance? Or is it more promising to influence chance and force luck? The complex issue of minimizing chance on the pitch may be the area where key advances in game development will be made in the coming years. At this point, old soccer wisdom meets scientific knowledge, but which paths will lead to success remains open for the time being.

The results of testing other theories from the long history of the game are clearer: should the fouled player really not take a penalty? How suitable is the coach's dismissal when it comes to stopping threateningly long losing streaks? Under what circumstances does an expensive team win titles? And are games really more attractive since the three-point rule was introduced in the 1990s? Science provides many answers, but this chapter also makes clear where soccer still wants to keep a few of its secrets to itself.

5.1 Is It a Good Idea, that the Fouled Player Takes the Penalty Shot?

There are those soccer phrases that are so hackneyed that they are only used by the clueless or as ironic quotes from a bygone era. If they want to be taken seriously, ambitious soccer experts would never say things like, "The cup has its own laws," or, "In soccer, anything is possible." Even though these statements still contain a fair amount of truth. But there are also supposed soccer wisdoms that not only seem dusty but have been exposed as false. For example, the phrase about the fouled player who had better not take the penalty himself.

It still happens that a player who has been fouled goes for the penalty himself and is unsuccessful, but in such cases, journalists and experts now quite consistently resist the temptation to reach into the mothballs of supposed truths. However, this has taken a long time. Until a few years ago, the assumption of the fouled player who had better not be allowed to take the penalty kick was a good example of the tendency, still widespread in soccer, to believe perceived truths rather than hard facts. Meanwhile, however, this example shows that findings of science can reach the grassroots and disprove firmly rooted myths. Penalty kicks are among the best-studied phenomena in the game, and the results are pretty clear.

Of 3768 penalties taken in the German Premier league, the Bundesliga between 1963 and 2007, exactly 74% lwere successful, and at least in the years between 1993 and 2005, the chance that the fouled player would score was almost as great as the chance that another player would be succeful the penalty kick. During that time, 835 penalties were taken by 229 different shooters from 30 different teams, scientists analyzed which player was fouled, which player took the penalty, and whether he scored. If the fouled player shoots himself, the probability of the penalty being successful is about 72%, while for other shooters it is about 74%. This tiny difference can be neglected from a practical point of view since it is within the range of random deviations (Fig. 5.1).

However, it seems to be is clear that other factors may very well play a role when it comes to choosing the right shooter: the age of the players, experience, individual hit rate on previous penalties, the minute of the game, or perhaps the score? All these aspects were considered in further analyses, but no correlation with the probability of success was found for any criterion. At best, a close look at the player's personality is helpful. The only thing that became clear in the statistical evaluations was that younger, less experienced players and also more successful goal scorers tend to take the penalty themselves when they have been fouled. But their chances of success always remain pretty much 3:1.

5.2 The Run that Does not Exist

Some research results can cause pain to the soccer heart because they lead to the loss of beloved theories. For example, it is hard to imagine the general discourse about the game without the phenomenon of so-called runs. Every player, every coach, and every fan knows this wonderful feeling of a winning streak that at some point develops its own special momentum: It just goes, no matter which opponent comes, everything feels easy, the self-confidence is there, and the luck, of course, too.

When players or teams believe they are on a roll, there seems to be no stopping them, and of course, there are all kinds of attempts to preserve this momentum. It is not uncommon for coaches to explicitly rely on those players who have previously been successful when choosing their starting eleven;

the old saying "never change a winning team" is also an expression of belief in such a series. A player or team is hot, feeling fired up from the success of the previous competition, and this elation provides the energy for the next victory. Some also say the athlete or team is in *flow* or has a *momentum*. In more scientific terms, the thesis sounds something like this: if there has been a series of positive results, then the probability of achieving another positive result increases, at least that is the hypothesis.

The question of whether such phases of increased chances of success actually exist has been the subject of legions of scientists for around thirty years because subjectively, every athlete and every fan has witnessed memorable series at some point. Roulette players believe that after a series of reds, the probability of black increases. This is nonsense, of course, because such series

Fig. 5.1 After ten goals from the spot, Arjen Robben misses his first penalty kick for FC Bayern. The most important one to date, of all things. (© Stefan Matzke/sampics/picture alliance)

in roulette come about exclusively by chance and the chance of red is always just as great as the chance of black.

The first insights into the phenomenon of the series in sports were provided by the U.S. psychologist Thomas Gilovich when he created the concept of the *Hot-Hand-Illusion*. Gilovich asked himself whether a basketball player who has scored three times in a row has a greater chance of being successful the fourth time than a thrower who has missed before. Hence the name *Hot Hand*. If the assumption were true, athletes might give the ball more often to such teammates who are on a streak because there would be a greater chance of basket success. But Gilovich showed that positive series occur by chance alone. There is no way to tell from previous throws whether a player is more likely to score or not. So, the run is an illusion.

For athletes and scientists alike, this was hard to believe, which is why numerous studies from different sports followed. And, of course, there were not always consistent results—in particular, volleyball has a special role because of the special structure of the sport (it is a sport without a time limit, unlike many other sports such as basketball, soccer, handball, etc.). But overall, in 2013, a group of psychologists were able to summarize and state in a large-scale study: Gilovich was right, with exceptions (like volleyball). The run is an illusion, a distortion of perception. Positive runs come about because chance wills it, but they tell us nothing about the outcome of the next event. But because the phenomenon in soccer feels so impressive, resistance stirred. Soccer is different, more special. Perhaps soccer has its own rules, and what has been studied in basketball and other sports cannot simply be transferred. It must exist, the run.

So, in the 1990s, English scientists studied the top 12 goal scorers and their scoring streaks in the Premier League, including Alan Shearer, the longtime center forward for England's national team who scored 422 goals for his clubs and the national team. But they, too, found no evidence of a statistically verifiable run by a striker. There is no increased likelihood of scoring goals just because the player has scored a few times before.

The same conclusion is reached by studies of winning streaks that soccer teams sometimes get into. In his book *Der perfekte Tipp (The Perfect Tip)*, Andreas Heuer dryly stated, "The concept of a run is thus invalid." He examined the results of all seasons of the German Premier League, Bundesliga from 1987 to 2012 and concluded that the probability of a win does not increase if a team had previously won several times in a row. The physicist took a closer look at all constellations in which teams had won two or four times in a row. Longer positive series cannot be seriously investigated statistically because they simply occur too rarely. Even a winning sequence of four games in a row did not occur that often during the study period of 25 years, namely 374 times.

A run would be characterized by the fact that the probability of winning the fifth game now is greater than it would be without this back story with the small winning streak. The result is astonishing to any soccer fan, but it is just as Gilovich has already described in *Hot Hand Research:* When a team has won twice in a row, the likelihood that it will finish the third game victorious does not increase at all. And even more surprising: a winning sequence of four consecutive games even leads to a slightly lower probability of winning again in the fifth game. So, the magical forces of success that those sometimes feel who are involved during long series don't really seem to help them win the next game either—or as Gilovich would put it: no *Hot Hand* in the Bundesliga.

5.3 Chance, Fate, Luck, and Bad Luck

Scottish defender Steve Nicols may have changed soccer history when, on May 26, 1989, a ball bounced against his stomach and from there accidentally at the feet of his opponent Michael Thomas. Arsenal Londons FC's Thomas suddenly found himself alone in front of Liverpool goalkeeper Bruce Grobbelaar and scored to make it 0–2 for the Londoners. It was the second minute of stoppage time, sometimes called *injury time* on the final matchday of a season that would go down in the history books. Thomas' goal knocked Liverpool off the top of the table, gave Arsenal their first league title in 18 years and, in retrospect, marks a new dawn. Soccer historians argue that this moment laid the foundation for the Premier League's global success today. It was "the night soccer was reborn," wrote the *Guardian* 20 years later (Fig. 5.2).

Before this breathtaking season finale, English soccer had hit rock bottom. Stadium disasters and fan violence had damaged its image, the standard was not good, and many people had turned away in disgust. Not only in England. The 1989 drama from Anfield Road in the season finale reminded millions of the game's power to fascinate, including media mogul Rupert Murdoch, who shortly thereafter began spending millions on TV rights. This money made the English Premier League the richest soccer league in the world. Author Nick Hornby created a literary monument to Arsenal's last-minute title in his best-selling book *Fever Pitch*, which was later made into a film, and helped pave the way for the game's rise to the center of

Fig. 5.2 Goal for the championship in stoppage e time on the last matchday: Michael Thomas scores for Arsenal FC. (© Empics Paul Marriott/dpa/picture alliance)

European societies. Without the ball bouncing off Nicols' stomach, none of this might have happened.

This example shows how strangely inscrutable soccer is governed by the whims of fate, by completely unpredictable coincidences. There are deflected balls, and goals that are preceded by three or four uncontrolled ball contacts. Sometimes a small unevenness in the turf makes the difference between victory and defeat. Clubs can have the luck of the draw, bad luck with injuries, and of course, there is the famous so called *Bayern-Dusel* ("the team of Bayern Munich has always luck") in Germany. Coincidence is omnipresent and therefore a highly interesting field of research for science.

In the meantime, researchers have well documented how great the influence of such more or less uncontrollable situations can be on the course and outcome of games. To this end, an attempt was first made to define chance, which is not at all easy. After all, the belief that luck can be influenced is deeply rooted in the thinking of many soccer players. Somewhere, this vague assumption may be true,, but it cannot be verified scientifically and should therefore not play a role in the study. Rather, by way of simplification, all actions or situations that precede a hit, but which cannot be trained at all or only poorly, were defined as random.

The search was on for goals that had previously touched the post or crossbar, for deflected balls that landed in the goal, for goals that were preceded by rebounds, and for assists on goals, such as the one from Nicols to Thomas. According to this definition, the chance is involved in around 45% of all goals in the German Bundesliga—a result that impressively documents how many aspects of the game cannot be planned because they do not depend on the skills of the players. Other results show that 35% of all ball contacts contain a random component, "the result of a soccer match thus results from the concatenation of coincidences in chance processing and goal scoring," is the radical conclusion of German researcher Andreas Heuer.

Through elaborate calculations of goal differences, he even comes up with a random share of 86%, at least when looking at individual Bundesliga games in isolation. This value drops to 30 to 40% when the entire season is examined because coincidences cancel each other out and the better teams win more often. But the influence of the uncontrollable remains enormous. The main reason for this amazing power of chance is probably the fact that the ball is harder to control with the feet than with the hand. And indeed, soccer is one of the games where studies have found the highest proportion of chance.

This is also shown by an analysis of a total of 7,263 goals in the English Premier League during the 2012/13 to 2018/19 seasons. Here, the scientists considered a further nine situational variables of random influence, including season, match day, match location, match situation, number of goals, or team strength. The researchers were able to identify a random influence in almost every second goal (46%). In addition, the proportion of random goals is more pronounced for weaker teams when the score is tied and depends on the exact match situation. In other words, whether the goals come from the game in progress, from corners, free kicks, or penalties.

It is also interesting to note that the proportion of random goals has fallen from 50 to 44% over the seven seasons. This could be related to the fact that match preparation is becoming increasingly professional and data-based, or that players are becoming better trained technically and tactically. Within the analyzed data set of 2,451 matches, more than 60% of all matches ended either in a draw or with a goal difference of one goal. Thus, a single random goal can be enough to significantly change the outcome of a match. Thus, chance is not only highly relevant for scoring goals but also plays a crucial role in the outcome of the match. Coaches and game analysts should therefore include chance as a crucial factor and further acknowledge the differences between performance and success. Coaches could even consider deliberately creating uncontrollable situations to provoke chance influences in the goal-scoring process.

Now, one might assume that team games like handball or basketball would actually be more attractive and the more popular spectator sports given this finding. Who likes to watch gambling? But exactly the opposite is the case. The fact that coincidence plays such a significant role opens up the possibility for weaker teams to develop strategies to challenge their luck. For example, by hitting a particularly large number of high balls into the penalty area, where a powerful striker causes a ruckus and, in the end, a random ball may somehow be poked into the goal.

Really good teams—the best examples were FC Barcelona and Manchester City under coach Pep Guardiola—on the other hand, try to avoid random situations as much as possible. High and long balls to a big player in the penalty area are not part of the Spaniard's repertoire, and even corner kicks are often taken short. Here, it's all about minimizing chance and controlling as much as possible. After all, you can also look at it this way: Around 55% of goals are scored without a chance component, so teams still have a large part of their destiny on their foot.

5.4 New Coach, New Luck?

In Germany Volker Finke is still the record holder in the Premier league, who coached his club, SC Freiburg, without interruption, namely for 16 years from 1991–2007, 5843 days, although Freiburg was certainly not exclusively successful and also experienced second league times with Finke as a coach. The team was relegated with Volker Finke, but also promoted with Volker Finke. Incidentally, the world record holder is probably Fred Everiss, who was in charge of the English club West Bromwich Albion without interruption from 1902–1948.

Such coaching fidelity is rather rare, however. Robert Körner of the German team 1. FC Nürnberg is the record holder in the Bundesliga, if you look at the list from the other side. He took over the team from Max Merkel at the time and coached Nürnberg for a whole 2 games in March 1969. Over the past 20 years, the average length of time a coach has stayed with a league club has been almost 680 days, or less than two seasons—if you follow the data from transfermarkt.de.

It is more the rule that coaches are fired before the end of their contract and often during the season, usually with the hope of club officials and many fans for a sporting upswing. As was the case in England three decades ago. In the 1972/1973 season, the supporters of English second-division club FC Sunderland had to endure a fabulous series of defeats. Ten games in a row were lost, and it was no wonder that relegation was imminent. But then Bob Stokoe was appointed as the new coach after the dismissal of soccer coach Alan Brown. The team earned ten wins in a row, did not get relegated, and won the FA-Cup final against Leeds United at the end of the season. Of course, Bob Stokoe went down in the annals of English soccer as a coaching legend. After all, his story at Sunderland FC exemplifies the kind of effect soccer officials want to see when they decide to suspend their head coach during a period of failure (Fig. 5.3).

Often it is simple logic that underlies such a move: The old coach has lost the trust of the board, the players, and the fans, he is responsible for the team and its performance, and someone has to take the fall for the failure. Just like a secretary in a government who has a scandal in his or her office, the reflex in soccer is to call for personnel consequences. There is no simpler solution, which publicly demonstrates leading power of the management.

It is striking that at locations where a feverish newspaper landscape generates external pressure and fuels the mood against a coach, action is taken particularly frequently according to this mechanism. In recent years, however, those responsible have weighed up their dismissals of coaches with greater care. In the meantime, discussions are usually held with the leading players before such a step is taken to gain insights into possible conflicts

Fig. 5.3 Winning the FA-Cup with Sunderland in 1973 after a change of coach: Bob Stokoe. (© PA/empics/picture alliance)

between the team and the coaching staff. More and more often, the focus of the analysis is also on the content of the work. And aspects such as injury misfortune or possible misjudgments about the quality of the team are also considered. After all, club managers are reluctant to be accused of giving in to media pressure. Such behavior would be a sign of weakness. Some German clubs, such as SC Freiburg, Werder Bremen, Mainz 05, or Borussia Mönchengladbach, even try to distinguish themselves as particularly coach-loyal and thus reason-driven locations, which certainly works. But even there, there are occasional premature separations, because the dismissal of the coach remains a widespread measure against failure overall. From 1963 to 2021, there were around 500 changes of a coach in the German Bundesliga, an average of around eight per match year. A closer look at these statistics, however, reveals a trend: since the mid-1980s, coaches have been dismissed significantly more often during the current season than in the first 20 Bundesliga seasons.

The exciting question now is whether this personnel measure actually triggers the desired positive effect or at least increases the probability of achieving the targeted improvements in results. There have been some very good scientific studies on this worldwide, but also for the Bundesliga, since the 1990s, such as the one by Roland Singer, a former German professor of sports psychology in Darmstadt, who was probably the first worldwide to point out that a serious assessment of the question must always include suitable control groups, for example, teams that have not fired the coach. For more than a decade, scientists such as physics professor Andreas Heuer, Bernd Strauss and others looked at the effects of coach dismissals as part of an extensive study. The study examined 154 coaching changes (interim or bridging changes were excluded) within the match years 1963 to 2009 and between the 10. and 24 matchday to include pre-history and aftermath. Ten games each before and after the dismissal were included in the analysis (Fig. 5.4).

For comparison, the results of many clubs over more than four decades were examined that had held on to their coach despite being similarly unsuccessful or successful as the clubs that replaced their head coach. Thus, there were different comparison groups and evaluations, always with the same result: In the figure, those control teams that lost twice but did not fire the coach are compared with those clubs that fired coaches. Although there may be a slight improvement in the points and goals situation in the short term, the effect is also apparent if a coach was not dismissed. This is because, in purely statistical terms, a win is sometimes achieved again after long periods of failure. Statisticians speak of "statistical regression to the

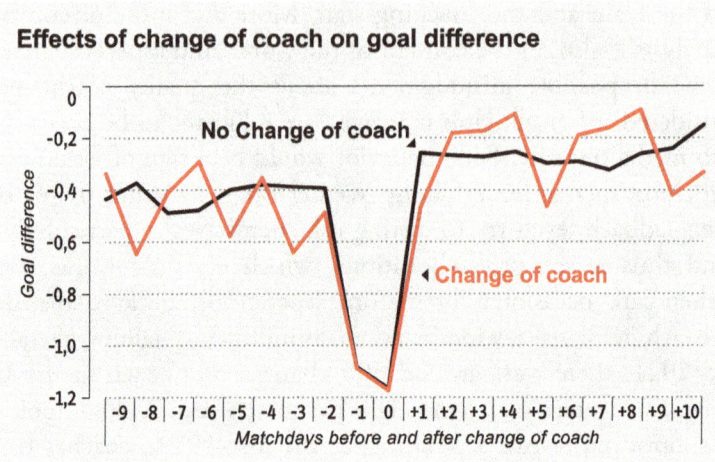

Fig. 5.4 The red line shows the performance of teams whose coaches were dismissed during the season (between Matchday 10 and Matchday 24). For reasons of comparability, this point in time of the sacking is shown as "0" in the graph. The match days before and after each change of coach are then considered. The black line indicates the control teams that had a comparable poor performance record (lost at least two games) but had not fired their coach. The goal difference in each match (goals scored by the home team minus goals scored by the away team) is presented here as a measure of success. The performance trends of the teams, whether with or without a coach's dismissal, run parallel. This is also the case if the points scored by the teams are considered instead of the goal difference

mean" in such situations, a statistical artifact, which sometimes leads to erroneous conclusions in the case of statistically less experienced people. Taken all coach dismissal studies together, also those which came sometimes to other conclusions (but then often accompanied by methological flaws): In essence, this reported result above is also what previous studies using comparable methodology had already found for the German Bundesliga but also for other league (e.g. the Netherlands).

The fact that some coach continues to be fired every few weeks in the major premier leagues is also because of factors that have nothing whatsoever to do with the work of the coach. For example, club managements want to document their determination or demonstrate their ability to act in a crisis. In addition, the change of coach repeatedly serves as a means of appeasing the fans or the media, and sometimes it is purely an act of desperation. Because as a rule, the managing council, the board, or the sports director also come under criticism when the suitability of the coach is discussed.

Of course, it can be right to dismiss the coach but to look for the responsibility exclusively in the coach after four or five defeats (that is usually the time when the coach is questioned at the latest) is usually wrong. It is not the last match results that should be the deciding factor for a dismissal, but deeper causes. If a coach is not doing his job properly, if he is not sufficiently qualified for his tasks, or if an irreparable conflict has arisen with the team, these are more convincing reasons than mere results.

However, the best measure against a dismissal is, of course, success, although even trophies and titles do not protect against an involuntary change of coach. FC Bayern decided in 2013, when Jupp Heynckes won the triple, the biggest success in the club's history to date, to hand over the important post to Pep Guardiola. And when Heynckes won the Champions League with Real Madrid in 1998, he was curiously not allowed to continue either. It was years before the club subsequently won the Champions League again.

5.5   Does Money Score the Goals?

One of the most frequently quoted phrases from the stately trove of soccer wisdom stands for a major misunderstanding. "Money doesn't shoot goals," the German Otto Rehhagel (former national coach of the highly successfull Greek national team) said during his time as coach of the German club of Werder Bremen, and at the latest when he achieved the feat of becoming German champion in 1998 with 1. FC Kaiserslautern, which had just been promoted from the second division, the phrase suddenly meant: "You can also achieve great things with a team without super-expensive world stars and leave FC Bayern behind." In Munich, Rehhagel's aphorism was always taken as a provocation, and after the highly paid world star Arjen Robben scored twice in his first game for the record champions, Karl-Heinz Rummenigge, then chairman of the Munich board, defiantly said, "Money does shoot goals!".

The background of Rehhagel's word creation was quite different. At the time, he wanted to discourage his superiors in Bremen from hoarding large sums of money in their saving accounts; the reserves were to be spent on players. Actually, what he meant was, "Money in the bank account doesn't score goals." But the misinterpretation is much nicer, of course, because it raises one of the core questions of modern soccer management: can success be bought if only enough money is invested? (Fig. 5.5).

Fig. 5.5 Hoping to buy titles: Self-deprecating Manchester City fan. (© Simon Stacpoole/Offside/picture alliance)

The answer is yes; at least up to a certain point. That's what analyses of the correlations between budgets and league positions show, as another study of the four English leagues showed in 2020. The fact that a club with many players who have a high market value usually does better than clubs with fewer resources can be shown statistically. For example, a look at the final German Bundesliga table for the 2020/21 season shows that there was only one club in the top seven that unexpectedly broke into the phalanx of market value leaders in this sense. That was the team of Union Berlin in seventh place with a market value sum of 82 million euros calculated by the specialist portal *transfermarkt.de*. In the market value table, 1. FC Union was thus only in 17. place. This is a very unusual jump because the market value of the Berliners reached just two to three percent of the volume among the 18 clubs in the league in mid-2020 (then 3.82 billion euros as of July 1, 2020).

For Bayern Munich, the German subscription champion, a market value of 858 million was calculated that season. This was more than five times as much as ten years ago. By contrast, Dortmund, third in the points table, had a market value of around 628 million euros and Leipzig, second, around 574 million, so the two were quite close. The lowest sums were shown by Arminia Bielefeld with 56 million euros and, as mentioned, Union Berlin with around 82 million euros. Whereas Bielefeld managed to stay in the league (with difficulty in 15. place) and Union, yes this cannot be said often enough, achieved extraordinary success with seventh place. So, it's entirely possible to be relatively successful with more modest (and perhaps then more creative) means. The counter-example was Hertha BSC in 2021, the self-proclaimed "Big City Club" only finishing 14th despite a three-digit million sum provided by an investor. It seems that it is important to use investments in a planned manner in a longer-term development process to achieve sustainable success on a sound economic basis. Bayern Munich is the prime example of how this works.

The exact position in the table cannot be predicted at all, but the table region usually can. However, the market value of the upper echelons of the table makes them even more predictable than the lower echelons. But what is the explanation for the fuzziness of the prediction? What are the secrets behind surprises like the championship of 1. FC Kaiserslautern in 1998 or the seventh place of 1. FC Union in the 2020/21 season?

For one thing, chance could play a role, which is also involved in many goals (cf. Sect. 5.3), and chance is, after all, difficult to predict. In addition, the differences in market value between the smaller clubs in the second half of the table are nowhere near as great as at the top. In this respect, the smaller clubs are more similar than the teams in the top half of the table. It is therefore much more complicated to make predictions against the backdrop of market value in the lower tier or even in the second Bundesliga.

If a club with a 333-million-euro market value, say, increases its value by another 30 million, the effects are completely different from a scenario in which a small club like FC Augsburg suddenly competes with a team whose market value increases by 80 million, which would amount to a doubling. Bayern Munich could expect this ten-percent increase to have at best a homeopathic effect on its points tally. For FC Augsburg (if it could afford it), a considerably better season could be expected. The physics professor Andreas Heuer, who has already been mentioned several times, formulated this more or less like this more than ten years ago with a rule of thumb: a doubling of market value leads to about ten additional points in a season, so the market leaders have to invest an incredible amount more to achieve similar point gains than those who maintain comparatively inexpensive teams.

Some time ago, a German research team from Karlsruhe examined all matches from three seasons (2014/15–2016/17) in terms of numerous performance factors. For market value as a success factor, they determined that when a team's market value increases by one million euros, the probability of winning increases by 0.03% for a home team and 0.05% for an away team (at least in the three seasons analyzed). That doesn't sound very relevant. But let's play with the numbers for a moment, and assume for the 2020/21 season that Dortmunds BVB's market value would have been 858 million euros instead of 628 million euros (the same as Bayern), or 230 million euros more. Then, according to the calculation of the researchers from Karlsruhe, eight to eleven points more would have been possible. It would then have been close for Bayern, who were champions with 78 points, while BVB was third with 64 points.

It is therefore important to exploit one's own potential as optimally as possible through wise investments and measures that are commensurate with market value, such as the ambitious promotion of young talent and intelligent selection of coaches and players. Money is important, but not everything; it must be invested prudently.

5.6 Basking in Reflecting in the Glory of Others

Quite fundamentally, all people try to shape their self-presentation in such a way that a positive impression is created in their environment. We dress and behave differently at the opera than at a rock concert, and of course, visitors to a soccer stadium also feel such a need for self-presentation. They want to distinguish themselves as supporters of a particular club. It can seem quite strange to see one's boss, whom one usually knows only in a shirt and tie, at soccer on a Saturday wearing a jersey that is also precariously tight. However, such encounters are not uncommon in stadiums around the world.

The reason for this strange urge to disguise lies in two very basic needs: the attachment and the power motive. The connection motive is closely linked to identification, the connection with the team, and the club. People demonstrate that they belong and are part of a positively valued group in the hope that the positive group characteristics will rub off on them. The so-called *Die-Hard Fans,* who are particularly unconditionally attached to a club (and these are by no means exclusively Ultras, but go far beyond that)—we have already talked about this in other chapters—often wear their symbols all over their bodies and demonstrate their affiliation in everyday life as well. More discrete supporters are content with a scarf when visiting the stadium or a simple bumper sticker. What they have in common is the hope that other people will ascribe positive values of the club to them as well.

However, the methods used to demonstrate solidarity are by no means necessarily viewed positively by all fellow fans. For example, the actions of a violent supporter can lead to great recognition in a certain reference group, while the majority vehemently rejects fisticuffs on an opposing fan. In addition, belonging to a group can cause the greatest disapproval among rival factions. It is not necessarily to be expected that characteristics that Liverpool FC fans ascribe to themselves, and which for the most part still stem from the tradition of the working-class milieu, will also be viewed positively by Chelsea FC supporters from one of London's trendier neighborhoods.

All this is obvious, while the second important motive for publicly displaying one's attachment to a club is somewhat less obvious: it concerns the demonstration of power and influence. Often, stadium goers strive to show those around them that they represent something special. The opportunity to be admitted to VIP lounges in the context of sporting events is reserved only for selected individuals; certain people enjoy the feeling of being particularly important to the club, for example as a sponsor.

Such needs play a significant role in the marketing of expensive business and box seats, because people who are allowed to enter the VIP lounge show those around them that they have influence, are powerful, and usually are also wealthy. On the other hand, people only go to the atmospheric standing-room stands, where there is a lot of singing and often even more drinking, if they are particularly devoted fans. This is another way in which many supporters gain the recognition of others; they are something special.

Incidentally, the power motive is also relevant for that fraction of fans who seek violent confrontations. These people not only prove to their reference group that they are strong and fearless, they also show a broad public that they influence the media, which report on them in a prominent position. Thus, being associated with a soccer club can satisfy a wide variety of needs, and the game can be of interest to all groupings as a stage for self-expression: Here, people have the opportunity to bask in the glory of others.

Almost all visitors to soccer matches, *Die-Hard-Fans* or not, try to show their closeness to a particular club by symbolic means, they want to show the outside world: Look, I'm connected to success and you can trust me to be successful. This increases their self-esteem. This phenomenon is called *BIRGing*, "basking in reflected glory". The term comes initially from Robert Cialdini, who conducted a famous field study with his colleagues in 1976. He found that U.S. students, from the colleges he studied, often wore clothing that indicated their connection to the university (such as varsity sweaters) in their lectures and seminars if their own college's American football team had won the previous weekend. If, on the other hand, their team had lost, the university's T-shirts, sweaters, and caps with the corresponding symbols tended to be left at home.

In Germany, this could be observed very well during Jan Ullrich's first Tour de France victory in 1997, when vast quantities of yellow winners' jerseys went over the counter. Cialdini and his colleagues also noted that *BIRGing* and the connection to successful people can even be found in language: "We won," but "They lost." This phenomenon also appears regularly outside the fan scene and sports, as in 2005: the headline in the *Bild newspaper* when German Cardinal Ratzinger was elected Pope Benedict XVI read: "We are Pope."

Another ritual of *BIRGing* is taking a picture of oneself with a famous star, one's idol that one has met, or a team, either as a selfie or photographed by others. People from all walks of life (fans, journalists, scientists, and everyone else) like to do this as soon as the opportunity arises—and sometimes people look for the opportunity, for example, waiting for an idol in front of the hotel. Besides the souvenir and memory value, this way a symbolic connection with successful others can be shown.

In fact, *BIRGing* occurs in the most astonishing forms, as German Eckhard Freise has also experienced. In 2000, the professor of medieval history in Wuppertal was the first to win the million in the German version of *Who Wants to Be a Millionaire,* whereupon within a few days some 1,800 high school graduates in Wuppertal inquired how to get a place to study history there. Clearly, many prospective students here also felt the impulse to bask in someone else's glory.

Or here's a very recent example: The streaming service *Netflix* launched the impressive miniseries *"Queen's Gambit"* in 2020, an incredible global success with already more than 60 million viewers within a month of its release. The series is about the rise of Beth Harmon, a fictional chess player, to become a grandmaster. Apparently, many people wanted to *BIRG*, of course, with scarves and caps this did not work. What happened was that shortly after the broadcast, chess boards and other utensils needed for playing chess were sold out in many stores. The German newspaper *Frankfurter Allgemeine Zeitung* headlined this phenomenon on its website on 19.1.2021: "Chess is the new toilet paper", alluding to the sell-out of toilet paper a year earlier at the start of the pandemic.

But back to soccer: another form of this need can usually be observed around really important games. Prominent politicians love to be photographed with famous soccer players on such occasions. Who doesn't remember the pictures of former German Chancellor Angela Merkel cheering on the German team? Her joy was probably genuine, but most politicians are well aware that such appearances in a soccer context can boost their popularity and they hope to increase their election chances (Fig. 5.6).

Another aspect of the multi-layered need to associate one's own person with success, prominence, and importance becomes visible when spectators go to great lengths and spend a lot of money to witness very decisive matches or particularly rare sporting events live. Being an eyewitness to something unusual also boosts one's self-esteem. In the U.S., for example, it is often said that about a million people claim to have seen Joe Louis' second boxing match against Max Schmeling live in Madison Square Garden

Fig. 5.6 Shining in the glow of world star Kilian Mbappé: France's President Emmanuel Macron. (© Liewig Christian/ABACA/picture alliance)

in 1938. In reality, however, only 20,000 spectators fit into this New York event hall.

Thus, many people try to portray themselves as successful by presenting a common characteristic of the successful and of themselves in public—they thus engaged in *BIRGing*. This feature is often very ephemeral, sometimes used only briefly, and often represents only a symbol. The advantage of this type of ephemerality is that it allows for a quick turnaround should the successes fail to materialize. This mechanism includes the fact that "we" were victorious, while "they" lost.

In soccer, many people quickly disconnect after initial failures—not the *Die-Hard-Fans*, of course. Such supporters are called *Fair-Weather-Fans*, meaning that they break off the connection with the club or athlete who is no longer successful relatively quickly (which, by the way, also has a nice name: *CORFing*, "*Cutting off reflected failure*"). They look for a new club or another sport to indulge their need to bask in the glory of others. *Die-Hard-Fans*, however, remain loyal to their teams even after long lean periods and can be clearly distinguished from *Fair-Weather-Fans*.

5.7 Winning is Not Everything

In the mid-1990s, the former German internationally well-known coach Jupp Heynckes truly did not have a reputation for being a visionary. During that time, this great coach initiated Eintracht Frankfurt's long time decline by suspending stars Anthony Yeboah, Jay-Jay Okocha, and Maurizio Gaudino in a fit of "disciplinary fanaticism", due to not-following the team rules. And when Heynckes won the Champions League with Real Madrid in 1998, Spanish writer and Real fan Javier Marias wrote: "I don't find the coach Jupp Heynckes very clear-sighted." Today, no one speaks in such disparaging terms about the former soccer coach from Mönchengladbach, who also had smart things to say during his time in Frankfurt. For example, in 1995, when FIFA, the soccer world association, decided that in the future three points would be credited for victories instead of two, he announced with suspicion: "I prefer the old system because the games don't get any better with the new rule."

Heynckes was to be proved right, but the rule-makers saw it differently. "The goal of soccer is to score goals, we want to make soccer more attractive, and we are unanimous in our opinion that this is how it will work," said Joseph Blatter, FIFA's secretary general at the time, whose vice president

Guillermo Canedo even quipped, "We are preparing for the next millennium!" The basic idea was that teams would be more likely to push for a winning goal if the score was tied during the course of the game because the incentive to win a game is higher if three points are credited in the standings rather than just two. This would reduce the proportion of draws and increase the number of goals scored, was the economic argumentation. Numerous studies on the consequences of the changes, however, indicate that hardly anything has changed in the way the games are played.

In the German Bundesliga, 25.9% of games ended in a draw before the rule change (1963 to 1994/95); between 1995/1996 and the 2018/19 season (i.e., before the Corona season), the figure was 25.6%.

If we look at shorter periods and the number of goals overall, the conclusion is similar: the hoped-for effect failed to materialize at all in the Bundesliga.

And of course, it's worth looking beyond the borders, since the three-point rule was introduced worldwide. Maybe the Bundesliga is just a special case and it only doesn't work here. Clearly, the findings will vary depending on the league, but overall it can be said that the three-point rule did not lead to the expected effects, simply because the incentive of three points is still too low, and there should be more points, at least four. This was determined a few years ago in the most comprehensive and detailed study to date on this topic by a team of researchers from Münster, among them Bernd Strauss and Andreas Heuer, in which 20 years before and after the introduction of the three-point rule were examined in 24 leagues.

This study revealed all sorts of curious things about points awards and their effects. In Bulgaria, for example, for 3 seasons in the 1980s, if the score was 0:0 at the end of the match, neither team received a point, so such a draw was not "rewarded" with a point for both. This unusual rule had enormous effects: the number of goals increased massively during these three years, and draws were much less frequent. Nevertheless, this rule did not catch on, neither in Bulgaria nor was it taken up elsewhere.

Of course, the introduction of the three-point rule remains a major structural intervention in the complex system of soccer, with consequences that are difficult to assess. In groups of four, for example, as in the World and European Championships or the Champions League, the incentive to play for a draw could even increase because, with so few points to be awarded, it is always important to prevent the opponent who is threatening to pull away from you in the table from winning. And in the Bundesliga, it is sometimes also a matter of avoiding defeats, not only because the point won can be significant, but also because the media echo and the mood in the upcoming training week develop completely different facets after a defeat than after a draw.

This psychological principle, that avoiding losses is often more important than winning, ironically comes from a Nobel Prize-winning economist, Daniel Kahneman. Coaches are also typically not fired after a series of draws, but they are fired after a series of losses. It's better not to lose than not to win, or in other words, winning isn't everything, with or without the three-point rule.

5.8 Need for Explanation, Evasion, Self-Deception

Perhaps the most beautiful words about the feeling of powerlessness that soccer players sometimes experience on the pitch were formulated by the former German player Jürgen Wegmann, a striker who played for Bayern Munich and Borussia Dortmund in the 1980s and 1990s. With his "First we had no luck, and then bad luck came along," the former striker created a classic soccer aphorism that is often used as an example of the rhetorical helplessness of the professional guild. On closer inspection, however, the statement is not so silly at all. After all, there are always soccer matches whose course feels exactly the same for the players and fans of the losing team.

In any case, this is an attempt to find the cause, which players and coaches are forced to do week after week in the interview zones of this soccer world. And bad luck is a very popular explanation. Because with this argument, the pros can conveniently absolve themselves of some of the responsibility. However, many match progressions require other analyses, which is why very different explanatory strategies exist for victory or defeat: a team's special abilities, excellent training, injuries, the referee, the club's right or wrong purchasing policy, an individual mistake, the weather conditions, the condition of the pitch, the coach who has worn himself out, or vice versa, the coach to whom the fans attribute magical abilities, and much more (Fig. 5.7).

Basically, two dimensions of this type of explanatory concepts are distinguished. One level allows us to distinguish between causes that are internal and external to the actor, while the second level describes stability over time. Some causes are constant over time, while others are changeable (constant and variable). Combining both dimensions results in four variants:

Fig. 5.7 Communicator with patience: star coach Carlo Ancelotti. (© Benjamin Cremel/DPPI Media/picture alliance)

- Attempting to explain performance in terms of an athlete's skills is a stable attribution of cause within the actor, for example, when fans, the board, and the players explain the team's successes in terms of the coach's skills.
- Jürgen Wegmann's "theory" is rather a variable cause explanation outside the actor. The sentence "You also need game luck." is a modern variant of his famous statement. It is given for the moment, but at the next game, completely different explanations are used.
- One's own form on the day and the current physical condition is considered to be causal factors that lie within the player and are variable ("In this game, the team gave everything.").
- The task difficulty and the quality of the opponent is the outside and stable factor ("The opponent was too strong for us.").

It is interesting to note that these attributions of causes are by no means always based on rational considerations; rather, they follow certain patterns and distort reality. For example, to protect or increase self-esteem.

However, these patterns can change depending on whether athletes, fans, or coaches have just experienced success or failure. Positive events tend to be attributed to stable causes within the actor (such as one's ability) to increase and maintain one's self-esteem. In contrast, after failures, the naming of causes that lie outside the actor and are variable accumulates. In many cases, such biases are deliberately used for specific psychological effects.

Victories, for example, can be a balm for a footballer's soul, even though they can be explained primarily by the weakness of the opponent, who may also have been massively disadvantaged by the refereeTo strengthen the belief in one's own abilities, however, people also like to refer to their qualities after such games. And after bitter defeats, the danger of falling into a spiral of self-doubt is averted by referring to instances outside the player. To the referee, an accumulation of bad luck or the overpowering opponent, for example.

This kind of reality distortion, however, runs the risk of overlooking the true causes of failure. In reality, players, coaches and officials like to publicly formulate explanations that lie outside the player in order to analyze the real reasons behind closed doors. Sometimes these are weaknesses of individual players who should not be publicly exposed. It is not uncommon that reality is deliberately and consciously misrepresented or obscured with the help of excuses.

The mechanism of repeatedly explaining successes with one's own outstanding abilities can also be risky. Too much self-satisfaction makes people fed up and uncritical and tempts them to stop trying to improve. For such situations, it is good when admonishers from the club step forward to ground the players (and fans), which amounts to everyone taking a rational look at success. The mechanism of explaining one's own performance with causes that contain only half the truth is therefore dangerous on the one hand, but at the same time, it can be used for one's own purposes. And it can be observed not only among players, coaches and club executives.

In many cases, it has been found that sports journalists use their reporting to enhance or maintain their self-esteem, especially if they are closely associated with the team. For example, because the club the journalist is reporting on is his favorite club or the coach is his idol. Even then, successes tend to be explained in terms of being within the player and stable (i.e., having special skills). Legendary in this regard, Rolf "Töppi" Töpperwien, a former German TV-journalist, is the one who commented on the most German Bundesliga games with 1444 appearances and maintained a close relationship with the former German legendary coach Otto Rehhagel. When the longtime coach of Werder Bremen arrived at the airport with the team after winning the European Cup in 1992, Töpperwien said with pathos: "Now Otto Rehhagel is stepping onto German soil!" You can hardly get more hero worship than that.

5.9 "There Are Phases When It's Absolutely Clear that You, of All People, Score that Decisive Goal."

Fredi Bobic is fascinated by the magic of runs in soccer, which every player knows and loves (Fig. 5.8). Or, if it's a negative run, fears. As a striker, Bobic was able to study the mechanisms of this phenomenon particularly extensively. He scored 108 goals in 285 German Bundesliga games and ten goals in 37 international matches. In the mid-1990s, he formed the famous "magic triangle" with Krassimir Balakov and Giovane Elber at VfB Stuttgart. Later, as manager of Eintracht Frankfurt and Hertha BSC Berlin, he discovered very successful strikers such as Sébastien Haller, André Silva, or Luca Jovic.

Mr. Bobic, You Scored Five Goals in Your First Five Bundesliga Games. Did Your Career Start on a Roll Right Away?
I think so. Having a run like this is a great feeling you don't appreciate as a young player. You don't really experience it consciously, you don't think much about it, you're just happy. I think the happiness hormones contribute a lot to the amazing security that characterizes such phases.

Long runs of success or failure always have a touch of magic about them. Why does the ball first bounce off the inside post into the goal many games and then back into the field of play for weeks? Do you also puzzle?
Sometimes I have the feeling that things are predetermined, and I don't mean that in a religious way. There are phases when it's absolutely clear that

Fig. 5.8 Former goal scorer, now manager: Fredi Bobic. (© Frank Hoermann/SVEN SIMON/picture alliance)

you're going to score that decisive goal. Sometimes it almost seems as if a striker's run even affects the opponents, who suddenly make very strange mistakes.

And then at Some Point It's Over. How Does a Run End?
Footballers who succeed at almost everything tend to simply do a little less and less. No active player will ever admit that, but I can put it this way now: You're full of confidence and at some point, you're also convinced that things will continue like this as a matter of course. Then the run ends quite abruptly.

Are There Methods to Prolong the Good Phases?
Be more diligent. The trick is to really work with high concentration every day, even during the week. You have to remain resistant to the omnipresent adulation.

That Sounds like a Very Reflective Process. But One Hears Again and Again that Too Many Thoughts Tend to Do Harm.
I'm always fascinated by strikers who think a lot and still do the right thing. Like Lionel Messi. He has the ball, looks, and thinks about how he can put it in the goal in a particularly beautiful way. I was a striker who did that without much thought: Goal angle or grandstand roof. When things are going well, the ball ends up in the corner.

What Occupies a Striker During the Phases When the Ball Lands on the Roof of the Stands?What Occupies a Striker During the Phases When the Ball Lands on the Roof of the Stands?
As an older player, you don't have nearly as much self-doubt as you do as a young player. You know it will come back if you work hard enough. For young players, this situation is often very stressful. You read the bad reviews, and on TV they count how many minutes you didn't score. You're the focus and then you're running alone toward the goal and you actually already know that you're going to hit the post.

Besides the Run of a Striker, There Are Amazing Series of Successes of Teams. Do They Work According to the Same Mechanisms?
There are many parallels. This feeling of ease in everyday life and the knowledge that nothing can go wrong is very similar.

6

Red Light and Yellow Fever

© Abaca Christian Liewig 95978/dpa/picture alliance

The era in which German players' wives like Bianca Illgner or Gaby Schuster appeared as representatives of their husbands' interests is long gone. Nowadays, many wives and girlfriends of the stars present themselves primarily as influencers in social media. Their husbands' business is mostly handled by male specialists. And the days when footballers' secret excursions into the red-light district made headlines are also a thing of the past. The salacious and extremely popular tabloid topic of footballers' wives/footballers' affairs has fallen victim to the process of professionalization. Meanwhile, research has even been conducted into how sex the night before matches affects players' performance.

Without prejudging the answer to this question: the wrong jersey can have more fatal consequences than a night of love before the game. Red represents qualities such as aggressiveness, the will to dominate, and the desire to win. This is probably the reason why judges in sports such as taekwondo, boxing, or wrestling judge the wearers of red sportswear differently than their opponents in blue. This is precisely why Jürgen Klinsmann, as former German national coach, wanted to ensure that the national team would play in red in the future. Reason enough to take a look at the effects of jersey colors in soccer.

The associative link between the color red and aggressive behavior suggests that teams wearing red jerseys receive more yellow cards, something that no one has yet investigated. Instead, there are other mechanisms, as complex as they are surprising, by which the referees are guided in their yellow decisions.

6.1 The Audience Shows Yellow: The Impact of Spectators on Referee Decisions

Research into the specifics of home games has shown that home advantage diminishes as the professionalization of soccer progresses. Moreover, spectators tend to overestimate their influence on the course of soccer matches, although in reality, the players are less and less irritated by the crowd. Many professionals even find it particularly motivating to play in the hostile atmosphere of a foreign arena. These findings must be disillusioning for fans, but they could take comfort from another research result: with the referees, there is an important authority on the pitch that can be influenced by the audience, and quite often the referees do not even notice this.

This is shown by experiments conducted by British and German scientists on the effects of noise in the stadium on certain decisions. In one study, video was used to present 56 foul scenes to 20 referees from the German Football Association, half of which had resulted in a yellow card in real life.

Some scenes were played with loud crowd noise, others with a very muffled sound. Now each referee was to make his decision. As in the real game, that is, spontaneously and immediately. The remarkable result: in the scenes with a high noise level, the referees decided more often on a yellow card for the away team than in the identical situation without noise.

This result suggests that referees unconsciously interpret the reaction of the audience as an indication of the severity of a foul. The results of another study by the Cologne research group also fit in with this. Here, 1,530 first-division soccer matches were analyzed for the effects of crowd noise on referee decisions (measured as percentage utilization of spectator capacity, considering stadium construction). The analysis of these data also suggests a correlation between crowd behavior and the frequency of yellow cards against the away team (Fig. 6.1, 6.2).

Accordingly, visiting teams are punished with an average of around half a yellow card more per match than home teams. And in football-only arenas, the rate even increases to three-quarters of a yellow card per game. In stadiums with a running track (of which there were still a few during the study period), on the other hand, the rate is somewhat lower, presumably because the audience is further away from the referees due to the athletics facilities.

Fig. 6.1 Charged with emotion from the stands: players and referees. (© Hahne/Eibner-Pressefoto/picture alliance)

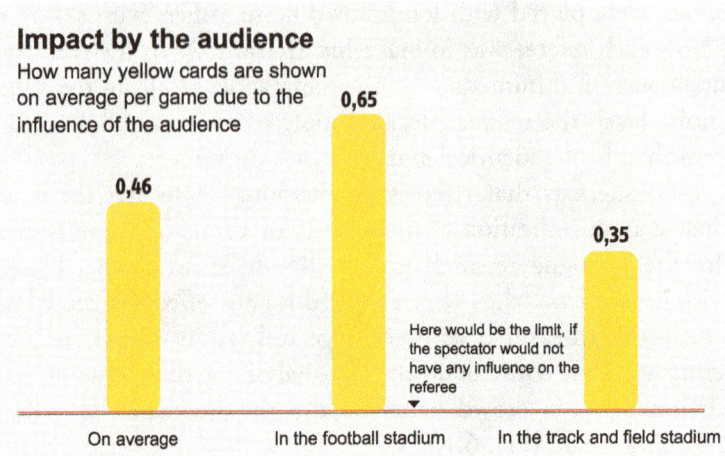

Fig. 6.2 The bars show how many additional yellow cards are shown on average per game due to the influence of the audience. The red line shows where the limit would be if the spectators did not influence the referee. In other words, if the home and away teams received the same number of yellow cards

Thus, in particular atmospheric soccer stadiums, more yellow warnings are issued against the away team.

It is even possible that a loud shout from the crowd after fouls has a greater influence on the game than all the cheering with which the fans otherwise support their club. However, whether these referee decisions actually result in a measurable scoring advantage for the home team as a result of the crowd's noise is unclear.

6.2 When the Referee Gives Yellow

One of soccer's oft-quoted legends is that referees who hand out yellow cards early in a game gain respect from the players. Teams are warned after such a time penalty and holding back, is the obvious logic on which the theory is based. Television commentators lovingly keep this myth alive, but the nature of soccer is not quite that simple (Fig. 6.3).

In reality, the opposite is more likely to be the case. If a referee already sanctions rule violations with warnings in the first quarter of an hour of a match, the likelihood increases that a particularly large number of players will see cards in the further course of the game. On average, about one yellow card more is shown in such duels, while the number of yellow cards

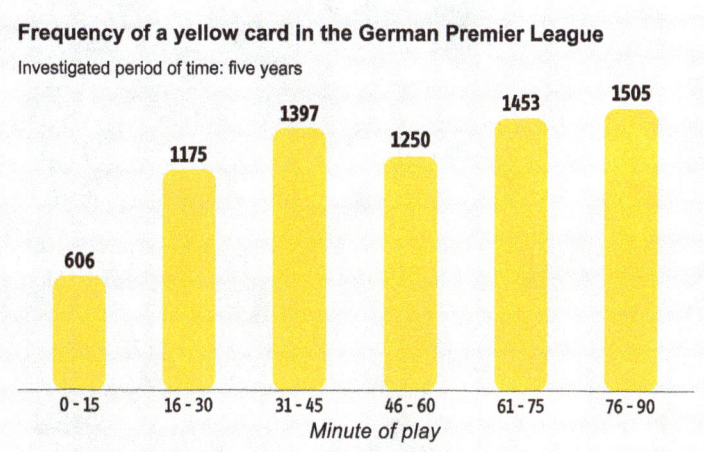

Fig. 6.3 Frequency of a yellow card in the Bundesliga. (This fig. was taken from Memmert, Strauss, & Theweleit, 2013, p.122)

decreases the longer the referee goes without this type of punishment in the first half.

This finding is astonishing at first glance, but its cause is easy to understand. If a yellow penalty is given early on, there is a danger that the range of offenses sanctioned with a card will be widened. A referee who gives yellow cards for comparatively harmless fouls during the first few minutes to take the harshness out of the game is forced to give the same penalty for later violations that are similarly rough. An effect that can have fatal consequences.

Driven by this mechanism, for example, the quarterfinal match between Portugal and the Netherlands at the 2006 World Cup really went off the rails. Referee Valentin Ivanov cautioned Mark van Bommel and Khalid Boulahrouz as early as the 2nd and 7th minutes, after which all fouls of equal (or greater) severity also had to be punished with yellow. Then, after a horrible foul on Cristiano Ronaldo was also only sanctioned with a yellow midway through the first half, the yellow card category was disproportionately broad. Both in terms of harshness and the insignificance of the foul.

This could only have been avoided if the violent foul on Ronaldo had been punished directly with red, thus shifting the entire scale (no yellow, yellow, red) downwards. Valentin Ivanov, however, used the scale he defined very broadly (yellow for weak and very hard fouls) consistently throughout the game, which in the end resulted in 16 yellow cards (including 4 yellow–red cards). In contrast, no player saw an outright red (Fig. 6.4).

Fig. 6.4 The escalated game: referee Valentin Ivanov struggles to keep order. (© sampics Photographie/sampics/augenklick/picture alliance)

Overly drastic penalties in the early stages are therefore more likely to escalate a match than to make players more conscientious about observing the limits of the rules that are pointed out early on. It's no wonder that referees are much less likely to resort to yellow cards in the first quarter of an hour than in the other quarter-hour blocks during a match. In addition to pragmatic reasons such as the fact that there are no replay fouls at the beginning, this finding must be explained as the result of calibration in the referees' judgment. This process could be demonstrated in a series of experiments conducted by the Cologne working group.

For example, referees judge foul scenes during the course of a game differently than when the duels were played to them as a single scene. In the first case, offenses at the beginning of a match were often not punished with a card in order to avoid the dilemma that the colleague from the Holland-Portugal match got into. As an isolated scene, on the other hand, the same situation was consistently punished by referees with a yellow.

In another experiment, referees were again presented with foul situations for evaluation, this time test subjects did not know in which phase of the game the scenes belonged. Half came from the first quarter of an hour, the other half from the section between the 60th and 75th minutes. In fact, the referees were more likely to deviate from the actual decisions (of the referees in the match) in their decisions for or against a yellow card if the scenes came from the first quarter of an hour. In contrast, the judgments for late-game scenes were very similar.

Accordingly, at the beginning of a game, in the best case scenario, a yardstick for yellow cards exists and is retrieved from memory. A yardstick for the game has yet to form and align. Referees thus develop a judgment scheme for their decisions at the beginning of a game and use it throughout the game, but this judgment scale must first be developed.

6.3 Sex Training Session

There may still be many soccer players who think the same way as the former German goalkeeper Toni Schumacher did when he wrote his best-selling and insider book "Anpfiff When it starts" in 1987. Buto professional today would express so openly the idea of a sexual all-round care for soccer players, who during many days of the year lodge as an all-male group in some team hotel. "If we're overcome by love lust, we should call in escorts to help us, (…) who are under medical supervision," said the former national goalkeeper. In any case, that would be "better than fleeing to the nearest town and catching foot-and-mouth disease in some whorehouse." Schumacher advocated "sex with only one residual risk: getting your eyes scratched out at home."

The Cologne veteran has not been heard from, nevertheless, visits to brothels by professional soccer players have become rare. The risk of being photographed by someone on a mobile phone camera and publicly exposed is far too great. However, there are always stories about scantily clad female visitors in hotel rooms, and when such a case comes to light, it's not just a question of how the female partners at home will react. Among fans, but also among players and coaches, there is always a discussion about whether sex before the game has a positive or negative effect on the competition.

To find out, it is useful to differentiate the physical and psychological sides of the sexual act. There are not many studies on the physiological effects of sex before a match, but there are some with a fairly solid body of knowledge. If the sexual activity does not take place just before the match, it is harmless from the physical side. The loss of calories is limited (200–300 cal depending on the intensity) and can easily be compensated by a cereal bar. Continuous fatigue is not a concern for well-trained athletes—the pre-game warm-up alone is probably more strenuous. In one study, married athletes were asked to perform standardized strength tasks each morning a few days apart. However, they were asked to spend the nights before differently. On the first night, the athletes had domestic sex, which was the experimental condition. In contrast, in the control condition, they did not engage in sexual activity before performing the strength tasks and experienced a quiet night. The next morning's performance was identical, regardless of whether or not they had previously copulated.

But even in more recent studies in which endurance tasks, such as intensive runs on a treadmill, were completed, there was no difference. In a particularly carefully conducted experiment over a longer period with six different tasks and parameters, there were also no differences between the groups with and without sexual activity within a period of 24 h before the exercise. Maximum oxygen uptake, reaction times, balancing results, or measured strength parameters remained unaffected by sexual activity.

Not even the sometimes expressed fear, with the exit of the ejaculate aggressiveness, would be lost due to the loss of testosterone, is tenable. More than the sexual act itself, the accompanying circumstances probably influence the physical condition. If alcohol is involved, smoking, lack of sleep, or muscular tension, performance may indeed suffer. Otherwise, neither negative nor positive effects are expected.

The psychological consequences of sex before a soccer match, on the other hand, have not yet been systematically studied, so we can only speculate about such effects. But it can be assumed that different effects may result depending on the athlete's personality and state of mind. For athletes, it is important to reach the optimal activation level in competition to develop the available performance potential. All body systems should be in a state of competition: the athlete is not tired, but he is also not anxious, his brain activities are oriented to the competition, and his heart is not racing. Too little activation is bad, but so is too much. Exactly where the individual level lies for each athlete, however, varies widely.

For some footballers, doing certain activating things before a match will therefore be beneficial to performance, and sex could certainly be one of them. However, it would then be important that the act does not lead to negative feelings, such as a guilty conscience toward the partner or the fear that intimate details will become public. Such emotions can have a negative effect on performance. Whereas similar effects cannot be ruled out in other activities; after all, watching a horror movie or reading an exciting book can also lead to bad feelings and a sleepless night.

From this point of view, it is quite possible that pre-match sex can have a performance-enhancing effect if it is embedded in professional competition preparation tailored to the athlete and his or her psychological status before the competition. This realization is certainly one of the reasons why many teams now define specific days before and during major tournaments when players' girlfriends and wives are allowed to come to the hotel (Fig. 6.5). And if the couples do not have sex during these hours, the soccer players still have another opportunity to act out sexual needs: the game.

At least this is suggested by the reflections formulated by the well-known German philosopher Gunter Gebauer and football fan in his "Poetics of Football". "The erotic and sexual charge of the game of soccer has sunk so deeply into the self-image of masculinity that the (male) lovers do not even notice it. They are entirely under the effect of their imaginations," writes Germany's leading sports philosopher. "For them, the goal line is not just a chalk line on the turf, but an extraordinarily sensitive boundary that, depending on which side you are on, triggers the desire to violate it, to penetrate it, or, conversely, to defend it, to protect it, to preserve its integrity. The ball in

Fig. 6.5 Now present at all tournaments: partners of national players like Cathy Hummels at the 2016 European Championship with Mats. (© Arne Dedert/dpa/picture alliance)

the net is a triumphant image, it wriggles, it strikes, it is in the holy of holies." It sounds like a successful soccer game can certainly satisfy sexual needs.

Incidentally, Toni Schumacher felt very similarly during the many hotel nights during the big tournaments: "I put a cheese cover over my love life during this time and think firmly of my goal: to become world champion, the best goalkeeper in the world. There's no time for pleasure and excitement."

6.4 The Winner Wears Red?

Most FC Schalke 04, a traditional German club supporters can think of a number of reasons why their favorite club has been trying in vain to win the title of German champion since 1958. Coaches, referees, and the soccer god are among the prime suspects in the search for those responsible for the continued failure. The thought that the shirt color might play a role, on the other hand, hardly crosses anyone's mind when investigating the causes. Schalke fans love their royal blue. But it is striking that since the introduction of the German Premier league, the Bundesliga in 1963, only 1 team with blue shirts has been able to win the championship trophy (namely the Munich Lions in 1965/1966).

One of the reasons for this amazing phenomenon is certainly the fact that FC Bayern Munich does not wear blue. But sports scientists have long been researching whether certain jersey colors are associated with better performance. Mostly the color red is in the center, from which a quite special signal effect seems to proceed, as evolution biology found out. In relationship situations, the color red is associated with eroticism and attractiveness; in dangerous situations, red is a warning to be careful; and in conflicts, the red color signals aggression, the will to dominate, and the desire to win. In the latter case, these are things that are important in sporting competition and can thus influence performance positively, but also negatively under certain circumstances.

The connection between athletic success and jersey colors had already been described by the English evolutionary biologists Russell Hill and Robert Barton in a statistical analysis that attracted worldwide attention and was published in the journal *Nature in* 2005. The two researchers found out that martial artists (boxers, wrestlers, and Taekwondo fighters) had an advantage, especially in close fights during the Olympic Games 2004 in Athens, if they competed in a red jersey and not in a blue one. It is important to know that the athletes in these martial arts only wear red or blue jerseys, which are drawn before the fight (Fig. 6.6).

As is common in science, there was intense debate around the results and how to explain them. Is it the fighters themselves who feel more motivated

Fig. 6.6 Red advantage: Taekwondo fighters are more likely to win if they are assigned the right color. (© Zac Goodwin/empics/picture alliance)

and aggressive in red? Does the cause lie with the opponents in blue, who look at a fighter dressed in red and then act more despondently? Or does the red advantage go back to the judges and their judgment bias and favoritism of red fighters? By the way, this last finding, which a team from Münster, Germany determined in a taekwondo study in 2008, is confirmed in a current study. According to this, the red advantage in taekwondo disappeared on the international stage the moment the world federation introduced electronic scoring a few years ago. In this respect, this is a good example of how digital support systems can be used to eliminate possible distortions of judgment by fighters and referees—but more on this in Sect. 7.4).

In pure combat sports, therefore, advantages can be derived for the red shirt carriers, at least if there are no electronic aids. However, in soccer as a complex sport with many components, a negative effect with a negative attribution for red as a hardness signal could also result, or positive and negative effects could be mixed.

Incidentally, the then German national coach Jürgen Klinsmann had also heard of the 2005 study by Hill and Barton and introduced the red shirt as an alternate jersey for the German national team. Shortly before the 2006 World Cup, he even advocated a red home jersey (switching from white into red).

But he scrapped this plan again after an outcry of indignation was heard. Who knows, maybe Germany would have been world champion 2006 (and not third) in a red jersey, but it's not very likely if you look at the latest analyses.

In 2008 a British study has been published, which seemed to show that there was a red advantage in the three English leagues. For this, Hill, Barton, and colleagues analyzed the supposed red advantage for soccer matches between 1946 and 2003 in the top three English soccer leagues, and they concluded that the advantage is extremely small at best. Teams wearing red jerseys won about 53 percent of their home games, while wearers of blue jerseys won only 51 percent of the time. Most impressive, however, was the finding that 60 percent of English champions wore a red jersey, but this has a lot to do with the fact that the main color of Arsenal FC, Manchester United, and Liverpool FC, three of the biggest clubs, is red.

For a long time, not even the small color advantages from the English league could be proven for the German elite league, and there were no clear results on possible influences of the jersey color on the results in the Bundesliga. The same applies, by the way, to the question of whether jersey colors (white or red) have an effect on the success of penalty takers. Result: no red advantage.

In a new large-scale study by researchers from Cologne and the USA, the question was put to the test once again for soccer. The authors examined the English league with more data and over longer periods. They also incorporated results from six other European leagues between 1999 and 2019, including the German Bundesliga (and Portugal, Spain, the Netherlands, France, and Italy). No differences in performance regarding the color of the jersey can be detected, neither in England nor in the other six leagues, in any of the leagues studied.

Fans can therefore continue to hope that at some point a team in a blue jersey will become champion again.

6.5 "A Soccer Match is like a Painting."

Urs Meier from Switzerland was one of the best referees in the world for many years before ending his career in 2011. He refereed the World Cup semifinal between Germany and South Korea in 2002 and the Champions League final in the same year, where he also refereed several semifinal matches. Today, he is one of the brightest experts among former referees because he not only has the rules in mind but also the people on the pitch (Fig. 6.7).

Fig. 6.7 Former world-class referee Urs Meier. (© Stephan Persch/picture alliance)

Mr. Meier, Unlike Their Colleagues in Many Other Sports, Referees in Soccer Have a Great Deal of Freedom to Implement the Rules Themselves. Does that Make Sense?

There are already places where uniformity is needed. When it comes to must fouls, must yellow cards, or must red cards, all referees should make the same decisions. On the other hand, match referees have their own personalities, and that personality plays a role in their work. Every game has its own character; I like to say that a soccer game is like a painting that sometimes needs a little more yellow, sometimes more red, and sometimes nothing at all. Good referees sense what kind of game they are officiating.

However, the gray areas in the rules often lead to conflicts and to the feeling among players, coaches, and fans that they have been treated unfairly. Time and again, decisions are made one way and another in almost identical situations.

Whenever we are in the gray area, the referee's job is to put his own touch in there. Some referees tend to be safety types, who don't even try to run a game properly because they know that once they've really galloped off with the 22 horses on the field, they'll lose control. And some referees can let the horses run and catch them again several times in one game. That is a question of quality and personality.

How Does the Search for the Right Line Work for Soccer Games, Which Can Develop Very Differently?

What I like best are referees who can read the teams, and I maintain: there's still a lot of room for improvement in refereeing at this point. I loved going into the teams' dressing rooms an hour before the games to feel what was going on there: what are the players like? What's happening in that team?

How are they sitting there? How are they interacting with each other? You see the coaches, I loved that. After this ritual, I often knew exactly what to expect on the pitch.

There is a study that shows that yellow cards in the early stages of a game often lead to a particularly large number of cards being shown later on. Does it make sense to use cautions sparingly at the start of the game?
No, that's the wrong approach. The players want one thing above all at the beginning: they want to know whether the referee is capable of managing the game or not. A foul happens, and every foul has a shade, let's take a scale from one to ten: ten is brutal and straight red, eight is yellow, seven is just before yellow, and so on. Now a foul happens, that's a three, and then there has to be a reaction like a three: a calm whistle, foul, free kick, done. Then comes a foul in category six then the whistle must sound differently and perhaps there must also be a speech. With a seven, it's even clearer: now you're really at the very edge, so there has to be some gesticulation. And with yellow, it's yellow. The players want to feel that. And when they feel that he's at the right level, then that gives them a sense of security, then the players know: three is three, six is six, and eight is yellow. Then it's relatively easy to manage a game. Game management means creating clarity.

However, Handball Situations Remain Particularly Difficult Even for Many Clearly Whistling Referees. No One Seems to Be Able to Say Definitively What is a Hand and What is not.
This has a lot to do with training and understanding the game. Many referees lack the feeling for what normal hand and arm movements are in dynamic processes. They don't feel this because they may not have played soccer themselves, because they've never gone into a sidetrack, because they've never turned away from a shot from close range. These are exactly the areas that should be practiced with the referees in training. They need to bump into an opponent in the air in a header duel and pay attention to what their hands do then. Many don't even know what happens to the bodies in the dynamics of the game. And then the video assistant comes in and shows these freeze frames or excerpts that don't even show the whole movement. That can't work.

Why Do Federations Keep Changing the Interpretation Guidelines When It Comes to Handball, Which Can Differ from Season to Season, from Country to Country, and from Competition to Competition?
This is a big problem and is due to the failure of FIFA and the IFAB rules board to provide clarity. Take the idea of the Germans whistling handball

for a few years if the arm was used to "increase the body area". This all came from people who have no understanding of the body, and who don't want to trust referees to answer the only two relevant questions.

What Are These Questions?
Does a player play hand with intention? Is his movement natural or unnatural? If the arm just falls, that's part of the body. It's unnatural if I have to put the arm behind the body. This has nothing to do with the increase in the body surface area. Only if referees can't be trusted to read the game and the movements, such auxiliary constructions have to be introduced, like the increase of the body area or the idea to show fewer yellow cards at the beginning. Better would be good training.

7

Perception and Deception

© David Klein/ZUMAPRESS.com/picture alliance

Slow motion is a wonderful thing. Soccer has become such a fast-paced game that many things can hardly be seen clearly by the naked eye. For the spectators but also the referees. After years of debate, this insight has led to the most important decisions of the referees in many professional leagues being reviewed and, if necessary, corrected by video assistant referees.

Studies show impressively that it is simply impossible to evaluate all situations correctly without such aids. To be at least almost always right, abilities would be necessary that neither the human sensory organs nor the brain areas that process information can afford. Perception takes place not only through the eyes and the ears but also through the brain and can be quite distorted from time to time.

Such deceptive maneuvers of the brain sometimes lead to bizarre mishaps in players, and of course, this knowledge can be used deliberately to throw opponents off the scent. When an assistant referee hastily raises the flag or a striker overlooks a completely free teammate, there are often deceptions involved that no one can be blamed for. With the help of this knowledge, goalkeepers sometimes even manage to tempt penalty-takers to shoot in a certain corner.

7.1 How to Make the Goalkeeper a Penalty Killer

For decades, the goalkeepers of this world have been puzzling over how their chances can be improved when a shooter challenges them to a penalty kick duel. Some goalkeepers create extensive databases to find out which opponent prefers to shoot where, and at some point, it was even investigated how the color of the shirt affects the chances of success. But there is a surprisingly effective and very simple trick, as sports scientists from Paderborn and Cologne have discovered.

Experiments have shown that it is possible to induce the shooter to shoot into a certain corner. Specifically, the effects of gestures and the keeper's position in the goal on the penalty taker were studied. Experienced soccer players and soccer novices each took 54 penalties and were confronted with different starting positions and behaviors of the goalkeeper. The results are remarkable.

Even a small shift of the goalkeeper of about ten centimeters to the left or right, which is not consciously perceived by the shooter, causes novice soccer players to aim into the supposedly open corner in three out of four cases (75%). This effect is even more pronounced in players who have been actively playing soccer for years; they choose the corner offered in four out of five cases (80%). The perception of gaps is better trained in these subjects. The temptation to shoot at the slightly open side is reinforced if the goalkeeper also points with his hand to the corresponding corner (Fig. 7.1).

7 Perception and Deception

Goalkeepers can therefore manipulate the shooter through their behavior in such a way that at least the probability of a penalty being held increases. The recommendation to the goalkeeper could be something like: "Offer the shooter a corner by standing about 10 cm from the center on one side of the goal, jump off in time, and you'll hold almost every shot."

However, this trick is only one of many promising goalkeeper strategies for the penalty kick situation. For example, analysis of numerous penalty kicks has shown that the longer a shooter has to wait to take the shot, the more likely he is to miss. For the goalkeeper, this means that his chances improve if he manages to delay the shot to leave the shooter in his stressful situation for as long as possible (Fig. 7.2).

In addition, if goalkeepers succeed in attracting the attention of the shooter, for example by gesticulating, the likelihood that the shooter will shoot the ball close to the body in the goal increases. People unconsciously

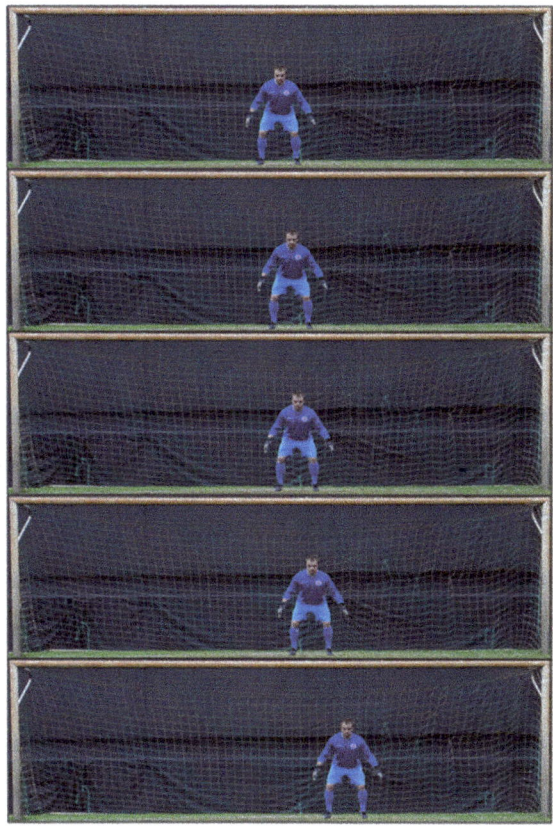

Fig. 7.1 Goalkeeper moves slightly away from the center of the goal

Fig. 7.2 Thanks to a note full of secret knowledge, successful in the penalty shoot-out of the 2006 World Cup quarterfinal against Argentina: German goalkeeper Jens Lehmann. (© Michael Hanschke/dpa/picture-alliance)

direct their motor actions toward moving objects. Helpfully, there is also an important key signal that can be used to identify which corner of the goal the shooter is aiming for. The biomechanics of the human body means that in most cases the tip of the foot of the supporting leg indicates the direction in which the shooter is aiming.

Sometimes, however, it is simply advisable to remain standing in the middle of the goal. Basically, goalkeepers always need to act, that is, to be active. They feel that simply standing still is passive. They often fear that staying in the middle of the goal will give spectators, journalists, coaches, and teammates the impression that they are not very committed or "sporty". Statistically, however, more and more players shoot into the middle of the goal. The strategy of standing still is therefore simply a third option that the goalkeeper should take to heart from time to time, even if it is difficult for him psychologically.

And most recently, an evaluation of many penalty kicks has shown that right-footed players, from their perspective, tend to shoot into the left corner of the goal, and left-footed players, conversely, into the right corner of the goal.

7.2 The Blind Spot

It is truly not a laudable place that the almost forgotten attacker Youssef Mokhtari takes in the collective memory of the supporters of German Club 1. FC Köln (Cologne). The German-Moroccan was under contract with this team for less than a full year, and that has a lot to do with that memorable 71. minute in a match against a rival from the neighborhood, FC Schalke 04 in the fall of 2005. The Cologne team, once again acutely threatened by the outbreak of a major crisis, was leading 2:1 when Mokhtari stormed alone toward the Gelsenkirchen goal. Matthias Scherz and Lukas Podolski were running along, a simple cross pass and the game would have been almost certainly decided. But the attacker refrained from making the pass, missed the goal, and created a scene that many observers retrospectively declared the key moment of the entire season.

Schalke 04 scored the equalizer, the Cologne team lost the remaining games until the winter break, coach Uwe Rapolder was fired, manager Andreas Rettig resigned, and a few months later the club was relegated. And in the end, almost everyone in Cologne agreed that everything would have been different if Mokhtari had played across.

Coach Rapolder was so incensed that afternoon that he immediately took his player off the field and after the game told him to write an essay on altruism, egoism, and social skills. Rapolder later explained that he had only wanted to make a joke, but Mokhtari wrote the text. "I wanted to do everything right and became the dork," the player said, summing up his state of mind and claiming that he had not seen his teammates. "If it had been like that, of course, I would have played. Anyone who knows me well knows that I'm not a selfish person." But, of course, no one believed him.

However, it is possible that the cause of Mokhtari's failure lies in a phenomenon called inattentional blindness: blindness due to inattention. Only when attention is focused on a specific area the information available in the field of vision is consciously absorbed and processed. And it seems that very specific attentional processes are required for this.

Experiments have shown that an unexpected object is often simply overlooked when attention turns to another object. In Mokhtari's case, for example, the goalkeeper and the corner of the goal he wanted to hit. It even happens that an unexpected object is overlooked when it moves right through the center of the visual field of view, as the two U.S. psychologists Christopher Chabris and Daniel Simons showed in their famous gorilla experiment: they had a man in a gorilla costume run through a basketball game and presented the videotaped scene to 200 test subjects. The subjects were given the task of counting the passes. And in fact, more than half of the test participants did not notice the gorilla at all. Although he was moving through the middle of the field (Fig. 7.3).

Fig. 7.3 Imposing yet invisible: the gorilla in the famous "Selective Attention Test". (© Malte Krudewig/dpa/picture alliance)

Many viewers are apparently so intensely occupied with their pass-counting task that no more attention capacities are available for perceiving unexpected things. If you search *YouTube* under the term combination "Gorilla Experiment Basketball", you will find a small video that you can show to a friend or colleague. With the task of counting the passes of one team. Most likely, the friend will simply overlook the gorilla, who also stops in the middle of the picture and drums his fists on his chest.

In soccer, the discovery of the phenomenon led to the realization that attention can be specifically controlled by certain cues from coaches. Experiments on tactical decision behavior by the Cologne research group showed that the focus of attention can be specifically influenced by the simplest variation of instructions and that this has a direct impact on the quality of tactical performance. With a large attentional focus, unexpected and possibly better solution variants can be perceived, used, and learned.

By the way, there are other real-life situations in which this form of blindness due to inattention can occur with dramatic consequences. While talking on the phone in the car, we overlook children who want to cross the street. And in court, it is not uncommon for two witnesses to disagree about what objects were at the scene of an accident—even though both were present and claimed to have observed the accident closely.

7.3   Referee Offside

Wrong decisions by referees make soccer "human and therefore emotional," Joseph Blatter liked to argue during his tenure as president of FIFA, the world soccer governing body when the soccer world was once again discussing a particularly momentous faux pas by a referee. Again and again, experts, players, coaches, and fans called for technical evidence for the referees, but Blatter believed that the introduction of video evidence, and even the use of goal-line technology, would "strip the game of its human face."

In the meantime, FIFA has changed its stance. The question of whether a ball was in the goal or not is no longer disputed at all, and the introduction of the Video Assistant Referee (VAR) has also meant that incorrect decisions on offside situations have almost disappeared. Plans by legendary coach Arséne Wenger, who coached the English Club Arsenal FC for a long time and then became director of global soccer development at FIFA, even envisage completely automating the determination of offside situations. In any case, the introduction of technical evidence was overdue, especially in offside matters.

Previously, the proportion of offside errors in games at major tournaments such as the World or European Championships was estimated at between 10 to 25%, and on closer inspection, this is not surprising to anyone. After all, the Cologne working group was able to prove that only 72% of offside decisions are correct if the angle of vision of the linesman to the passer and passer-receiver is less than 35°. The error rate becomes even more dramatic when the angle of vision increases to more than 35° (for a long ball to the striker near the offside line), in which case the decision is even tantamount to a coin toss (the error rate is 42%). This cannot be in the interest of fairness in soccer. Since the vast majority of the world's competitions in smaller soccer nations and at the amateur level will continue to have to do without VAR, it is worth taking a look at the causes of the many incorrect offside decisions.

To correctly recognize an offside position, the assistant referees on the sidelines must have several moving objects in view at the same time. Objects that are also moving relative to each other. The assistant with the flag tries to keep an eye on the player with the ball, the ball itself, the defenders, and the addressee (or sometimes even several possible addressees) for the pass. Studies show that the eye needs 130 to 160 ms at a time to switch back and forth between two objects; a sprinting player can cover more than a meter in that time.

In addition, one-half of the pitch covers a large area, so that the assistant can only perceive many actions peripherally. When a long pass is played, it will almost always be difficult for him to clearly see whether an attacker is offside or not at the moment the ball is passed. Basically, there are currently two common theories on the causes of errors in offside decisions.

One explanation attributes certain errors in detecting the offside position to the fact that people generally tend to see a moving object not where it actually is, but a bit further ahead in space, this is shown by psychological experiments (Fig. 7.4).

This effect can be experienced impressively on the Internet at http://www.youtube.com/watch?v=DUBM-GG0gAk. And according to the second theory, incorrect offside decisions are caused by the linesman not standing exactly on the offside line. In this case, his perspective is distorted because his "perceived offside line" does not correspond to the actual one (Fig. 7.5).

So far, it is not entirely clear to which of these two explanations incorrect offside decisions are actually attributable; both probably play a role. What is known, however, is that assistant referees who are particularly good at peripherally perceiving stimuli that are far apart (the passer, the last player in the defense, and the player who may be offside) have an advantage in their search for the correct decision. However, the high tempo, large spaces of the pitch, and complexity of the game make truly informed decisions almost impossible in some situations. Especially since there are other factors influencing offside decisions in soccer.

Contrary to what one might think, assistant referees, for example, made fewer errors when they were farther away from the field and thus had a more

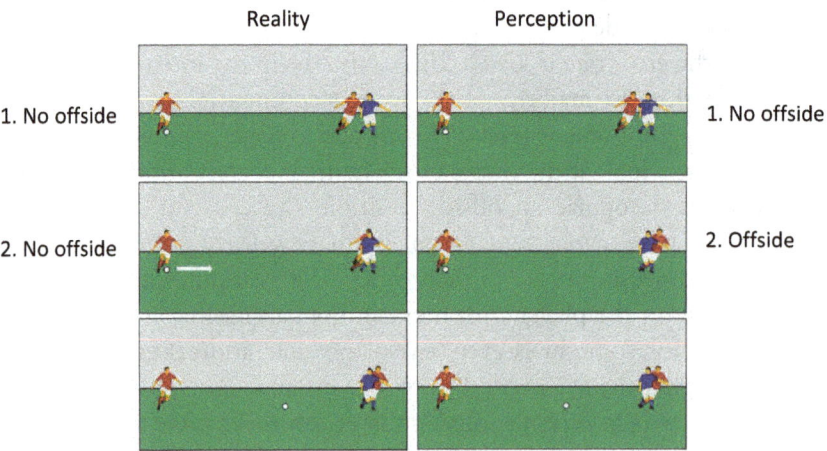

Fig. 7.4 The assistants tend to see moving objects (here the striker in red) not where they actually are (reality), but a bit further ahead in space (perception)

Fig. 7.5 Depending on whether the assistant referee is standing exactly on the actual offside line or not, he incorrectly decides on offside (top) or correctly on no offside (bottom)

advantageous (smaller) viewing angle to the action. This pattern holds even when we consider individual differences in the attention window (i.e., the ability to perceive multiple objects simultaneously) of referees. The position of linesmen directly on the pitch, with a correspondingly smaller viewing angle, may even explain fan complaints in some situations: It is actually easier for spectators further away from the pitch to make the correct offside decision because they sometimes look at the game from a more favorable angle.

Furthermore, the contrast of the jerseys is relevant for the frequency of offside judgments in soccer, as the Dortmund and Cologne working group found out. The assistants on the line raise their flags more often when strikers wearing Schalke 04 jerseys (blue jerseys, white shorts) move along the offside line than in comparable situations with strikers wearing Borussia Dortmund jerseys (yellow jerseys, black shorts). The reason for this could be that the brightness contrast between the figure and the background is higher for the Schalke players. In fact, when analyzing all German Bundesliga duels between these clubs between 2013 and 2021, players from the German team Schalke 04 were (supposedly) offside more often than their colleagues from BVB-team, the greatest rival from Dortmund. And in these clubs' matches against all other teams in the German Bundesliga during the 2019/2020 season, there were also more whistled offside decisions against Schalke 04 and fewer for Borussia Dortmund. Taken together, the results suggest that more offside judgments are made against teams with higher visual conspicuity, i.e., with greater figure-background contrast.

7.4 The VAR—Cursed Be Justice

From today's perspective, a debate that took place before the introduction of the video assistant referee (VAR) in professional soccer seems downright absurd. Skeptics feared an increasing lack of discussion if a technology helped to ensure that the referees always made the correct decision at the end of a thorough investigation process. Moreover, traditionalists worried that emotions so significant to the fascination of the sport, such as anger over unjustly suffered defeats or joy over completely undeserved successes, might suddenly disappear. What a colossal mistake! Since the introduction of VAR in the year—initially in 2017 on a trial basis in the German premier league and other competitions, for example, and from 2018 in the globally applicable set of rules—there has been more dispute and debate than ever about the work of the referees. Many fans have the feeling that things are even more unfair than before, but this can easily be refuted.

A large study by Werner Helsen's team at the Belgian Katholieke Universiteit Leuven, which examined 3,477 games, showed that, although not all, a large number of incorrect decisions could be corrected (Fig. 7.6). In total, the video assistants intervened 1,251 times during the analyzed matches in Germany, Italy, England, Portugal, Australia, and the USA. The experts in front of the screens were able to correct mistakes made by their colleagues on the pitch 864 times—an enormous gain in terms of fairness. In addition, there were 184 clearly correct decisions that were thoroughly reviewed and confirmed, i.e. remained correct. Unfortunately, 29 correct

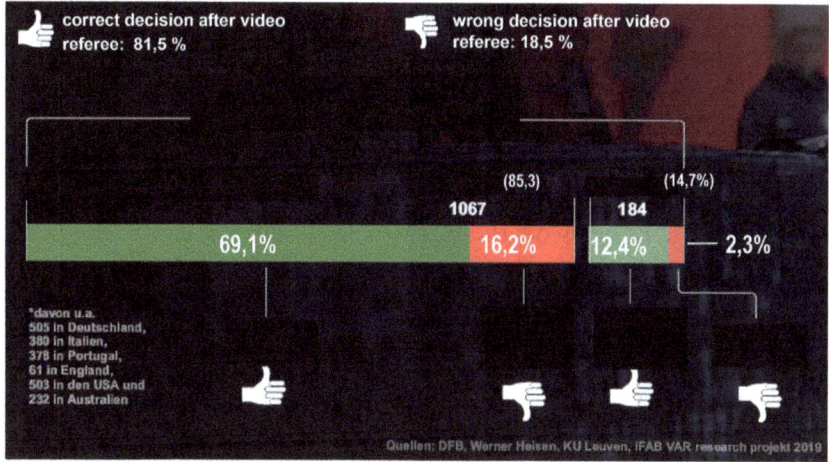

Fig. 7.6 Statistics of worldwide VAR decisions

decisions by the referee on the field were also corrected by the final VAR review; these must therefore be classified as incorrect.

However, these evaluations contain the potential for debate, because even the best experts sometimes argue about when a bad decision is clear enough for VAR intervention and when a decision can just about be defended. Jochen Drees, who manages the VAR project of the German Football Association (DFB), once said a wise phrase: "The video assistant is not there to turn a bad decision into a better one, but only to enable referees to review and assess the images on the monitor in the review area if necessary in the event of clear and obvious misjudgments."

It is precisely this restraint that is often very difficult for referee teams. Even with scientific analyses, there is a danger of categorizing bad but just defensible decisions that are corrected as correct interventions. Attempts to adapt the handball rule to facilitate its implementation using TV images also caused a lot of trouble. The attempt to create clarity by using auxiliary linguistic constructions such as "increasing the body area" or "the hand is above the shoulder" failed miserably.

In the meantime, the question of intention is back in focus: there are now "two criteria in which a handball in soccer by a defender is punishable," the DFB announced on its homepage in the summer of 2021: "First, if a player brings his hand or arm to the ball with an intentional movement. Or secondly: If the player by his body posture pursues the intention to stop the ball." Many referees still find it difficult to implement these rules. But it is not only the scope for interpretation that annoys many spectators; the period of uncertainty during which the reviews are underway is perceived as at least as disturbing.

In a study of 2,195 official matches in 13 countries, VAR analyzed 9,732 reviews for potential match-fixing incidents; a review was completed in an average of 22 s. Reviews on the pitch took an average of 62 s (N = 534); VAR-only reviews (N = 261), i.e., not reported back to the ref, took assistants 15 s. Prediction odds of making the correct decision after a VAR intervention were significantly higher than for the original referee decision, with accuracy increasing from 92 to 98%.

And yet there is a great deal of disagreement about whether the introduction of the technology was sensible and right. The opinion of the professionals is just as heterogeneous as the attitude of the public toward technology. Some supporters welcome the gain in objective justice, while others are annoyed by the many VAR interruptions or filled with the subjective feeling that the hope for more justice has not been fulfilled. However, according to the survey conducted by Werner Helsen's working group, a majority of referees, players, and coaches believe that the professional and moral standards of the sport have improved as a result of the introduction of the technology. Referees expressed the most positive views, followed by coaches and then players. In addition to the gain in fairness in individual players, the prospect that the application practice will reveal weaknesses in the rulebook, such as precision deficiencies in the soccer handball rule, and lead to improvements in the long term is also welcomed.

The performance of the VARs, on the other hand, is problematic, as they repeatedly make mistakes. If the referee on the pitch has doubts about the judgments of his colleague in front of the screen, he feels compelled to look at the images again in the review area, which can lead to lengthy stoppages in play. A confident referee of high quality might tend to reject any review of his own in the review area on the sidelines, while a referee of low quality might exploit VAR technology to confirm every decision.

It is undisputed that constructive cooperation among referees will always be and remain very important. Just as in the teams that play soccer against each other, different skills are required in the referee teams. The on-field referee, for example, needs the ability to set the right impulses in communicating with the players. The VAR, on the other hand, needs a sense for the camera angles from which a disputed scene can be judged most clearly. In the UEFA competitions, specialized VARs are now in place, while in the national competitions in Germany or Belgium, almost every referee also has to act as a VAR, whether he has the necessary skills or not. Apart from technology, it is always the human factor that makes the difference (Fig. 7.7).

7.5 The Big Disadvantage

Many surprising factors influence a referee's decisions: the audience, the course of a game, limited perceptual abilities, and more. Perhaps the most surprising result, however, came from a study in which referees were shown scenes of footballers in duels who differed in height and who were lying on the ground at the end of the duel.

Subjects were asked to make immediate judgments as to how the athletes fell, as in the real game: Foul? Swallow? Or a fair duel? This showed that the taller player in each case was significantly more likely to be declared the cause of the foul, while shorter players were more likely to be thought of as foul victims. This suggests that height is unconsciously interpreted as an indication of who uses unfair means in a duel. And a further evaluation, in

Fig. 7.7 Moments of greatest tension: A referee reviews a disputed scene. (© ESTELA SILVA/EPA/picture alliance)

the context of which the impressive number of 123,844 fouls from soccer matches in the first Bundesliga, the Champions League, and soccer world championships were evaluated, strengthens this thesis.

Analysis of this immense amount of data revealed that referees were more likely to consider the taller player to be the foul causer, while the shorter soccer players were more likely to be awarded the free kick. However, it must be added explanatory to this result that the size difference between the foul causer and the foul victim was relatively small on average. On average, the difference was only about one cm. This difference is hardly perceptible for a referee in the game. Therefore, the sizes of the players were again considered separately, and it was found that as the differences increased, so did the probability that the action of the larger player would be whistled for foul play. If the difference between the athletes is more than ten cm, the smaller player's probability of getting the free kick is still almost 60%.

This surprising result can be explained by the following considerations: The perception of height is always associated with strength, power, and aggression. Conversely, weakness is associated with attributes such as low, small, and closeness. There are evolutionary biological reasons for this: Children also experience adult superiority through differences in height, and the same is true between children and physically taller adolescents. In our world, strength and power are firmly anchored with "up." For example, stock market prices go up, leaders in the German soccer league rank at the top, and gold medal winners stand highest on the podium.

For smaller players, this finding indicates that they are more likely to be able to push the boundaries of what is allowed in their duels without the whistle being blown, while tall soccer players tend to appear threatening and aggressive and are therefore more quickly perceived as foul players (Fig. 7.8).

But there is something even more astonishing to report about body size and referees in soccer. In a recent analysis of data on the four professional English soccer leagues, the body size of the referees themselves was correlated with the awarding of yellow and red cards and fouls. It was found that while there was no relationship to the number of fouls, there was a very strong relationship to the awarding of yellow cards. Smaller referees gave more yellow cards than larger referees in all leagues.

An explanation? The authors of the study suspect that the increased number of sanctions could be a consequence of the *small men effect*. In other words, compensation for the lack of height.

7 Perception and Deception 137

Fig. 7.8 Unequal duel: the tall Antonio Rüdiger against the short Lorenzo Insigne. (© Robin Rudel/Pressefoto Rudel/picture alliance)

8

Pressure and Failure

© Norbert Schmidt/picture alliance

There is always a result after the final whistle of soccer matches, but that is often it with the certainties. The 90 or 120 min often raise further questions, some of which will be answered on the following pages. How could Germany, on that autumn evening in 2012 against Sweden, first celebrate the very highest art of soccer for an hour, only to lose a 4–0 lead in the closing stages? Were the Germans suffering from a phenomenon called *social loafing* at the time? What madness drove Zinedine Zidane to his fatal headbutt against Marco Materazzi in the 2006 World Cup final? And why do the English always fail in penalty shootouts? Psychology does not provide definitive answers, but it can provide clues as to how these unforgettable moments came about.

The more important a soccer match is and the more pressure builds up, the harder it is for many players to really unleash their own potential. Matthias Sammer explains in an interview how world-class athletes can succeed in activating the very last percentages of their performance power in decisive moments. Because the fact that soccer matches are decided in the mind is particularly true when it comes to the big titles. This is when small things can have an impact on historic dimensions. This is shown not least by the detailed analysis of the penalty shootout from the 2012 Champions League final carried out by Norwegian sports psychologist Geir Jordet.

In the championship final 2012 played in Munich between FC Bayern and FC Chelsea, the venue may also have played a role. The more important a match, the more likely it is that the supposed home advantage will become a serious problem, as the following pages will also show.

8.1 Penalty Shootout is not a Lottery Game

Jupp Heynckes will probably forever be one of Germany's greatest soccer coaches, having won a number of major titles, including the two legendary Champions League triumphs with Real Madrid in 1998 and FC Bayern in 2013. But Heynckes also bears some of the responsibility for a traumatic defeat: Munich's lost penalty shootout against Chelsea FC in the 2012 Champions League final (Fig. 8.1).

The *Süddeutsche Zeitung* described the dramatic showdown at the time as an "attack on the brand essence of this club" and further analyzed: "The penalty shootout, although it is always also a game of chance, has called into question much that is sacred to this club: the so-called Mia-San-Mia, the leading player, the mysterious Bayern gene, even the Bayern-Dusel—it has shaken the world view of the bosses that have functioned for decades." On this May evening, the Munich team lost—at least temporarily—its globally feared belief in its own mental superiority.

8 Pressure and Failure

Fig. 8.1 Who does not practice, does not become a champion. With coach Jupp Heynckes, FC Bayern loses the 2012 Champions League final due to a completely failed penalty shootout. (© firo Sportphoto/augenklick/picture alliance)

In retrospect, it seems almost negligent that Heynckes regards penalty shootouts as a "lottery game" and takes the view that this fine art, which was once one of the core competencies of top German teams, cannot be trained. Heynckes believes that the enormous pressure combined with the exhaustion after 120 min of play at the highest level and all the turning points, moments of success, and setbacks experienced in such a match cannot be simulated in training.

But that's not even necessary to prepare the players for extreme situations. After all, many significant things happen during a penalty shootout, that can be practiced excellently. From a sports psychology perspective, mental training can be used to develop cognitive routines that help reduce psychological pressure. The penalty taker can practice focusing his attention on certain nodes in the penalty shootout, such as taking a certain number of steps during the run-up or setting up the standing leg before the shot.

In addition, there are strategic factors that a soccer player can pay attention to. Dominant body language during preparation for the penalty kick associates in the goalkeeper's subconscious the image of a positively dominant opponent who will convert his penalty kick. Research shows a clear link between the person's schemas stored in the brain and the reaction to body language. Even the slightest signals of dominance or submissiveness activate stored ideas. Associated with this is the corresponding assessment as well as one's own reaction. To a person perceived as dominant, the counterpart reacts submissively and vice versa.

There are also soccer-specific techniques that can be called up in extreme situations after well-structured training. For example, it is recommended that players decide where exactly they are going to shoot before they shoot and that they stick with this decision. At best, in the first phase of the run-up, the gaze is directed at the target, for example, down to the left of the post, and, as the shot progresses, at the ball. If possible, the shooter should also avoid having his or her standing leg pointing toward the targeted corner.

These are all minor details, given the pressure of a grand finale that can never be adjusted, but minor details are known to be decisive when a game is on a knife's edge.

In recent years, three new aspects of the penalty shootout have also been investigated by the Cologne working group of Daniel Memmert:

- the influence of the overall strength of the team on success in the penalty shootout.
- the feasibility of a prediction model for penalty shootouts
- the existence of a penalty-specific home field advantage.

For this purpose, a sample of 1,067 penalty shootouts from 14 cup competitions was examined, and team strength was estimated using betting odds. The results show that stronger teams win significantly more penalty shootouts compared to weaker teams. However, team strength appears to have only a moderate influence, as a predictive model suggests that the probability of winning even for very weak teams against very strong teams is about 40%. Related to the team strength as an influencing factor, then, penalty shootout outcomes are not pure lottery, but they are still very much randomized. Therefore, it seems to be advantageous for weaker teams to focus on a draw against stronger opponents, as their probability of success during a penalty shootout is much higher compared to a normal match. In contrast to the robust evidence for a home advantage during the normal match, the results also show that there is no home advantage during the penalty shootout.

8.2 The Fear of the Englishman at the Penalty Kick

"Oh no, not again!" lamented the *Daily Star* after England lost the final of the 2021 European Championship, once again on penalties (Fig. 8.2). This time, it was particularly dramatic against Italy. "For Gareth Southgate, it had to be the penalties," wrote the *Guardian*, because the coach himself has been an icon of England's penalty trauma since failing to score against Germany in the semifinals at the European Championships 1996. At the continental tournament 2012, England had failed in the quarterfinals in the same way, whereupon the *Independent* lamented full of fatalism: "Failing from twelve yards has become synonymous with England in recent years. Like black cabs, the monarchy, and self-deprecation." So now Marcus Rashford, Jadon Sancho, and Bukayo Saka had failed with their attempts in the European Championship final at home in Wembley Stadium.

Coach Southgate later said that he had nominated the players who were most confident in training. Three very young professionals without much experience, who had hardly played in the tournament, Sancho and Rashford had even been substituted for the penalty shootout. He had apparently simply ignored the question of whether this extreme situation could be compared with training kicks, thus adding a particularly grueling chapter to the great English penalty epic. "Coach Southgate has sinned against the psychology of the game," was the verdict of the *Süddeutsche Zeitung*.

Fig. 8.2 Typical England: Jadon Sancho misses the penalty kick in the 2021 European Championship final against Italy. (© Paul Ellis/ASSOCIATED PRESS/picture alliance)

Since the worldwide introduction of the penalty shootout in 1976, the English national team has been on the penalty spot nine times at World and European Championships, and the "Three Lions" have only been successful twice. That sounds like a disastrous record, especially since the Germans are often cited as a counterexample, winning six of their seven penalty shootouts at major tournaments. But can it be deduced from this that English shooters are actually worse than players from other nations? Therefore Cologne sports scientists evaluated all 696 attempts scored in matches and penalty shootouts during the World and European Championships between 1976 and 2018, as well as 4,708 match penalties scored in five of Europe's top soccer leagues (England, Germany, Spain, Italy, and Holland; 2006/07 to 2015/16 seasons).

At major tournaments, a total of 72% of attempts on penalties (473 penalties) landed in the net, while the figure for match penalties was 79% (223 penalties). In the European leagues, 71% of the 4,708 penalty kicks were converted during the same period. The leaders in penalty kicks at major tournaments are the Germans, who were successful in 85% of their 46 kicks. The success rate of England's shooters in European Championship and World Cup penalty shootouts was below average at 61% on 40 attempts, but statistically, this figure does not deviate significantly from the rate of penalties converted overall by all nations. When it comes to penalty kicks taken out of play, the English—probably to the surprise of all adherents of the "penalty curse" theory—actually perform better than average, with 90% of the ten penalties taken at major tournaments and 75% in the European leagues.

With regard to nationality, differences can be seen, but none of them are statistically significant. Conversely, this means that English players are not actually worse penalty takers than footballers from other countries. It's only in the more acute situations after 120 usually dramatic minutes in the knockout phase of a World Cup or European Championship that footballers from the island are not as accurate as players from some other nations. And because spectators tend to remember just such highly emotional penalty shootouts, English tournament history may lead them to believe that these events occur more often than is actually the case, according to a renowned theory in cognitive psychology—the availability heuristic.

Nevertheless, it cannot be ruled out that there are other influencing factors that could affect the performance of English penalty takers. In addition to the often-cited pressure from the English tabloid press, one possible explanation would be that English national players are influenced by the ubiquitous stereotype and are then actually more likely to miss. Psychological findings on the so-called *Stereotype Threat* show that such stereotypes have been shown to negatively influence the performance of the stereotyped group.

The reasons for the failure of the players from the chalk point have been discussed often and much, and of course, there is no comprehensive explanation. However, science has provided some pretty interesting approaches that could lead to the causes. Astonishingly, there seems to be a correlation between team status, and failure from the penalty spot. By team status, the standing of the players in the world at the time of the penalty shootout is meant. Surprisingly, it was the most notable players, who took less time preparing for the penalty shootout and were less successful than players from teams with lower team status. In particular, the stars from England (but also Spain), who are always particularly in the spotlight at major tournaments, failed conspicuously often from the spot. Research suggests that this may be related to the poorer self-regulation strategies of these players.

This term describes the ability to control yourself and act with particular awareness. Experiments show that players should by no means turn their backs on the goalkeeper after placing the ball on the spot. Shooters who move backwards to their starting position facing the goalkeeper have a much greater chance of success. This behaviour conveys a certain strength, the shooter stays in the stressful situation, does not dodge, and will prevail. The goalkeeper also believes that the player is strong and confident and is likely to score. English footballers most often turn their backs on the goalkeeper and already show some weakness here.

In addition, players should take their time and not start running as soon as the referee blows the whistle. It is more promising to wait a while, take a deep breath, focus, and only then start running. English players take the least time of all nations between the referee's whistle and hitting the ball. The reasons for this behaviour, however, are obscure.

8.3 "Haste Increases the Likelihood of a Miss-Kick."

Geir Jordet is a professor at the Norwegian School of Sport Sciences in Oslo and a specialist in many aspects of sports psychology. In addition to his scientific work, he advises various European soccer clubs on how to use knowledge of psychology most effectively in practice. The behaviour during a penalty-kick is only one small aspect of his work, but no one can dissect the great penalty shootouts of soccer history more meticulously than Jordet (Fig. 8.3).

Fig. 8.3 Geir Jordet

Mr. Jordet, for many years German teams had a reputation for being virtually unbeatable in penalty shootouts in major international competitions. Then came the 2012 Champions League final, in which Bayern Munich lost to Chelsea FC. Against Englishmen, of all people, who actually never win in these final deciding games. What was going on there?

Basically, this penalty shootout already started with the penalty kick, that Arjen Robben missed in the 95. minute, in extra time. If you examine this penalty, the first thing you notice is that Robben had to wait longer than two minutes until it was clarified whether there was a penalty at all. Only then could he begin his preparation for the shot. Then, after placing the ball on the spot, he had to wait another ten seconds for the referee to give the go. Our analysis of historical data shows that the chances of scoring drop to 60 to 70% when the shooter on the point has to wait longer than three seconds for the referee's whistle.

The Penalty Shootout Started Well for Bayern. Philipp Lahm Had Missed Against Real Madrid in the Semifinals, but He Scored in the Final. What Did He Do Better?
His body language was much calmer. He took his time to put the ball on the spot. And although he reacted quite quickly to the referee, his gaze was always fixed on the ball. Against Real, he looked at the referee while waiting for the whistle. I had the impression Lahm was in much less of a hurry in the final than he was in Madrid.

Mario Gomez and Manuel Neuer Were also Successful, then Came Ivica Olic, Who Shot Very Weakly. What Did You Observe About Him?
His shot is typical of problems, that we have found occur, when players rush too much. He took very little time to place the ball on the spot, this

behaviour clearly statistically increases the probability of a missed shot. Then he had to wait seven seconds for the referee's whistle. You could really see how difficult it was for him to wait, he takes a step towards the ball as if to encourage the referee to finally give the signal. And when the referee then blew the whistle, Olic had already started his run-up. Such behaviour very often leads to missed shots. All in all, the shooter gave the impression that he just wanted to get the annoying affair over with.

The decisive factor, however, was Bastian Schweinsteiger's penalty, which landed at the goalpost.

This miss can't be explained very well with my usual analyses. He takes enough time to put the ball on the spot, he takes his time after the referee's whistle, precisely this behaviour actually increases the chances of getting a good shot. In terms of shot preparation, there is not much difference from the decisive penalty that Schweinsteiger converted in the semifinals against Real Madrid. However, he seems to have opted for a different strategy. Against Real, he seemed to have known where he was shooting before he took his shot, and the execution was characterized by great determination. Against Chelsea, he interrupted his run-up movement to look out for the goalkeeper. It always seems strange to me when someone changes the way he executes, even though he was successful last time.

Can You Explain This Change in Strategy?
Perhaps Schweinsteiger's behaviour during Robben's penalty in extra time is significant in this context. He was sitting in his own sixteen-meter area with his back to the action. It seemed as if he wanted to avoid the stress of the situation. This avoidance strategy is fine as long as you don't take the shot yourself. One could conclude from Schweinsteiger's behaviour that the stress he feels in such situations is extremely high, probably higher than for others.

8.4 The Zinédine Zidane Enigma

There is probably no great footballer in the world who ended his career with such a dramatic punchline as Zinédine Zidane. The Frenchman, who at the turn of the millennium was probably the best player on the planet, having won almost every major title, was playing his last game, appropriately the final of the World Cup 2006. Zidane had played a great tournament, and with a victory for his French against Italy he could have crowned his breath-taking career, it would probably have taken a few hundred years for a truly great footballer to achieve such a perfect farewell again. But then Zidane rammed his head into the chest of Italy's Marco Materazzi in extra time (Fig. 8.4). He saw the red card, France lost, and the midfielder's career-ending, while incredibly spectacular, was also quite sad. The soccer world struggled to compose itself in the face of this incredible turn of events and then began its search for explanations for the self-destructive act.

Particularly, psychologists were in demand, who could serve with a highly regarded theory on the phenomenon of self-control. This term describes the ability to stop automated action tendencies, emotions or attention processes and to initiate alternative action processes instead. Unfortunately, this requires a certain amount of energy, for example when people want to control their hunger impulse at the sight of a delicious buffet because they have resolved to lose weight. Or when runners actually intended to go jogging, but simply find it more comfortable on the couch. In soccer, it can be observed time and again that players are haunted by some incriminating event, such as anger over an opponent's painful attack. The term "Revanchefoul" describes a form of lost self-control.

Zidane was insulted by Materazzi in that 110. minute, and for some reason he could not control his emotions at that moment. Often the mechanisms of self-control are compared to the way a muscle works. If the muscle has been strained too long and intensely, then it has no more strength. People's self-control actions are based on a limited self-control resource, which can be described as a store of force that provides fuel. The capacity of this force store may be temporarily depleted.

People with depleted self-control (triggered, for example, by anxiety, fatigue, or a great deal of great built up anger) are less able to concentrate, less able to manage their emotions, react more aggressively to provocations, are less persistent in unpleasant tasks, and get frustrated more quickly. In

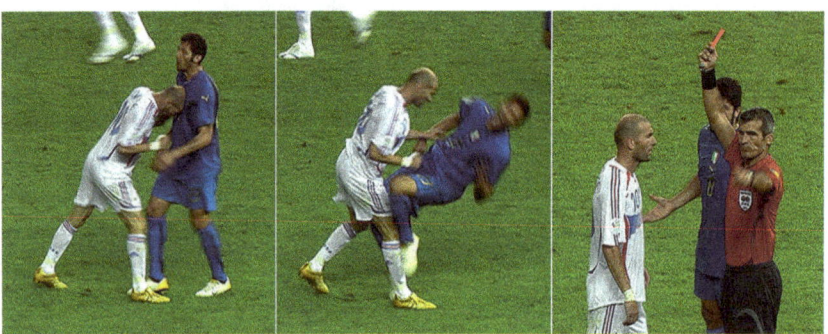

Fig. 8.4 On the road to immortality: Zinedine Zidane's last act as a professional soccer player. (© DB WDR/dpa/picture alliance)

contrast, individuals with greater self-control stores are less susceptible to stress, have fewer physical and psychological complaints, are more socially integrated, more conscientious, and perform better academically and athletically. They also react less impulsively and less aggressively. Partly, the ability to remain calm depends on personality. However, there is some evidence to suggest that self-control can be improved through certain forms of training or targeted regeneration of depleted memory through relaxation exercises or music, for example.

Zidane lost his cool more often than not, seeing a total of twelve red cards during his career. It is possible that in the extreme situation of the World Cup final, which was also to be his last game as a professional, he had to summon up an enormous amount of self-control on a very fundamental level. He managed to do this until the 110. minute, then his resources were exhausted, and several factors came together: He was physically tired, psychologically possibly disappointed as he had missed a great chance a few minutes earlier, afraid of not becoming world champion at his farewell. Then came Materazzi's insult, which led to the inner explosion. That is at least one theory, although there are also completely different explanations for the headbutt.

That evening, Belgian novelist and director Jean-Philippe Toussaint was among the spectators in Berlin's Olympic Stadium watching the final, but he didn't get to see the most famous scene of the match until the next day in a recording. After all, most of the spectators on site were following the ball, which was entirely somewhere else when Zidane committed his inconceivable act. Instead, Toussaint collected some impressions that the millions in front of the screens saw nothing of.

For example, he claims to have observed that the French captain repeatedly "unintentionally signalled his intention to leave the pitch and return to the dressing room" during extra time. As the clearest indication of this flight reflex, Toussaint cites Zidane's captain's armband, "which he keeps clumsily adjusting," which can certainly be interpreted differently. However, that such an experienced player is unable to solve a problem with the armband is surprising. And in its entirety, the theory in Toussaint's little booklet entitled *Zidane's Melancholy* provides a lot of witty reflections on the spectacular headbutt.

Although Toussaint has emphasized in various interviews after the publication of his text that it is a literary essay that makes no scientific claims, his psychoanalytical argumentation is not without charm. After a missed header chance just before the final boundary violation, Zidane's "eyes were finally opened to the defensibility of his incompetence" Toussaint writes. "Now all of a sudden the form opposes him—unbearable for an artist. One knows the intimate bonds that link art to melancholy. And unable to immortalize himself with another goal, he immortalized himself in our memory."

Elsewhere, the Belgian author provides another possible motive for the act of madness. With his act of destruction, Zidane had refused a happy ending and thus prevented himself from becoming a kind of superhuman myth: "With him there was always this impossibility of ending his career, of doing it above all in beauty, because to stop in beauty means more than just stopping, it means becoming a legend himself: To wave the World Champion trophy means no more and no less than to accept one's own death, but to screw up one's own exit leaves all perspectives open, the future in the dark and thus alive." Of course, no one (probably not even Zidane himself) can know how accurately Toussaint's reflections approach the truth. But the Belgian delivers an impressive painting of how complex, convoluted, and self-destructive psychological processes can be, which in the end become momentous deeds.

8.5 When the Nerves Fail

Only one last round of 18 holes was missing for Greg Norman in 1996 to win the Masters in Augusta (USA), the most important golf tournament in the world. At the start of the day, he was a very comfortable six strokes ahead of his opponent Nick Faldo, a gap that should normally be easily enough for one of the best golf professionals of his time to win. But Norman squandered his comfortable lead. Sports journalists later spoke of one of the worst days of failure ever experienced by a top athlete. The Australian not only forfeited his clear lead but ended up losing the tournament by a five-stroke margin to Faldo after failing in situations that were actually grotesquely easy for an expert. Norman couldn't even begin to play up to his normal level of performance.

That day will always be associated with that helpless sense of failure that Timo Werner is also well acquainted with (Fig. 8.5). The German striker of Chelsea FC has the reputation of being one of the biggest squanderers of chances in Premier League history. On Youtube, there is a video titled "Only Timo Werner can miss these chances", with a truly spectacular collection of unused opportunities. At first glance, such missteps seem rather puzzling; apparently, it happens even to top performers like Norman, Werner, and many others to fail in the circumstances of a special moment to solve what is actually a very simple task for them. Norman failed in the face of the greatest triumph of his career, and Werner probably suffers from ever-increasing

Fig. 8.5 Failed to score again: Timo Werner at Chelsea FC. (© Frank Augstein/ASSOCIATED PRESS/picture alliance)

pressure as supporters freeze in fear of the next miss every time he gets a chance. Exactly what mechanisms are behind this kind of failure, however, remains an interesting question. Not only for the athletes themselves and their fans but also for psychologists like Roy Baumeister, who researched the causes of suboptimal performances by skilled athletes, even though they are maximally motivated at that moment. Baumeister coined the term *Choking under Pressure*—failure under pressure.

In sports, there are various factors that can affect athletes in a specific situation: for example, the competition itself, the importance of a performance to be achieved, a final, a match that decides whether a team is relegated or stays in the league, the presence of spectators, the amount of the reward, the expectation of critical media coverage, and much more. We have summarized this in Fig. 8.6 and also shown what consequences these pressure factors can have psychologically and physically.

And at least it should be underlined: In this chapter, we are talking about the failure in a specific stress-inducing pressure situation of great performers who are also maximally motivated. Psychologists then speak of this as a "state". In another situation, this can then be quite different again. If the pressure is experienced as permanent and the stress is permanently present, this can have very serious psychological or even physical consequences. The

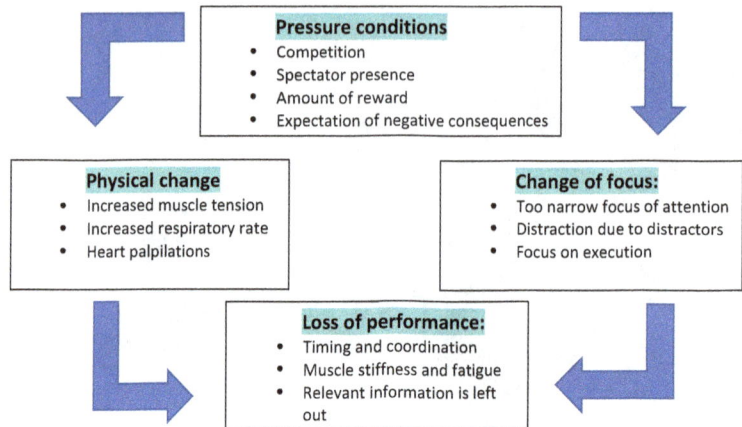

Fig. 8.6 The origin and consequences of choking under pressure

open reports of Ralf Rangnick or, more recently, Max Eberl give a very good impression of the consequences that permanent pressure and chronic stress can have (see Sect. 4.2).

But what goes on in the minds and bodies of players like Werner when they fail in individual important situations? Werner once reported great self-doubt, in the meantime downright wondering about his high standing among Chelsea FC supporters. He says that sometimes he doesn't know why the fans support him so much because he is a striker who wants to score goals but misses chances. It is difficult to fathom the deeper reasons for the poor coordination of this professional who is actually very gifted in movement. Whereas there is scientific data that can be used to describe the phenomenon in more general terms.

The failure process is characterized by the fact that on the one hand, there are direct physical changes, such as an increased heartbeat and increased muscle tension. And that on the psychological side, serious changes in attention can occur, for example, the athlete tends to be distracted, but also that he pays too much attention to himself and thinks about how his own movement should be executed. Even an experienced soccer player can then no longer correctly perceive whether there is perhaps a bump in the field or how quickly the goalkeeper rushes over.

So the chances of success grow when good soccer players do not think about how the ball is best to be hit now. The focus should be on the goalkeeper and on the goal, while the movement is executed automatically. However, this only applies to experts who have a very good command of the relevant sequences. All experienced car drivers know this: braking, clutch …

everything is automated, but if you start thinking about these sequences when reversing into a parking space, you quickly get confused.

Now, it can be argued that pressure is an integral part of the daily lives of the best soccer teams, which is why, according to this theory, the very biggest clubs would have to fail permanently. After all, they are doomed to win all the time if possible. But apparently some athletes and teams handle pressure better than others. The golfer Norman, for example, has repeatedly failed at decisive moments in major tournaments, while the tennis pro Novak Djokovic, for example, has been particularly efficient at important moments throughout his career. Possibly, because he is used to the permanent pressure and has developed routines for dealing with this situation.

And in fact, there is also the exact opposite of *choking*, which in psychology is called *clutch performance*, and which describes a particularly good way of dealing with pressure situations. The term itself has been around for a very long time. It was first used in the *New York Times* in 1929. But it's only been in the last decade or two that sports science has been looking at it more intensively. It is important to note that it is not a skill, but always a momentary state, with some players reaching this state more often than others. Sometimes it is also associated with the phenomenon of "flow," of being absorbed in an activity, and it seems that some players just attract and enjoy this state in such pressure situations, like Michael Jordan or Dirk Nowitzki, who succeeded several times in decisive actions seconds before the end in very significant moments.

Athletes who rarely or never get into such a state can at least take comfort in the fact that they can be trained to cope with such pressure-stress situations—and that failure can first be avoided. The first thing to do is to recognize which forms of pressure can occur in a competition. In addition, one's own performance expectations should be reconciled with public perceptions. After all, players who doubt while the public expects a world-class performance provide an excellent breeding ground for *choking* (Fig. 8.6). It is good if players are not confronted with unknown situations in the decisive competition, which can be avoided by practicing certain stressful moments during training or in preparatory games. Automated rituals or even routines that have been developed beforehand help to keep physical phenomena such as one's own heartbeat under control in standard situations such as a penalty kick. Fixed, familiar actions help people not to think about the consequences of their actions and to call up automated movement sequences.

A good example of how to deal constructively with such a situation was provided by the German team at the 2006 World Cup, where the young team and its inexperienced but creative and innovative coach Jürgen

Klinsmann were under incredible pressure. Thanks in part to the help of sports psychologist Hans-Dieter Hermann, it was possible at that time to prepare the team psychologically for the tournament and the expectations, whereupon the players were able to transform the pressure into additional energy.

He doesn't want to reveal what measures the sports psychologist used to prepare the team for the special situation at the time, but when he recalls 2006, there is immediately an undertone of enthusiasm in his voice. "Of course, one of our tasks was to take advantage of the special position of the host," Hermann recounts, "and we also clarified whether we have to take pressure of it. But there was a squad, a generation of players that fit that moment exactly. They wanted that experience exactly like that, they soaked it up, they enjoyed it." So there's that, too, whereby Per Mertesacker told us after his career how glad he was when the tournament ended and the pressure was off.

8.6 Social Loafing

It took former german coach Joachim Löw quite a while to understand what had happened in the German national team's 4–4 draw with Sweden in the fall of 2012. The match, in which Germany was already leading 4–0, has probably been the most puzzling drama in recent German soccer history. "I can't find an explanation for it at the moment either," was the key sentence of the astonished national coach's analysis in the obligatory television interview after the final whistle. The man was as perplexed as everyone else who had seen the German team transform from a breathtakingly performing world-class collective into a confused losing force within a few minutes (Fig. 8.7).

However, a few weeks later Löw did knew more. The team had "performed at a world-class level for half an hour—and then I see some of our players in the video analysis who don't move at all for half a minute," the national coach complained in an interview with the *Frankfurter Rundschau* after a process of extensive reflection. "The defensive players didn't offer themselves at all," Löw said—a typical case of *social loafing*.

Basically, this phenomenon can always be observed where team performances are made in which the contribution of the individual is not or cannot be made transparent. There are quite astonishing studies on this: If you give a person the task of pulling as hard as possible on a rope, you can measure his performance. If two people pull on a rope, it can be observed that

Fig. 8.7 Everyone stays away: Zlatan Ibrahimovic during the 4:4 between Germany and Sweden. (© Christina Pahnke/sampics/picture alliance)

each person uses only 93% of the strength of a single rope puller, with a group size of three only 85% and with eight people only 49% each. So it seems that team athletes generally tend to rest more or less unconsciously when they know that others are helping.

Even when preparing for a task, this social loafing can be observed, namely when people can assume that it is a group task. If they believe (this thought alone is enough) that they are about to be challenged alone and that their performance is to be closely observed, then they prepare more intensively. And if some group members suspect that other teammates are socially lazy, they are even more inclined to do less themselves—a fatal vicious circle.

However, such social loafing is normally hardly noticeable in soccer, either to the group members or to the fans. If this were different, then the players could not afford this kind of underperformance, as it would immediately attract attention. Even in the extreme case of the Sweden international match, Löw only knew about it after extensive video study. Apparently, at the time, the players simply believed that they couldn't lose anymore, they felt incredibly strong after 30 min of magic soccer and a 4–0 lead, and then massive *social loafing* unconsciously set in. Every player walked a few steps less, and chance then certainly played its part in the spectacle.

One way of mitigating social loafing in high-performance soccer is offered by the modern analytical methods used to measure individual behaviour, such as running distances, running intensities and the number of sprints. The fact that players know exactly how their personal performance is being recorded, and that submergence in the group is thus hardly possible, has a motivating effect. Beyond the strategic insights that coaching staffs generate from match data, just knowing how data is collected should reduce the risk of social loafing. In the Sweden game mentioned above, even this knowledge didn't help, but this extreme experience and the subsequent realization are among the birth moments of that very homogeneous team that won the World Cup title in Brazil two years later.

8.7 Tired Bodies, Tired Minds

It didn't take Jürgen Klopp long to search for explanations for an unusual series of failures in January 2021. "Mentally exhausted" were his players, and this condition was known to "not lead to the best legs," said the Liverpool FC coach after a 1–0 defeat against Burnley FC (Fig. 8.8). It was the fifth league game in a row that the then reigning champions had failed to win. The chances of defending the title were fading, and at the end of the season, Liverpool just managed to qualify for the Champions League thanks to a feat of strength in the season finale. After two very successful years with the Champions League win in 2019 and, even more, significant for many fans, the first league title in 30 years in 2020, the mental strength was lacking for another feat. Liverpool FC suffered from a phenomenon whose mode of operation Philipp Lahm had already succinctly described ten years earlier.

In the late summer of 2010, the Bayern Munich captain spoke out and lamented his woes in a major newspaper interview. Lahm was actually healthy, the new season had just begun, but he did not feel recovered. "Nothing hurts or anything," he reported, "you're actually top motivated again, but somehow you lack the drive." Lahm had three weeks of summer recovery behind him, but the long preseason with a lost Champions League final (0:2 against Inter Milan) and the World Cup in South Africa was far from over: "At the end you have so much behind you, which was incredibly exhausting, and suddenly it starts all over again. You have to perform again, from the first to the nineteenth minute, for a whole year. It's like a mountain at that time."

Lahm and his FC Bayern subsequently had a difficult year. After eleven match days, they were only ninth in the Bundesliga, with Borussia

Fig. 8.8 Exhausted and injured: Jürgen Klopp with Mo Salah. (© FrankHoermann/SVEN SIMON/picture alliance)

Dortmund as the champions. The usual explanation for such problems is that the seasons after major tournaments are particularly tough for a club with many international players. And most experts, when they hear these words, think first and foremost of the physical fatigue that can be the result of constant strain. Klopp's and Lahm's statements, on the other hand, suggest that mental exhaustion can have at least as great an impact on performance. After all, the psyche also needs regeneration times, experiences have to be processed, and there has to be an anticipation of new challenges.

Relevant for planning a functional recovery is not only the type of exhaustion (physical or mental), but also the question of whether long-term or short-term stresses have led to fatigue. Short-term stresses can have quite different characteristics, such as problems in the private or business environment that need to be solved in a timely manner. Even birthdays can sometimes lead to reduced performance, as shown by a study from 2021, which examined the running performance of 1,040 Bundesliga field players in 2,142 games. On average, the soccer players covered 11.1 km and 63 sprints in 90 min. However, if the game was played the day after a player's birthday, fewer sprints were registered among the pros who had something to celebrate the night before—a short-term strain, apparently (birthdays only come once a year), even if the study cannot clarify what the actual causes are.

Knowing about short-term stresses and how to remedy and avoid these performance-impairing influences are important aspects of the work of coaches and sports psychologists. But: short-term stresses come and go; long-term ones stay and often have more serious effects. This is also due to the fact that people's mental state is difficult to plan for. Sometimes mental overload can disappear quickly, even during periods of short successive competitions. In other cases, however, mental fatigue results from what many scientists call *overtraining*, a prolonged period of too much physical training or exertion that results in significant drops in performance.

With early diagnosis and the right countermeasure, these overloads can be compensated and quickly reversed. If, on the other hand, the state of overload persists for a longer period of time, a chronic decline in performance often follows—a so-called *non-functional overload* reaction. If no countermeasures are taken during this time, there is a high risk that even the third stage of exhaustion will be reached: the so-called overtraining reaction (which, as described above, can also be triggered by many competitions in quick succession). This can have massive consequences, including depressive symptoms.

In a very detailed study over a longer period of time with 94 junior soccer players from the first Dutch junior league, among them members of the youth selection teams, it was shown that already two months before the diagnosis of an overload reaction, which is reflected in significant reductions in performance, reduced values of mental recovery appeared, as a result of a lack of balance between recovery and stressful events. In the study, the classic symptoms of a prolonged overload reaction were evident in 7.4% of the participants, i.e., a severe drop in performance, an increased experience of stress, and a higher heart rate. If no countermeasures are taken against this type of exhaustion, a return to old performance levels is at great risk. A Belgian study, which examined the exhaustion of soccer players in the adult sector, shows how massively the performance of players is affected in some cases. Here, the scientists concluded, that 30 to 50% of professionals suffered from an overload reaction during a season.

One reason for this could be that the dosage of recovery phases is often based almost exclusively on knowledge of the physical processes in the body. The rest that the head needs is rarely considered. And the competition calendar with national league, international club competitions, and national teams leaves little room for scope of application anyway. Usually, the best players have to compete at the highest level and with full concentration every three days over a long period of time, which can be too much to maintain performance over the long term. Even several sports medicine studies show that even one important, high-stress competitive match can lead to very short-term physical consequences (dehydration, glycogen balance) and significant mental exhaustion.

The usual solution to the problem is a broad squad that makes it possible to give all players sufficiently long rest periods. But only the really big clubs can afford to do that, and their coaches must also have the courage to spare key players in phases when victories are urgently needed. That is a fine art. But coaches are also well advised to ensure from the outset that training strengthens the mind and body in equal measure. Last but not least, this includes regeneration phases with sufficient sleep and good quality of sleep. There is a lot of knowledge on the mechanisms of recovery, as shown by an extensive collection of articles by Michael Kellmann and Jürgen Beckmann published in 2021.

Incidentally, Philipp Lahm had to play all Bundesliga and Champions League games for Bayern in the season mentioned at the beginning of this article. It was one of the weakest seasons in the career of the future world champion.

8.8 Clap Your Own Team to Defeat

Every soccer fan knows those uplifting moments when a magical connection is formed between the crowd and their own team. When, after a successful move or a few won duels, the crowd becomes a powerful entity, inspiring the home team and intimidating the opposition, contributing to a period of footballing dominance. Such experiences are memorable, and often the memories of these sweet moments eclipse the daily grind at the stadium. Because, of course, soccer spectators also experience home defeats time and again, for which, of course, they never feel partly responsible.

Probably the most memorable example of such a home defeat in front of a large crowd is the 1950 World Cup final in Rio de Janeiro between Brazil and Uruguay, which took place in the famous Maracana Stadium. Needless to say, the match was sold out with 197,000 spectators; never has a World Cup match been played in front of a larger crowd, and the people in the Maracana were certainly not quiet. But Uruguay won 2-1, Brazil lost its home World Cup, and when Ghiggia scored the winning goal, "a silence broke out in the stadium, the most thunderous silence in the history of soccer," Uruguayan writer Eduardo Galeano wrote in his book *The Ball is Round and Goals Lurk Everywhere*. A crowd can apparently also paralyze its own team (Fig. 8.9).

And what applies to the whole team can also apply to individual players. One of the most famous and at the same time most momentous misses from the penalty spot in the league came from Michael Kutzop, then a player for Werder Bremen in 1985/86. Michael Kutzop had successfully completed all of his nine penalty attempts earlier in the season and stepped up again to take a spot kick in the penultimate game of the season against Bayern Munich. All the advantages seemed to be on his side—it was a home game, the fans in the stadium supported him, and he himself was full of confidence, he said later in the *ZDF* interview. The special thing: It was a special

Fig. 8.9 The loudest silence in soccer history: World Cup final 1950 in front of 200,000 spectators in the Maracana. (© dpa/picture alliance)

pressure situation. It was the 89. minute, the score was tied, and Werder would have been German champion with a successful penalty kick. The result: Kutzop missed, and the ball just touched the right goalpost. Munich goalkeeper Jean-Marie Pfaff had long since moved to the other corner, and some television commentators suspected that Kutzop had thought too long about the shot, and the game ended in a draw. SV Werder lost its match on the last matchday, Bayern became champion and Kutzop again scored eight penalties in a row after this momentous miss.

The economist Thomas Dohmen describes this scene as an impressive example of blunders in extraordinary pressure situations, although apparently all the advantages lie with the athlete, the home crowd supports him, he can actually do it and the player is sure of himself. In his very detailed statistical analysis of all penalties in the first division from 1963 to 2003/2004, he shows, in a completely different way than one might expect, that away teams are more successful at taking penalties (75.83%) than home teams (73.59%).

Basically, most players and spectators tend to believe that the home team benefits from a loud crowd in a full stadium. For a long time this was also the common assumption in science. The support of a team by its audience stimulates the players to try harder and at the same time creates a social rejection for the away team. All this is expressed in the rituals of the audience, in cheering for one's own team, and in chants.

However, this assumption is now scientifically difficult to sustain. Many research studies show that the absolute number of spectators, the capacity utilization of a stadium and also spectator behaviour have little or no correlation with the match outcome (Fig. 8.10). This was particularly evident during the 2006/07 season in Italy (i.e., pre-Covid times) when 20 matches were played without spectators (as a result of fan riots). A comparison between these matches, of the teams concerned, with those played in front of a crowd, showed: nothing was different. The home advantage was still there—at least in this small number of matches. It was irrelevant for the match result whether the stadium was empty or full, at least in this pre-Covid study.

In the Bundesliga, as elsewhere in European professional soccer (cf. Sect. 1.1), it became apparent, at least until 2018/19 in pre-Covid times, that it is hardly relevant how many spectators are present for victory or defeat. In figure 8.10, we have compiled the results up to 2011. In the decades leading up to 2011, we saw that while more and more spectators were coming to the stadiums, the home-field advantage in the Bundesliga

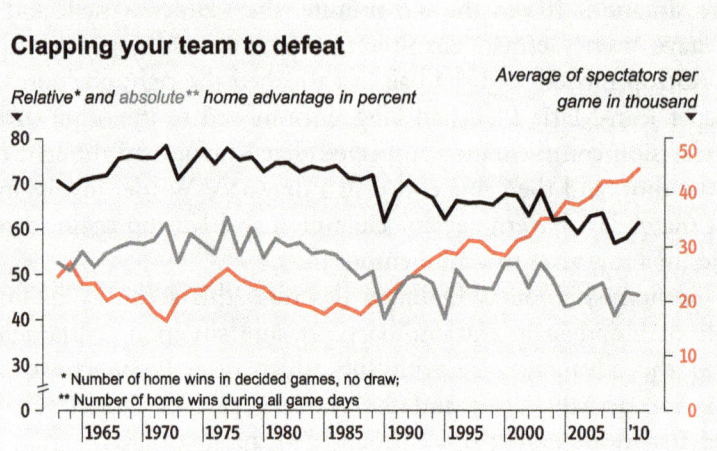

Fig. 8.10 The development of home advantage in the 1st Bundesliga from 1963 to 2011 and the development of the average number of spectators over the same period: The axis on the left together with the green line shows the average number of spectators in the respective season. The right-hand axis shows the home advantage. The blue line indicates the so-called relative home advantage (the share of home games won in the games decided, i.e. excluding draws). The red line shows the absolute home advantage, i.e. the share of home games won in all games. (from Memmert, Strauss, Theweleit, 2013; see p. 188)

nevertheless continued to decline as spectator numbers increased. While there were always more home wins than away wins in each season, as can be seen from the figure, there were significant seasonal fluctuations. Over the decades, the trend has become smaller and smaller for the home advantage in the 1st Bundesliga. Since 2011, it has fluctuated around the mean of 45.78% in the pre-Covid periods, i.e. up to the 18/19 season, from around 49% to 42%. The average attendance has always been above 40,000 per game from 2008/09 to 18/19 inclusive but has stagnated between 41,000-45,000 since then with a peak of around 45,000 in the 11/12 season. So, the home advantage is still there, but it was already getting smaller in pre-Covid times and even if you evaluate this with all sorts of complex statistical calculations: increasing audience does not lead to more home wins.

But wait: this can't be true, hasn't the Corona period with frequently empty stadiums taught us otherwise? Was not the home field advantage eliminated in the 2019/20 season with the onset of the pandemic because of the lack of spectators, as some studies and headlines tell us? No, this was not the case, at least this needs to be looked at more closely. Therefore, for this statement, it is worth taking a separate look and a separate chapter on home advantage in Covid times in our book (see Sect. 1.1).

Players always talk about the important role of the fans, especially when winning at home. This behaviour is the all-too-understandable impulse to praise those fans who supported you in a victory. However, hardly any footballer will ever publicly blame a crowd for social pressure, yet here lies the crucial point: if the importance of the crowd for home advantage is to be examined, positive and negative influences must be weighted. Positive aspects can be, for example, that the players' willingness to exert themselves is increased, which should have mainly positive effects. At the same time, the studies show that, under certain circumstances, there can be a loss of performance in one's own stadium, even though players and spectators are highly motivated. The technical term for this effect is *Choking under Pressure* (see section 8.6). On the one hand, players may believe they have all the advantages on their side at home (like the situation Michael Kutzop found himself in), which can lead to a loss of concentration on the essentials. On the other hand, for other players, this situation can lead to misgivings and self-doubt.

The classic study of *Choking under Pressure research,* already 40 years old, comes from two American psychologists, Roy Baumeister and Andrew Steinhilber. They claim that the expectation of success in situations in which the actor can gain a new, desired social identity (i.e., winning the championship, for example) can lead to performance degradation. In addition, the athlete's mind may already be preoccupied with celebrating the victory and what it would be like to be a champion. This diverts attention from the task at hand. In addition, as numerous subsequent studies have shown, the athlete may also suffer from unhelpful negative thoughts, such as the idea of what will happen if the championship trophy, which was thought to be safe, is lost. And how embarrassing it is to face the fans and the club as losers. According to the study, the probability of negative performance increases at the most important moments, even though the athletes are actually highly motivated and have a high level of self-confidence. As evidence, the two researchers cite World Series final results from 1924 to 1982 in baseball and NBA final and semifinal results from 1967 to 1982 in basketball. Meanwhile, with more and more data and more seasons, the effect has been shown to be absent in the NBA. Nevertheless, the two researchers are credited with establishing an entire line of research with this study. Many studies followed that looked at reasons for this failure under pressure, and training and counterstrategies have also been developed for professional athletes and teams.

At World and European Championships in soccer, the enormous expectations probably contributed a lot to the fact that the hosts of the major tournaments repeatedly fell by the wayside early on. Even the spectacular collapse of the Brazilians in the unforgettable 2014 World Cup semi-final, when the German team advanced to the final by a score of 7-1, can be explained by the tremendous pressure that weighed on the host nation. A colleague from the U.S., Edson Filho, described this team collapse, as he called it, in great detail in an article. And in the meantime, home teams are not only expected to defeat opponents, but also to shoulder a larger mission. Since 1998, no soccer nation has won a World Cup or European Championship on home soil.

8.9 "For the Very Greatest Successes, It's Important for a Team to Breathe, to Be Able to Operate Independently."

With very few exceptions, Matthias Sammer has been involved in all of German soccer's international successes since the mid-1990s: as a player (European champion in 1996, Champions League winner in 1997), as FC Bayern's sports director (Champions League victory in 2013) and as DFB sports director (European championship titles U17, U19, U20, U21), laying the foundations for the 2014 World Cup title. He particularly enjoys talking about the small difference that separates very good soccer players and teams from true champions (Fig. 8.11).

Fig. 8.11 Matthias Sammer. (© Bernd Thissen/dpa/picture alliance)

Mr. Sammer, this conversation is about border regions. About paths to the summit, about the last five percent of people's performance. As a European champion, Champions League winner and official at FC Bayern, you have repeatedly been on this high level. Does a feeling or a term spontaneously come to mind when you think of these areas?
Matthias Sammer: Yes, a relatively simple term that is not only positively afflicted and is no longer used so often: a deeply felt ambition that must feel good. People who want to activate that last five percent of performance should be sympathetic to this endeavour and not feel they have to fight against their own will.

But What's in Vogue at the Moment Are People Who Seem Casual Rather Than Ambitious. Do People with Such a Strong Will to Succeed Often Have a Harder Time Developing?
  That's a big issue with young people: types like that get into situations again and again where they ask themselves: Am I actually normal, when I might freak out after playing Ludo because I lost? The others are laughing again, but I'm pissed off, don't know what to do with myself. It just feels bad. It's an otherness that's not always easy to bear. Young guys in particular have ambivalent feelings because they sense that they are unusual. But in a process that, in the best case, is accompanied by people who recognize the character, who may even carry similar feelings, you can learn to deal with it. From the moment an athlete recognizes that few people have this characteristic, that he therefore often remains misunderstood, he can be at peace with himself.

You Sound as if You Yourself Have Had to Struggle with a Kind of Outsider Role Because of Your Ambition.
Absolutely, and in my case, there was also the red hair, of which I have a few less today. I have been confronted with this a lot, and have thought about it a lot. The word ambition also contains the concept of avarice, and in my eyes it's not far from avarice to envy. I asked myself: why do you always get so angry when others win and you don't? That also has something to do with envy, with a fundamentally negative feeling. But out of my envy of the better ones came the need to learn from the winners. I wanted that, too. It's important to allow negative feelings and also contradictions, to work with them instead of fighting against them.

People Who Are so Focused on Winning Are Quickly Said to Be a Bit Crazy. Is This Extreme Expression of Ambition a Form of Madness?
There's a fine line between genius and madness at this point, and the question is often: what's normal, and what's abnormal? I recently saw this documentary about Michael Schumacher, which is currently running on

Netflix. It shows a scene in which Schumacher rams Damon Hill at a crucial moment in the world championship fight, in an obviously deliberate action. I watched it and thought: sure, that's it. I think he knew exactly what he was doing. He was in a borderline area that is not far from madness, and that's where you sometimes overshoot the mark. It's not peace and quiet in this place, mistakes happen there, too.

Was It Fundamentally Easier to Approach Abysses and Endure Conflicts Back then, Because Headlines on the Internet and Debates on Social Networks didn't Follow Every Border Crossing?
That may well be. Great leaders have never been easy, and their actions always harbour potential for conflict. In sports today, people often talk about energies that leaders are supposed to develop or give. I then always ask: what exactly is this energy that you give? Often the answer is: a positive energy, everything has to be positive. I have always thought that energy comes from contradictions. It is a strength to allow contradictions in order to grow, but we think more and more often: no way! Contradiction immediately seems malicious, is quickly taken personally. Energy is demanded, but please on the simplest terms and preferably completely without conflict. This cannot work.

Working at the Highest Level Has Its Downsides. How Can a Balance Be Found Between Top Performance and Sufficient Rest?
The idea that something extraordinary is permanently expected of one can cause great anxiety. There is always the danger of moving above the line, and that not only breaks the individual, but also the others who are confronted with it. But you can also find the right balance. Great champions who play competitive sports at a very high level over a long period of time, Messi, Ronaldo, Djokovic, Nadal, they all need an equivalence to what they do every day for their profession. I think the art is to be really happy and satisfied with things outside of sports, with family for example. Accompanied by the feeling of having done everything possible, even in these phases, to create the highest possible probability of success. For coaches or managers that's even more difficult, because they still have a responsibility for others every day.

You worked with Pep Guardiola in Munich, who always wanted more in every game, no matter how unimportant, and even when the team was leading by three or four goals. Was the team able to take the necessary timeouts under this regime?
Pep is extremely ambitious, and he always wanted the perfection of beauty in the game. This was constantly recognizable in his appearance. The results

were also important to him, but the beauty and the philosophy, were still a bit higher. A lot was expected of the players, but at the same time they had more days off than they were used to from previous coaches.

The Really Big Games in the Champions League, Where the Last Percent Counts, Were Still Lost. Why?
Guardiola is certainly the most important driving force behind contemporary soccer. His possession game is debatable, but he is brilliant when it comes to changing positions. However, the conductor should realize that he is not the orchestra at the same time. I have the greatest respect for Pep and feel deep gratitude for the time we spent together, but in Munich, we failed to activate the last two percent. At the end of this fantastic process, he did not allow the team to grow in such a way that it could take the final steps on its own.

What Do You Mean?
For the very greatest successes, it is important that a team can breathe, that it can act independently. If a violinist breaks a string in a very important concert, the musicians must not look helplessly to the conductor and ask: What do we have to do now? The orchestra should continue to play in such a way that people don't even notice that the string has broken because, for example, the trumpeter steps in so that everything continues to sound completely harmonious. The great secret of leaders like Ottmar Hitzfeld or Jupp Heynckes was, that they enabled teams to achieve this form of independence. Pep was always right with his analyses; his measures almost always worked out exactly as planned. As a result, the team stopped thinking for itself a bit. But at the very highest level, there comes a point when players' own decisions are required.

Is This also His Problem at Manchester City, Where He is also Still Waiting for the Champions League Title?
In the final against Thomas Tuchel and Chelsea FC, he wanted to reinvent the game and had his team play without a centre forward and without a six. Sometimes, if you want to put a final i-dot and you have a pen in your hand and ink is still on it, you can say, Just put the pen down. That's all it takes.

What Worked Better in the year FC Bayern Won the Triple in 2013 Under Jupp Heynckes?
A year earlier, I joined FC Bayern as sports director and we asked ourselves: who are actually the faces of this team and my impression was: president

Uli Hoeneß and CEO Karl-Heinz Rummenigge, but neither of them played anymore. They were so dominant, and embodied the class and strength of the club. In the team there were Bastian Schweinsteiger and Philipp Lahm, who at the time had the reputation of losers because they lost their grand finals. And the individualists Arjen Robben and Franck Ribéry. Philipp and Basti also had the problem at the time that their advisors tried to portray the other as more important. Then there was Manuel Neuer, who had already won something: the 2009 European Under-21 Championship. But there was no clear hierarchy, as was evident in the penalty shootout in the 2012 Champions League final, when almost no one wanted to take the shots.

What Was the Solution?
I spoke with Manuel, Basti and Philipp and said: If you don't change anything, the team will be divided: a few think Basti is better, and a few think Philipp is better. As long as you don't speak with one tongue, you're the cause of division. Manuel Neuer's job was to make sure that the two stayed together in the process. That wasn't so easy at the beginning, because Ribéry and Robben were also hierarchically important—stars, but they often stopped when they lost the ball. The team was so pissed off and they didn't find a way to integrate these players. But after it was clear that Schweinsteiger, Lahm and Neuer stick together as leaders and the two stars realized: we are loved and wanted, but the other guys are the bosses, processes went off. There were then training sessions where Franck stopped, and Philipp shouted: Come back! When there were objections, Basti shouted: shut up, defend! Franck and Arjen, the two best were led differently and suddenly a team emerged. Right here we are talking about the last percentages.

What Does It Take to Be Accepted as a Leader on a Team?
I once read a beautiful sentence in the biography of Alex Ferguson, the long-time successful coach of Manchester United: "Good leadership is getting the percent out of your employees that they don't even know they have in them today." Today, I would put it a bit differently: The great art of leaders is to make decisions and give instructions, and to sense the resistance of those who may still be filled with scepticism and doubt, while knowing: The day will come when everyone understands. That is power.

The Term Mentality is Often Used for Performance in the Border Area, but It is not Easy to Grasp. Is This Term Suitable for Approaching the Phenomenon?
I think discussions about mentality in soccer are very German because German teams have had, for decades, not the best soccer players, but an

extraordinary amount of resilience. Whereas there's always the danger that you'll be considered an eternalist if you name these things. I try not to describe the components of winning with modern verbiage, but the art of analysis means finding the right words. Mentality is one of them. Every opponent had to expect that the Germans would somehow come back, because they always believe in themselves and get everything out of themselves. That was a fundamental part of our identity. Is that still the case today? No! This phenomenon is meant, when speaking of mentality.

9

Harmony and Drama

© Norbert Schmidt/picture alliance

"The bait must be to the liking of the fish—not the angler," Helmut Thoma, former head of programming at German TV station RTL, once said to justify formats that were accused of being too lowbrow. Any number of trash can be justified on this basis, including, of course, the voyeurism that characterizes parts of soccer coverage. The luridly colored fringe stories about the game, which have received more and more attention since the 1990s, have contributed a great deal to the current soccer boom. And who knows whether academics don't find a slap in the face at the center circle more exciting than the question of whether a coach switched to a 4–3-3 system in the 70th minute and thus had the winning idea?

It's clear that soccer would be nowhere near as entertaining without the controversies and conflicts pointed out by the media. The drama is as much a part of the concept of the gigantic entertainment machinery as the great goosebump moments, the experience of celebrating as part of a large crowd of like-minded people. A fervently singing stadium can be an unforgettable event. Music has been part of soccer for many years and may even have a fairly direct impact on the game.

As, of course, does the behavior of the referees, who allow leeway that sometimes stretches the rules to their limits. What is astonishing is that there are clearly recognizable mechanisms by which the impartial referees exhaust the possibilities of the rulebook: they engage in what is known as *game management*. Is it really more important for the referees to manage a game harmoniously than to enforce the rules?

9.1 The Pleasure of Conflict

The well-known German coach Jürgen Klopp, currently coaching the Liverpool team successfully, was mightily annoyed at the end of the press conference after Dortmunds BVB's Premier league match against Bayern Munich in May 2013. "90 min of soccer and not a single question about the game, I have to say: I take my hat off to you," he said to the journalists full of irony. On his face was an expression of deep contempt. Later at Liverpool FC, too, there were always these moments of confrontation with reporters when the successful coach disliked questions. In this case, the reporters had aimed exclusively in one direction: It was about a rather aggressive exchange of words that Klopp had had with Matthias Sammer, then FC Bayern's sports director, during the course of the game.

In fact, the sporting course of the encounter hardly played a role in the subsequent coverage, which was surely also due to the fact that Bayern Munich had already been determined as champions and Dortmund had already qualified for the Champions League. While the conflict on the sidelines provided a perfectly fitting image for the battle for hegemony in German soccer that the two clubs (who would also play a Champions

League final against each other a few weeks later) were engaged in. But did this total focus on an event with fairly trivial content, involving a sending-off for Munich's Rafinha, meet the needs of viewers and readers?

That's hard to verify, but Alfred Draxler, who has worked in leading positions at the influential German *BILD newspaper, Europe`s largest yellowpress,* for many years and writes mainly about soccer, believes: Yes! "We did what we should do as journalists: We have sharpened and personalized the events of the game to one topic, and the topic at that time of the season was the duel Dortmund vs. Bayern." It's understandable that a coach like Klopp, who loves to talk about soccer most of all, would be less pleased with such pointedness. And journalists also wonder whether they are living up to their standards of seriousness and balance when they put such a supposedly marginal aspect at the center of their stories. But there is much to suggest that in this case they have at least been able to satisfy the needs of the recipients.

Because "in soccer or in sports, all topics that evoke emotions are attractive," says Draxler. "That's the jubilation or joy with a winner, the sadness with a loser. And that's just sometimes the voyeurism in a conflict." This mechanism is human, certainly doesn't just apply to *Bild* readers, and can be scientifically proven.

In a particularly illustrative experiment on this topic, three different groups of viewers watched a recorded tennis match, but with different commentaries. One commentator gave the impression that friends were playing against each other, other viewers were told that they were "intimate enemies," and a third group was told nothing at all about the players' relationship. As expected, viewers found the version of the game that pitted the supposed enemies against each other the most attractive and enjoyable. Although everyone was shown exactly the same pictures and the tension of the pure competition was also identical.

One might now object that tennis is perhaps not as exciting as soccer, and viewers could use a bit more excitement around the game. Therefore, similar experiments were carried out with ice hockey and American football, and the result remained the same: viewers (men even more so than women) find the picture clips considerably more enjoyable when the reporters' comments emphasize the toughness of the game, the aggressiveness and the conflicts between the players and the teams.

At first glance, these findings may seem harmless, but of course the publication of quarrels and anger can greatly affect or even hurt those involved. And if there are interpersonal difficulties in soccer teams that become public, this can have a massive impact on the course of a season. In this respect, the realization that the enjoyment of the reception of sporting competitions is greater when the audience knows about personal conflicts or crises between athletes and clubs presents a challenge to reporters. They want to provide their listeners, viewers or readers with the most interesting stories possible, knowing that conflicts are particularly exciting, but at the same time they should be careful to treat the protagonists of the game with some consideration.

The portrayal of a brawl in a discotheque involving a professional soccer player is highly unpleasant for the people involved, but it certainly promotes sales for the reporting medium. This inevitably leads to conflicts of interest, for which every broadcaster and newspaper must develop its own solution strategies. The special thing about sports, however, is that there are conflicts whose presentation actually doesn't bother anyone.

Derbies between clubs that have been rivals for decades are always explosive and exciting, even if the clubs are currently languishing somewhere in no-man's land in the table. The conflicts between so-called arch-rivals are virtually celebrated by many fans and powerfully fueled by the reporting. And the memory of the legendary enmities between German coaches Christoph Daum and Jupp Heynckes, between Daum and Uli Hoeneß, the long-time manager of FC Bayern, who also liked to argue publicly with Willi Lemke, the former manager of Werder Bremen, still provides amusement today.

As long as they remain non-violent, most confrontations are exciting and thrilling, they make soccer more emotional, they put the spectator in a state of positive excitement. When things get really heated in a stadium, interest increases, but there is also trouble that can quickly destroy the appeal: Betting scandals, referee bribes, systematic doping of players and similar crises, paradoxical as it may sound, initially lead to a thoroughly attractive shudder. But only at first. At some point, a reaction of turning away results, because even the greatest pleasure in voyeurism cannot replace the credibility of a competition (Fig. 9.1).

9.2 The Magic of the Wave

Scientific knowledge permeates soccer at all levels, as almost all fans, journalists, coaches and the readers of this book know by now anyway. This also applies to the mathematical calculation of the *the Mexican Wave* with a rather complex formula—at least complex and incomprehensible for the non-mathematician. That's why we refrained from writing it down here, but yes, it definitely exists. And this mathematical gobbledygook actually

Fig. 9.1 English newspapers after the abandonment of an international match between England and Ireland in 1995. (© PA/dpa/picture alliance)

answers the question of whether and how spectators in a stadium come together to form a La Ola, a wave, and how it spreads.

However, American cheerleader Krazy George Henderson didn't know anything about this when, on October 15, 1981, on the sidelines of a game of the American League Championship Series, baseball's second division, he encouraged the Oakland crowd to perform the first wave in sports history. In any case, Henderson himself claims to have been the first, which other sources dispute. Be that as it may, what is clear is that the wave originated in the early 1980s in the United States, which is why the term *Mexican Wave, which is* widely used in some countries, is not entirely accurate. But it was at the 1986 World Cup in Mexico that wave first became known to a large international audience and began its triumphal march across the world (Fig. 9.2).

Fig. 9.2 Merging with the mass: A thousand hands, one wave. (© Herbert Rudel/picture alliance)

The principle is simple: the spectators infect each other, throwing their arms in the air one after the other, which results in a pretty looking wave of extremities flying in the air over the sea of spectators. However, not all visitors are immediately infected, and there are also those who reject the wave. There are active and inactive spectators. Active spectators must carry the inactive ones along in order for the wave to work, at least from a physical point of view, and it is precisely this process that is described in the mathematical model published a good twenty years ago by three physicists around the German professor Dirk Helbing in a world-famous paper in the journal *Nature*. The scientists consider the spectator as a cell in a so-called cellular automaton model; and from them also comes the said formula with which we started this chapter.

But why are many of the visitors to large events so fascinated by the little game that they enthusiastically jump in every time a group starts the ritual in a corner somewhere? The most obvious reason is probably that this is an excellent opportunity for even the more inactive spectators, who are not standing in the corner singing, to merge with the crowd without danger, and to synchronize with like-minded people. Moreover, spectators can be active during phases when not much is happening on the pitch.

However, the initial spark for such a synchronization process must come from an instigator. In most cases, it is smaller groups from which the contagion emanates, although by no means everyone in the fan blocks likes the wave. Among the purists in the stands, the Mexican wave is considered a typical feature of the eventization of soccer, and the accusation is: here, spectators are merely celebrating themselves and, in doing so, abandoning their concrete connection to the game. This is one reason why the phenomenon was somewhat less common in some stadiums, even in pre-Corona times.

For that part of the audience that tends to be more passive, and that is the majority, the wave, however, is a nice way to lose one's own individuality for a moment and become one with the masses, something that *die hard* fans, who sing along to every song and clap along to every rhythm, experience all the time anyway. In contrast to these forms of self-expression, however, La Ola can be better explained psychologically and mathematically, which ultimately also serves stadium safety.

This is because knowledge of the mechanisms behind such mass phenomena helps to understand how individuals behave in large crowds, which is important to avoid panics and to direct the flow of spectators in the stadium. Stadium architects and all those who share responsibility for the security of large events will benefit. Because what all these phenomena have in common is that they are about synchronization and the dissolution of the individual in the mass. As a rule, this process is extremely fascinating.

9.3 You'll Never Walk Alone

In sporting terms, the final minutes of the preliminary round match between Spain and Ireland at the 2012 European Championship had long since lost all significance. The favorites from southern Europe were leading 4–0, the job was done, and the TV audience was relaxed as the final whistle blew. Some viewers had already switched over, but these infidels missed one of the most memorable moments of the European Championship tournament. In the 87th minute, 20,000 Irish fans raised their beer-soaked voices and, full of pathos and pride, said the heartbreaking classic *Fields of Athenry*. It was immediately clear that this was a special moment, the more sensitive of Europe's TV commentators were silent for minutes, giving the TV audience a great experience. Touching, moving, kitsch at its best. And the sporty, chanceless Irish were suddenly the darlings of the European Championship.

It was a moment that reminded all those soccer fans who never make music in the stadium themselves that singing around soccer is more than just a pretty background noise against boredom. At a time when fewer and fewer people sing in church, when Christmas music comes from cell phones, and when many children say goodbye to the day with music from loudspeakers that helps them fall asleep, soccer is one of the last places where people sing with passion and fervor. Chants are a significant factor in the development of feelings at soccer, they shape moods, and of course the people in charge at Swiss television know that.

When fans fell silent during the first ten minutes of a derby between FC Zurich and Grasshopper Club from Switzerland in May 2013 in protest against planned repression with respect to national drug measures, Swiss television underlaid the images in its summary with an audio track recorded later in the match. "In order to make the report as attractive as possible, the fan chants were subsequently edited into the summary," a TV official said, explaining the minor media scandal. And when the Corona pandemic of 2020 caused empty stadiums around the world, some TV stations offered their audiences the option of underlaying the images with sound recordings from previous games. Including matching chants to the respective teams involved and reactions adapted to the respective game situation: Cries when a foul is committed, cheers when a goal is scored, murmurs when a chance is missed, and so on. The offer was gladly taken up.

So, music and song are a fundamental part of the stadium experience, but that was far from always the case. The first stand-alone song to make it into stadiums is the classic soccer song of all, composed in 1945 as the finale for a Broadway musical called *Carousel*: *You'll Never Walk Alone*. In 1960, legendary Gerald "Gerry" Mardsen and the band "Gerry and the Pacemakers" covered this rousing song and played it at Liverpool's Cavern Club. The song was well received and stormed the top ten played before matches at the stadium at *Anfield Road*. Then, when the song was suddenly off the charts, Liverpool's famous standing-room-only crowd, "The Kop," shouted to the legend, "Where's our song?" The stadium DJ knew what to do and played *You'll Never Walk Alone*. Since then, the song has been the club's anthem and began its triumphant march around the soccer world. In England, however, the song is still sung exclusively by Liverpool FC fans (Fig. 9.3).

Meanwhile, almost all clubs and fans have their own songs and chants that create a sense of specialness and community. For English behavioral biologist Desmond Morris, these are tribal rituals designed to drive players as members of their own group. The energies of such a vibrant atmosphere

Fig. 9.3 Cohesion in front of the famous stand "The Kop": Liverpool FC and the song *You'll never walk all alone*. (© Simon Stacpoole/Offside/picture alliance)

put those involved in the stadium into a comfortable state of excitement and mood, which, coupled with exciting action on the pitch, can then become an unforgettable experience. A deep, physically felt connection is created that is reinforced by the synchronized behavior of the crowd and choreography that matches the music. In a recent article, two South American musicologists describe this as a kind of magic, a special form of communication between players, fans and other participants that sometimes cannot be explained rationally.

This magic is particularly intense in the first minutes after important goals. People sing more often during these phases of the game than at other moments. This is what the two German music scientists Reinhard Kopiez and Guido Brink have found out, whereby the chants and the other acoustic signals of the fans tend not to result in an advantage for the home team (cf. Sect. 8.9). And this is also due to the fact that a charged atmosphere has a motivating effect on the guests. "I think it's awesome. I like being the bogeyman, it pushes me," professional players say time and again.

So, in addition to joy, there are other motives for singing, for example to revile an opponent, to overcome grief after conceding a goal or as an expression of anger after bitter defeats. And last but not least, the songs of the audience serve to bridge phases of boredom in the stadium.

In England, a count was made as early as the 1970s of the average number of songs and short chants heard during a match. 147 songs with a wide variety of messages were identified. Most of the time, however, the songs are about getting into a positive mood during the game and keeping people in a state of excitement. It is possible that this form of *mood management* even influences the game. A study at the Austrian University of Salzburg has shown that when guitarists play music together, their brain waves also synchronize, which harmonizes their playing. A group of researchers from Cologne and Hanover in Germany now wanted to know whether music also has a positive effect on the teamwork of soccer players.

To do this, they had two teams play against each other for 30 min, in the first third completely without music. In the second period, the teams played with wireless headphones through which they were played precisely synchronized music that German composer Matthias Hornschuh had written especially for this purpose. The tempo was 140 beats per minute, which corresponds to the average sprint speed of a soccer player. In the last ten minutes, the players each heard different pieces of music with completely different rhythms. The athletes themselves had no idea what the others were listening to and what was in store for them. And indeed, with the synchronized sound on their ears, the players were clearly better—the individual player passed the ball faster, and more players were involved in a passing chain.

But even that probably wouldn't have helped the poor Irish against the fine rhythmists from Spain, whose passing game in those years could develop a breathtaking harmony even without music to their ears.

9.4 Trapped in the History of the Game

Actually, impartial referees should perceive every game situation independently of the context and judge it according to the rules, but this intention seems to be practically impossible to implement in reality. The feeling that a referee has made a so-called concession decision, i.e. that with a certain whistle he is correcting mistakes that he previously made, is widespread in stadiums.

The concession decision, however, is only the most extreme form of a distorted judging system, and not infrequently the players and coaches involved, as well as journalists commenting on the game, even find this kind of faultiness somehow fair. Then they talk about "compensatory justice," although the term "double injustice" would be even more accurate.

It is a mechanism that is hardly surprising, because referees often learn during matches that they have made a serious mistake. Some are explicitly informed at half-time about the correctness of their decisions, and communication with the video assistant can also address decisions that may not have been completely wrong, but were unfortunate and therefore possibly unfair. In addition, the coaches and substitutes on the sidelines are quite quick to inform each other about any supposed disadvantages, and this is then sometimes shouted into the game or mentioned in conversations with the fourth officials, who are connected to the other referees via radio.

Research on the phenomenon of concession decisions in soccer also indicates that referees by no means succeed in evaluating all situations regardless of their antecedents. They make their decisions in the context of the game. Studies show, for example, that comparable foul scenes in the penalty area are judged completely differently depending on whether the same team has already been awarded a penalty kick or not. If a team has already been awarded a penalty kick, a second penalty is rarely whistled after another foul in the penalty area. If, on the other hand, the opposing team has already been awarded a penalty, the frequency of penalties awarded increases massively.

In a rather complicated experiment on this phenomenon, different groups of referees were shown several scenes from a game to be evaluated. The first group was shown two clear penalty situations for team A. Those subjects who had given the first penalty clearly tended to dispense with the second penalty whistle. In the pictures shown to a second group, the first of these penalty scenes was omitted. The result: 34 percent of the subjects who had not seen the first foul at all, i.e. who had not yet given the first penalty, reacted to the pictures of the second foul with a penalty decision. Thus, the omission of a scene alone led to an enormous difference in the evaluation of an identical game situation. This astonishing finding raises the question of whether any inner resistance prevents referees from whistling two penalties for one team in one match, and the answer is quite clearly: Yes!

For the other test subjects, the penalty-worthy situation for Team B was mixed in with the game clips shown. 42 percent of the referees who had already awarded a penalty to Team A considered the hard tackle in the penalty area to be a foul, while the same scene was only considered a foul by 23 percent of the referees who had not yet awarded a penalty to Team A either. Accordingly, the willingness to blow the penalty whistle increases if the other team has already been awarded a penalty kick (Fig. 9.4).

However, the reasons for this phenomenon are still unclear. Perhaps impartial decisions are made in the spirit of so-called *game management*. This

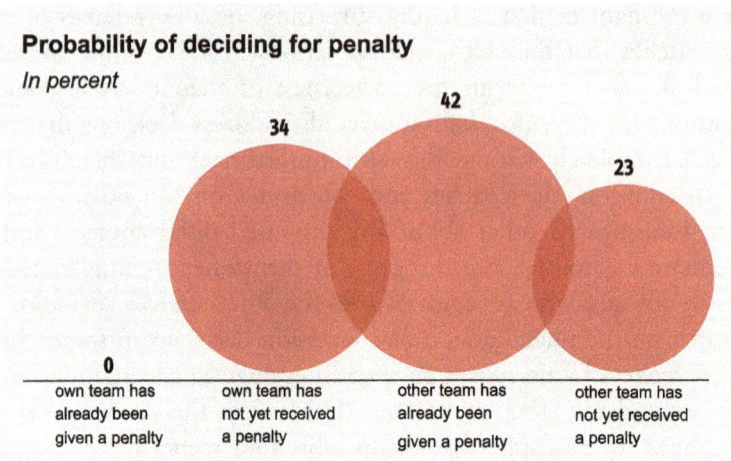

Fig. 9.4 The probability that a referee whistles two penalties for a team in one match is rather low. On the other hand, it is surprisingly common for a team to be awarded a penalty when the opponent has also previously been awarded a penalty kick

term refers to a feeling for the course of the game and the need to manage the match smoothly and fairly. Basically, good referees have a desire not to interfere too massively in the action; the old saying that the best games for referees are those in which no one particularly notices them will hold true for all eternity. However, when a referee whistles two penalties for a team, he significantly influences the outcome of the game, which contradicts his desire for inconspicuousness and restraint.

In addition, it is not uncommon for discrepancies to arise between strict interpretation of the rules and concern for fairness. When, for example, the whistle was blown in many close situations against one team or a team was awarded a dubious penalty kick, the experiment apparently grew the need to decide the other way around for the sake of fair game management. Coaches, managers and players know this, and they want to—and probably can—influence referees by complaining during games about an accumulation of perceived injustices.

Referee whistles therefore often only become comprehensible through their previous history, whereby conscious considerations on the part of the referees are not always involved. Rather, these are automatic processes in the course of which a certain prior knowledge becomes effective. And these processes can also ensure that the referees have inhibitions about whistling two penalties for one team in one game.

9.5 Goals with Handwriting

There is this wonderful dialogue in the film *"Looking for Eric,"* when Steve Evets, in the role of postman Eric Bishop, joins the unforgettable footballer Eric Cantona in a search for his "most wonderful moment of all". "It must have been a goal", exclaims Bishop, enumerating some of Cantona's most magnificent strikes, but the Frenchman only ever shakes his head. He can barely remember his many goals, he claims. At one point, the Manchester United legend says, "It was a pass." A pass to Denis Irwin, in a game against Tottenham Hotspur, "a gift, an offering to the great God of soccer," says Cantona, who plays himself in the fabulous film. His role is a fantasized psychotherapist for the unstable Bishop, who is not in control of his life.

"I tried in every game to give a gift to the audience", Cantona says. Successful passes, he says, are an act of communication, a contribution to a common work, and will always mean more to him than goals. Bishop marvels. Because, of course, even the preparation for a goal can be imbued with a special grace, nonetheless for most fans, artful goal finishes remain the most impressive moments of beauty. There are gorgeous-looking long-range shots that land in the corner, virtuoso dribbles that are refined into a goal, and many other circumstances, origin stories, or trajectories that give goals an exquisite aesthetic. And everyone can have their say here because as always when art is discussed, the matter is highly subjective. Which moments of soccer are truly beautiful? A rather astonishing study shows that apparently, the viewer's cultural background plays a decisive role in aesthetic perception.

For example, Philipp Lahm's 1–0 goal in the opening match of the 2006 World Cup, which Germany eventually won 4–2 against Costa Rica, was voted the most beautiful goal of the month by a wide margin, partly, of course, because it was a very important strike that gave the feverish host nation an initial rush of joy. However, an Italian research team would argue that this brilliant shot from the left edge of the penalty area into the top right corner would have thrilled the German spectators less if the trajectory had been from the right side into the left corner.

The scientists played Italian test subjects' soccer scenes with spectacular goals in which the trajectory of the ball ran from left to right in some cases. In other cases, the ball flew from right to left before landing in the goal. Now the subjects were asked to indicate how attractive and beautiful they found these goals. It turned out that shots from the left side that passed the goal line near the right goalwere perceived as significantly more beautiful. The scientists provided a surprising explanation for this finding.

Due to the course of the Latin script, which is widespread almost everywhere in Europe, movements that run from left to right (for example, also in the cinema when airplanes take off) are perceived as more harmonious and fluid in this culture. This sequence is virtually burned into the brain and shapes the perception even in situations that actually have nothing to do with the script. At first, this sounds like a rather daring explanation, but it could be verified quite easily.

If this assumption is true, people using a right-to-left trajectory would have to perceive the gracefulness of the gates differently, and this is exactly what happened in the study. The researchers presented the same material to people from the Arab culture and they found gates with trajectories from right to left much more beautiful. So the influence of the culture we live in is undeniable even in seemingly simple things like judging the beauty of a goal.

To substantiate this left–right effect, the same group of researchers then also presented boxing scenes to Italian and Arabians, who were now asked to assess when a punch was perceived as more violent. And indeed: Italians found punches from right to left much more violent and aggressive than punches from left to right, while Aribians judged exactly the opposite. Movements in the usual reading direction are thus generally perceived as more harmonious and less aggressive.

This astonishing theory is supported by the results of an American study by neuroscientists. Here, soccer referees (who came from cultures with Latin script) were asked to evaluate TV images showing tackles: Foul or no foul? One group was shown the images in the original direction of movement, while other test subjects were shown them mirror-inverted, i.e. in the opposite direction of movement. And indeed, tackles from the left to the right were less likely to be ruled a foul than actions with a movement against the usual reading direction. It would now be interesting to find out how the Japanese or Chinese judge since their writing runs from top to bottom.

10

Risk and Side Effects

© Norbert Schmidt/dpa/picture alliance

Thinking outside the box can be helpful, in life as well as in soccer and the well known coach of the Freiburg soccer team Christian Streich is particularly good at this. The longtime youth coach from the city of Freiburg, located in the German Black Forrest, who turned out to be a brilliant professional soccer coach for the premier league team in Freiburg after his move to the Bundesliga in January 2012, is an expert on all the fallacies, temptations, and aberrations that young players face. The side effects of the big dream of a professional career are often fatal. In an interview, Streich explains what kind of traps lurk at the sensitive transition from youth to adult soccer.

Many players have to realize much earlier that their career in a professional team is not going to work out, and that even the level of the players at lower level clubs will remain unattainable. And that obviously has to do not only with talent and training but with completely different risks. You need to be lucky enough to be born in the right month, otherwise, it doesn't help if the right stimuli were set in the very first years of life. Because it seems that children up to the age of seven should rather practice forms of play in which soccer competence emerges as a side effect, so to speak.

And all those who end up having to look for a profession other than that of a professional can always remain connected to soccer as fans. But that seems to be quite risky. It can be very nice to give your heart to a soccer club; some people as we know, base their entire life planning on the match schedules of the major competitions. But this hobby is not healthy for the heart.

10.1 Capricorn and Aquarius Prevail

For several decades, the dictionary publisher Pons has dedicated itself to the beautiful task of regularly selecting the word creations of the year, and in Germany Franz Beckenbauer was one of the very first winners in 2001. The multi-talented Bavarian captained Germany to world championship glory in 1974 and coached the team to world championship glory in 1990. He created the German term "Rumpelfußball" in a column for the German yellow press *Bild newspaper,* which means "scrappy soccer". It was a frighteningly accurate description of the disastrous state in which the national team and the best German players were trailing the developments at the top of the world around the turn of the millennium. The invention of the term "Rumpelfußball" was, in a sense, the rhetorical culmination of a development that saved German soccer, today we know that. After the disastrous performance of the German national team at the European Championship in 2000, when the DFB eleven was eliminated from a tournament with a shocking 0:3 against the substitute team of Portugal, for which coach Erich Ribbeck had reanimated the libero, which had become extinct in all halfway contemporary soccer locations, the realization matured that a few fundamental things had to change in German soccer.

In a hurry, the German Soccer Association (DFB) decided on a small reform, the most important consequence of which was the professionalization of the base system for talented players, before the great revolution swept over the soccer nation in 2002. On the one hand, all first- and second-division clubs were obliged to maintain professionally managed and well-funded performance centers, and on the other hand, since this moment of rethinking, enormous efforts have been made to find and optimally promote as many soccer talents as possible with the help of extensive sightings at various levels.

The first stage can be described as a kind of basic promotion and takes place in clubs, kindergartens, and schools. The second stage of talent development is based on support from the DFB support centers and the work of numerous elite soccer schools. The next step is elite support, where the youth departments of the licensed clubs and the junior national teams form the core of the support system. And the final stage of support, stage four, is then dedicated to the difficult transition to top-level soccer.

Presumably, the totality of these measures, with an elaborate tier system, is responsible for the German soccer upswing. However, it remains to be seen whether these upheavals can eliminate a rather astonishing injustice. We are talking about the so-called *Relative Age Effect*, which has been documented in various studies on a wide range of sports. This also applies to the first national soccer league.

When fixed cut-off dates are defined at the youth level to determine when players move up to higher age groups, children from certain birth months are sometimes massively disadvantaged. It would actually be reasonable to assume that roughly the same number of players from all months would arrive in the German premier league Bundesliga or the selected teams and that the birthday distribution would reflect the population as a whole. So, the chances of becoming a professional soccer player should not depend on which month the children were born. But this is not the case.

Analysis of the birthdays of more than 4,000 players in the first German premier league Bundesliga from 1963/64 to 2006/07 revealed a significant bias: the shorter a child was born after the cutoff date for transfer to the next higher division (previously August 1., since 1997 January 1.), the greater its chances of making it to the Bundesliga.

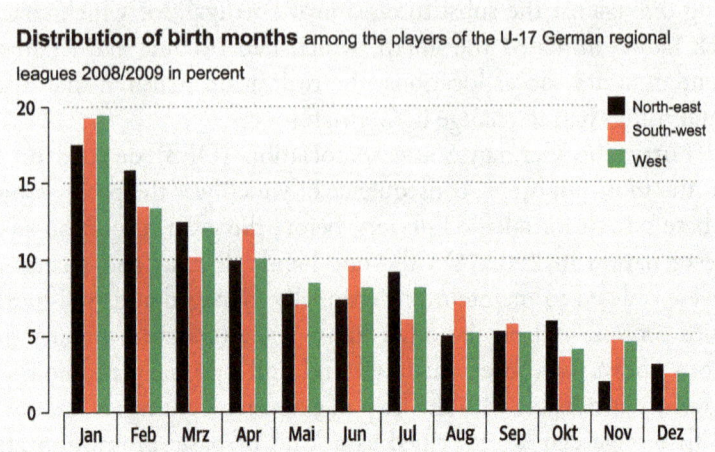

Fig. 10.1 Percentage distribution of the twelve months of birth from January to December among the players in the three U-17 national leagues (northeast, southwest, and west)

And this effect can also be impressively demonstrated at the junior level in the U17 first division, as another study shows. Here, 911 junior players from the 2008/09 season and their birthdays were registered; all of these talented players had to deal with the January 1. deadline in their young careers. Figure 10.1 shows the impressive result.

Almost 50% of the players were born in the first quarter, i.e. close to the cut-off date (Fig. 10.1). Accordingly, those with a birthday in December have significantly lower chances of a career that leads far up the ladder. The reasons for this probably lie in the promotion system and its cut-off date regulation. The older players (those born in the first quarter of the year) are often superior to the younger ones in physical comparison and thus have a better chance of taking important positions in the teams and prevailing in the end. In these early years, a few months difference in development makes a lot of difference. And because parents who are considering a successful soccer career for their child do the strangest things, there is certainly already the first offspring whose birthdays have been planned with the relative age effect in mind.

Birth data not only has the potential to open gates to high-performing cohorts but can actually lead to higher monetary value and thus income. It would be easy to mitigate the relative age effect if information about players' ages were properly considered in scouting and day-to-day training.

10.2 First Play, Then Practice

Many parents, or probably it would be better to say fathers, can't wait to send their young sons off to soccer practice. On the sidelines of the sports fields, where drills for four- to seven-year-olds are offered, ambitious people of all stripes gather and look at their boys with a mixture of pride and concern (and, more rarely, girls), who would often much rather be playing with sticks in the neighboring forest.

Of course, this is not possible because every training session is important for the career, many soccer parents believe. But they are mistaken. Today, it can be said with great certainty that, unlike youth athletes in individual sports such as track and field, gymnastics, or swimming, soccer players should by no means begin sport-specific training at kindergarten age. This is because the first years of life are initially about developing general coordinative, motor, and cognitive skills.

In addition, the age between four and seven is the most important phase for developing creative potential in dealing with sports play equipment. This is because correspondingly versatile thinking strategies can no longer be trained as efficiently in later training phases. Field reports of creative players indicate that childhood experiences with many different sports games increase the inventiveness and versatility of adult athletes. In addition, exercise biography studies of the German national team and Bundesliga players suggest that non-guided experimentation with sports games of all kinds in childhood had a positive effect on the creative potentials of later professionals.

Take for example the large scientific studies conducted by the Heidelberg and Cologne working groups over several years to investigate the influence of playing handball, soccer, field hockey, or general ball sports-related training on the development of creativity in children at the age of six. On the whole, the results speak in favor of cross-sport training to promote basic creativity components at preschool age and against overly specific soccer training (Fig. 10.2).

It makes sense to use different motor forms of execution (hand, foot, tennis, or field hockey stick) to prompt the children to repeatedly approach different tasks in a different—new—way (Fig. 10.3). This phase should then be followed by a period of sport-specific development, which is often not necessarily joyful. Increasingly larger training volumes are completed and techniques are repeated monotonously even under high stress until they are automated. Day after day, week after week. "We go to the training ground

Fig. 10.2 Star sign Aquarius: Leon Goretzka. (© Marcel Engelbrecht/firo Sportphoto/fi/augenklick/picture alliance)

so that we can show a little bit of lightness in the game on Saturdays," says Bundesliga coach Christian Streich, adding, "Only when you've gone far into detail like a madman before the match, you are sometimes rewarded with little moments of lightness. It's like a great musician who plays the violin—when he plays the violin lightly, everyone feels like they can fly a little. Then he's practiced like a pig."

Experts estimate around ten years or, in other words, 10,000 h of such sport-specific practice required to become a top international athlete. So, talent alone is by no means enough. And of course, not only professional soccer players have to go through these years of training, but also track and field athletes, weightlifters, cyclists or musical virtuosos, and many other artists who want to reach the top of the world with a very special skill. Unlike ball players, however, individual athletes do not require this high level of creativity. This is one reason why the peak of performance in sports such as swimming and gymnastics is reached in adolescence or in very early adulthood at the age of 15 to 20—after ten years of hard, monotonous practice. On the

Fig. 10.3 In the first years of life: better not just soccer. (© BERNHARD KUNZ/Fotoagentur Kunz/AUGENKLICK/KUNZ/picture alliance)

other hand, the best soccer players need creativity as well as technique and automaticity. The foundations for this are laid in childhood with the right forms of training.

10.3 Loyal, More Loyal, *Die Hard*

The outbreak of the pandemic and the long months of top-level soccer in front of empty stands were a tough break for all fans who want to go to the stadium regularly, but Silvia Krüger was hit particularly hard by the Corona restrictions. As a passionate supporter of the German team 1. FC Köln, she had followed all the compulsory matches of her heart's club in the stadium for 31 years. Both at home and away, more than 1,200 games. At the so called Betzenberg stadium in Kaiserslautern, she stood in the visitors' block with a fever of 40 degrees, and when her grandfather died on a Saturday morning in April 1988, she still went to the derby at archenemy Mönchengladbach and sang on the way home after the 1–0 away win: "Such a day, so wonderful like today." This makes her part of a very exclusive group that exists in many big clubs: the "watching all games fans" But then came the virus. At first, Krüger bravely accepted that an incredible series would now come to an end. "After all, this is force majeure. As soon as I can go back to the stadium, I will," she told the German newspaper *Kölner Stadtanzeiger*. But "when I heard the FC anthem in front of the TV, I still had to cry."

Krüger belongs to the fan group of so-called *Die-Hard-Fans* who never give up, just like Bruce Willis, who in the films of the same name lets nothing shake his resolve and his love. *Die-Hard-Fans* show a particularly high level of identification with their team or club. This group of soccer fans includes people who remain loyal to their team throughout their lives and possibly even beyond death (some clubs offer their fans a corresponding all-round package with associated funerals). They are the most loyal of all fans, whose everyday lives are highly influenced by soccer and a particular team. The british writer Nick Hornby, a devoted fan of the London soccer club Arsenal FC, described such a way of life in his bestselling autobiographical novel *Fever Pitch in a very impressive way.*

The Die-Hard-Fans are in contrast to the so-called *Fair-Weather-Fans*, who are attracted by success when the sun is shining at the club. As soon as the victories fail to materialize, they quickly move on and turn to another club, another sport or even a completely different leisure activity. That's why people often turn up their noses at *Fair-Weather-Fans* in the standing-room sections of stadiums, while *Die-Hard-Fans* like to think of themselves as supposedly "real" fans.

Therefore, their connection to the club is so close that they come to the stadium even when one game after another is lost, when the soccer is cruel to watch and an icy wind sweeps through a half-empty arena. *Die-Hard-Fans* invest not only money but, like Silvia Krüger, a lot of time for away trips. And they often see themselves as representatives of a fan culture that needs to be protected because in the eyes of people like Philipp Marquardt, it is threatened by commercialization, by the rules of conduct in modern stadiums and by the restrictions imposed by clubs.

Markhardt is a German team of Hamburger SV supporter and spokesman for the ultra-group "Chosen", and has rather elitist ideas about what can be subsumed under the term fan culture. "Public viewing is certainly not part of it," he is quoted as saying in an article on the German newspaper *Zeit-Online*, "it's an event put on by professional organizers to make a lot of money."

That's how some supporters think, but certainly not all *Die-Hard-Fans*, *who devote* energy and lifetime to being involved with their clubs. To avoid a misconception: The specific group of *Ultras* certainly belong to the group of *Die-Hard-Fans as well,* but the group of *Die-Hard-Fans* is much, much larger and goes far beyond that of *Ultras.* It is true that the entirety of stadium visitors is almost as heterogeneous as the population, and the question of who is now the custodian of fan culture is a highly controversial one. But for sociologists and sports scientists, *Die-Hard-Fans* are obviously interesting objects of research because they sometimes behave in a rather special way. Surveys have shown that these particularly devoted supporters fundamentally consider themselves to be special, and they also have a higher collective self-esteem than other people. They tend to behave more aggressively (especially verbally) toward fans of the opposing team than people with low identification, and they get into violent confrontations more often than other fans. Science thus confirms many clichés that circulate about particularly passionate stadium visitors, including how supporters feel about their clubs and their teams.

In this case, it is worth taking a look at the results of the Münster team Identification Project, which one of the authors of this book, Bernd Strauss, initiated over 20 years with many students and colleagues back in 2002 with the World Cup in South Korea/Japan and which is still running today. Since this event and the following World Cups (and some European Championships), among other things, the team identification of the German Münster citizens with the German national soccer team has been determined in street surveys during the tournament. Thousands have taken part over time, and of course these were not only *Die-Hard-Fans*, but also *Fair-Weather-Fans* or people who don't like soccer at all.

A brief reminder: the German team was finalist in the 2002 World Cup, third in the 2006 World Cup at home, fourth in South Africa in 2010, and world champion in 2014. Over the years and tournaments, there is a clear dependence of identification on success over time. Many people become fans of the team's success, and thus initially *Fair-Weather-Fans*. It also shows that over the last 20 years, the German team has earned the affection, that is, the identification, (at least until 2014), from tournament to tournament it has increased, often starting at the beginning of a World Cup where it ended at the previous World Cup, four years earlier. And the data also show that the identification of men and women is getting closer and closer. And last but not least, it can be observed that more and more female fans are becoming enthusiastic about the national soccer team.

Basically, as fans identify, their emotional reactions to success and failure become more intense, especially, of course, among *Die-Hard-Fans.* After victories, they show strong positive emotions; after disappointments, they feel bad. Fans who form a bond with their club risk feeling sad and down about a game that others are running, but this is also where the very big appeal lies (Fig. 10.4).

And one thing, in particular, characterizes *Die-Hard-Fans*: their (excessive) and often unrealistic optimism. In the Münster team identification project, this was demonstrated in a special way in 2018. Even if not everyone likes to remember, 2018 the World Cup took place, in which the German team was already eliminated after three games in the preliminary round. It was a major failure and could not be compared to the German team in all World Cups ever. In addition to the identification with the German team, the citizens of Münster were asked shortly before the first game (against Mexico, which was then lost), how high they think the probability is that Germany will be World Cup champion 2018. 56% was the mean, meaning a high probability was expected before the tournament that Germany would win the World Cup. Given the competition, even this was already very, very optimistic and hardly realistic. After the third game and the elimination against South Korea, the probability was once again investigated, but now they focused on the chances of the German team to win the 2022 World Cup in Qatar. The average probability was 47%, and very special contributors to this result were those who identified highly with the team, i.e. those who tend to be described as *Die-Hard-Fans*. At first glance, this value is astonishing, considering that the team had just been eliminated from the tournament the day before. But at second glance, it's understandable, because *Die-Hard-Fans in* particular don't give up their emotional connection and identification with the team so quickly, especially not after just three defeats. History teaches us that this high expectation of winning the

Fig. 10.4 Red up to the skin: fan of 1. FC Kaiserslautern. (© Eibner-Pressefoto/Neis/picture alliance)

2022 World Cup was much too high and the German national team failed again in the 1st round. Once again, the German team was eliminated after three games, highly disappointing and a disaster for all fans in Germany. But the same pattern of results as in 2018 occurred in dne surveys of the citizens of Münster: Again, it was the *Die-hard-Fans* who were very optimistic after the German team's elimination from the tournament that the German team would become European soccer champion in 2024—one of the core results of the survey of more than 2,500 Münster residents in the 30 days before and during the 2022 World Cup in Qatar.

But there is more to tell about fans and how identification interferes with everyday life, far beyond sports.

In one other survey, for example, German men reported greater life satisfaction immediately after national team victories during the 1982 World Cup than before the game. And in a study conducted shortly before the first Iraq war, negative sentiment among fans after their team lost games led them to believe that a U.S. war with Iraq and major devastation were more likely than after winning games.

Even the chances of their own personal success outside of sports are correlated by fans with high identification with the results of their teams. After supporters had witnessed a defeat of their basketball team live on the TV screen, they were more skeptical about their own performance in a task they had to solve afterward than people who witnessed a successful game of their team on the TV screen. And there is a whole host of other cognitive biases: Fans often explain their team's success in terms of personal (internal) factors, such as their team's strength or the athletes' abilities. When their own club loses, on the other hand, this is often explained by external (extrinsic) factors such as bad luck or weak refereeing. Their search for causes leads to distorted interpretations.

And finally: fans believe that they can help their team through their own actions and thus play a significant role in its success. They want to support their club with maximum means, and some fans use elaborate choreographies or visual aids such as confetti rain, Bengal fires and seas of flags to do so. Coordinated chanting with a lead singer – the capo, also plays a major role here. Outside of the game, they also try to influence the club's fortunes through concrete behaviour. For example, when a team bus is prevented from leaving in protest or spectators loudly demand that the coach should be sacked. Fans are firmly convinced that they can personally influence sporting events through their behaviour. In fact, this influence is rather small, but a true *Die-Hard-Fan* wouldn't be a fan if he didn't believe in himself and his impact: even beyond death.

10.4 Palpitations

Such a life as a soccer fan is a rather dangerous affair. Supporters who devote a large part of their lives to this passion are often on the road, at home matches, but even more so on away trips. The risks are already lurking on the way there or on the way back, on the highway, in the airplane. In addition, there are all kinds of dangers in the narrow, high-ceilinged arenas; falls, broken bones and other accidents can occur. Incidentally, this threat is much higher than becoming a victim of an act of violence by hooligans or other beating stadium visitors. In the following, however, we will deal with a health hazard that hardly anyone has in mind when they turn to the pleasure of watching soccer: the so-called cardiovascular event, i.e., heart attack or even cardiac death in the vicinity of soccer matches (Fig. 10.5).

Already on the journey to the stadium, many spectators are subjected to a great deal of crowding, in packed special trains, buses or streetcars, and in the stadium, it hardly gets any better. The cramped conditions in the standing stands of the big Bundesliga arenas are actually too frightening for many people to feel comfortable there for two hours. That's why it requires an excellent level of training. Older people are rarely seen in these seats anyway. The fact that many visitors consume alcohol while spectating feverish, suffering, hoping, singing, shouting and jumping doesn't make things any better. In addition, many fans simply eat an unhealthy diet. They eat too much fat and too much food, at least under certain circumstances, as a French study has found.

Marketing researchers looked at North American data from cities that are home to an NFL team (i.e., a professional American football team). They analyzed food sales in those cities (and for comparison, the cities that did not host a team) the day after Sunday games from food industry statistics and found that whenever the home team lost, food consumption of unhealthy food increased and decreased when the home team won. They were able to see the same pattern in subsequent experiments among French soccer fans.

In short, many fans—and this finding does not only apply to the most loyal fans in the standing room—are in a high state of excitement and stress. This can also be measured. During the 2010 World Cup in South Africa, physicians examined the saliva of Spanish supporters before, during and after they watched their team's final match against the Netherlands. Further samples were taken at public viewings, as well as from supporters watching the match at home. The first thing that stood out was that a significantly elevated concentration of the sex hormone testosterone was found (significantly

10 Risk and Side Effects   197

Fig. 10.5 Endangered hearts: The intensity of the game has its downsides—even for fans. (© Frank Hoermann/SVEN SIMON/picture alliance)

more in men than in women). This hormone is actually released in high doses when one's own social status or home territory has to be defended against attackers. In other words, in situations where dominance and increased aggressiveness are required. The purpose of this natural reaction is to provide additional energy.

In addition, the Spanish physicians detected a greatly increased concentration of cortisol in the saliva of the test participants, a sign of very great stress that the fans apparently experienced during the game. And as the duration of the final increased, so did the release of cortisol. Poorly trained people, possibly also with unfavourable eating habits, who smoke frequently and are drunk, can therefore get into a situation while watching soccer that many

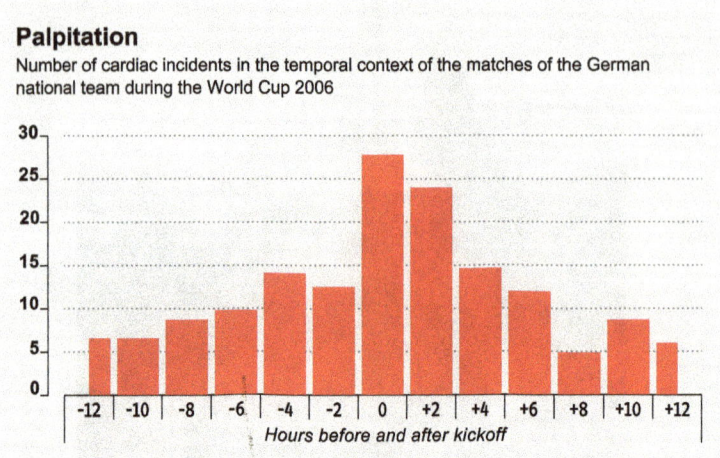

Fig. 10.6 Cardiovascular events in the temporal context of the matches of the German national team (mean values from seven matches) during the World Cup 2006. 0 denotes the start of the match. The negative numbers denote the hours before, the positive ones after

medical experts consider to be quite risky. And this assumption fits with the results of a study from 2006 (Fig. 10.6).

During the 2006 World Cup in Germany, the Munich Clinic investigated whether the excitement before, after and during the games could possibly lead to an accumulation of cardiovascular incidents. The medical experts wanted to know how many heart attacks occurred at which times on the match days of the German team. The astonishing result: there was a clear accumulation of heart symptoms around kickoff, and while the games were going on, the risk of heart attack was also increased.

On the one hand, the great excitement is perceived as positive. Emotions such as joy and sadness, feelings that can be felt immediately and physically, are beautiful and part of the fascination that fans feel towards the game of soccer. But like almost everything beautiful in life, this passion also harbours dangers.

10.5 Real Interest in Teammates Helps to Play Better Football

Christian Streich was one of the most successful youth coaches in Germany for many years. With the U19s of SC Freiburg, he won the German championship once and the German DFB Cup competition three times before being promoted to head coach of the Bundesliga team at the end of 2011. There, he consistently relied on players he had trained himself and launched a fairy-tale phase of success. Hardly anyone can find a better approach to young soccer players who still have to take a few last decisive steps to ensure that the dream of a professional career does not end in a major disappointment (Fig. 10.7).

Mr. Streichthey always say that the transition from the youth divisions to the adults is very difficult, with many highly talented players falling by the wayside. SC Freiburg is very successful at precisely this point. What's the secret?

First of all, we have the locational advantage here because it's easier to get into the first team than e.g. at VfL Wolfsburg where the professional squad is simply filled with prominent names. Less obvious, but very important, is the fact that the permeability among coaches is also high.

Why is that Good? You Could also Say that New Impulses from Outside Inspire the Work

The big advantage is that the players know very well how I and the other coaches think, also in the pedagogical-psychological area. There are

Fig. 10.7 Thoughtful developer: Christian Streich, the coach of SC Freiburg. (© O. Behrendt/contrastphoto/picture alliance)

fundamental things that players no longer have to learn if they have been trained with us. That frees up capacity for the real work. During the 90 min of training that we have every day, we try not to let any time go by because the ball reception or the sharpness of the pass are not so good. That's a matter of course for the players from our soccer school. It's about meticulousness, and the players have internalized that. New people who don't know us take longer to work on the things we really care about. With a consistent philosophy through all the teams in a club, it's more about little details like that than whether you play a 4–4-2 or a 4–2-3-1 system. It also helps enormously if we know the players as people and they know us.

It's Always Said that the Climate in Freiburg is Warmer and Warmer Than Elsewhere. Is that also an Aspect of the Success of the Freiburg Football School?
I don't know exactly. Maybe this image comes from the fact that we believe some form of interest in the teammates helps them play better soccer. It's important to us that the players and the coaches want to know what kind of people they're playing with. Because if that interest is there with a lot of players on the field, then that gives a stronger bond, then the team plays better soccer. It may still be the case that eleven players thrown together win against those who are bonded because they are simply better, but this social aspect is becoming increasingly important in an environment characterized by increasing individualization.

A Modern Variant of the Elf Friends Myth?
That's the funny thing. On the one hand, players let themselves be managed as individual athletes, and on the other hand, the family is becoming more and more important. The tattooed bodies of the players have grandma, dad, mom, wife and kids written all over them. But why do they have all the brothers on them? They just have a longing to have someone they can rely on. Clubs are changed, there are constant offers and options, which leads to the question: Where do I really belong?

What Do the Players Who don't Make It at Freiburg Fail at?
Most of them don't make it because there aren't enough jobs. There are a few spots, and a lot of people are competing for them. But for those who are strong enough, there's another very big difficulty in making the jump to the Bundesliga: These players were always regulars in their youth, they constantly played against Bayern, Leverkusen, and Stuttgart. Then they join our second team, the amateurs, and are constantly on the bench in their first year.

The Replacement Feels like a Crash?
Yes, and if they don't make the starting line-up right away, they think they're thousands of miles away from their goal. But they're really close. The truth is that one of them is playing because of a few minor problems, and the other is just barely sitting on the bench. Dealing with that, maybe continuing to work for another year or two, and staying patient is very, very difficult. The big question is what the players do in the two years they have to hold out. Whether they are really physically and mentally fit afterwards. Or whether they keep saying to themselves, "The world is unfair!".

Source graphics

Fig. 1.1 cf. Riedl, D., Staufenbiel, K., Strauss, B. & Heuer, B. (2014). The global home advantage in soccer: Status, developments and causes. https://psyarxiv.com/zaujy/

Fig. 2.1 Williams, A. M., Davids, K., & Williams, J. G. (1999). Visual perception and action in sport. London, UK: E. & F. N. Spon. (modified from Fig. 5.4, p. 160)

Fig. 2.1 cf. Hagemann, N., Lotz, S. & Cañal-Bruland, R. (2008). Wahrnehmungs-Handlungs-Kopplung beim taktischen Entscheidungstraining – eine exploratorische Studie. E-Journal Bewegung und Training, 2, 17–27. (Fig. 1, p. 20)

Fig. 2.3 Memmert, D. (2019). Fußballspiele werden im Kopf entschieden: Kognitives Training, Kreativität und Spielintelligenz im Amateur- und Leistungsbereich. Aachen: Meyer & Meyer.

Fig. 2.5 https://www.soccerbot360.de/

Fig. 2.10 Memmert, D. (Hrsg.) (2022). Spielanalyse. Berlin: Springer-Verlag.

Fig. 2.11 Memmert, D., & Raabe, D. (2019). Revolution im Profifußball. Mit Big Data zur Spielanalyse 4.0 (2. Auflage). Springer-Verlag: Berlin.

D. Memmert et al., *Mind Match Soccer*, https://doi.org/10.1007/978-3-662-68035-3

Fig. 4.5 cf. König, S. (2008). Die Strukturen der Sieger – Überlegungen zu einer Theorie der Mannschaftsführung in Sportspielen. In A. Woll, W. Klöckner, M. Reichmann, & M. Schlag (Hrsg.), Sportspielkulturen erfolgreich gestalten. Von der Trainerbank bis in die Schulklasse (p. 25–38). Hamburg: Czwalina. (modified from Fig. 1, p. 27)

Fig. 5.4 cf. Heuer A., Müller C., Rubner O., Hagemann N., & B. Strauss (2011). Usefulness of Dismissing and Changing the Coach in Professional Soccer. PLoS ONE 6:e17664.

Fig. 6.2 cf. Unkelbach, C., & Memmert, D., (2010). Crowd noise as a cue in referee decisions contributes to the home advantage. Journal of Sport and Exercise Psychology, 32, 483–498. (created according to data, p. 489)

Fig. 6.3 cf. Memmert, D., Unkelbach, C., Ertmer, J. & Rechner, M (2008). Gelb oder kein Gelb? Persönliche Verwarnungen im Fußball als Kalibrierungsproblem. Zeitschrift für Sportpsychologie, 15, 1–11. (created according to table 1, p. 4)

Fig. 7.1 cf. Weigelt, M., Memmert, D. & Schack, T. (2012). Kick it like Ballack: The effects of goalkeeping gestures on goal-side selection in experienced soccer players and soccer novices. Journal of Cognitive Psychology, 24, 942–956. (modified from Fig. 2, p. 6)

Fig. 7.4 vgl Fasold, F., Wühr, P., & Memmert, D. (2017). Response requirements affect offside judgments in football (soccer). Psychological Research, 83, 924–934

Fig. 7.5 cf. Wühr, P., Fasold, F., & Memmert, D. (2020). The impact of team preferences on soccer offside judgments in laypersons: a quasi-experimental study. Cognitive Research: Principles and Implications, 5(1), 1–24.

Fig. 7.6 cf. Spitz, J., Wagemans, J., Memmert, D., Williams, A. M., & Helsen, W. F. (2021). Video assistant referees (VAR): The impact of technology on decision making in association football referees. Journal of Sports Sciences, 39(2), 147–153.

Fig. 8.10 cf. Memmert, D., Strauss, B., & Theweleit, D. (2013). Der Fußball, die Wahrheit. (p. 188)

Fig. 9.4 cf. Plessner, H. & Betsch, T. (2001). Sequential Effects in important Referee Decisions. Journal of Sport & Exercise Psychology, 23, 254–339. (created according to data, p. 257)

Fig. 10.1 cf. Augste, C., & Lames, M. (2011). The relative age effect and success in german elite U-17 soccer teams. Journal of Sports Sciences, 29, 983–987. (modified from Fig. 2, p. 985)

References

1 Faith and knowledge

"Home advantage is nowadays no longer as significant as it once was ".

Beckmann, N. (2021). Statistical influence of travelling distance on home advantage over 57 years in the men's German first soccer division. *German Journal of Exercise and Sport Research, online first,* 1–9.

Bryson, A., Dolton, P., Reade, J. J., Schreyer, D., & Singleton, C. (2021). Causal effects of an absent crowd on performances and refereeing decisions during Covid-19. *Economics Letters, 198,* 109664.

Fischer, K., & Haucap, J. (2021). Does crowd support drive the home advantage in professional football? Evidence from German ghost games during the COVID-19 pandemic. *Journal of Sports Economics, 22*(8), 982–1008.

Heuer, A. (2012). *Der perfekte Tipp Statistik des Fußballspiels*. Wiley.

Pollard, R., & Pollard, G. (2005). Long-term trends in home advantage in professional team sports in North America and England (1876–2003). *Journal of sports sciences, 23*(4), 337–350.

Riedl, D., Staufenbiel, K., Strauss, B., & Heuer, B. (2014). The global home advantage in soccer: Status, developments and causes. https://psyarxiv.com/zaujy/.

Strauss, B., Staufenbiel, K., van Meurs, E., & MacMahon, C. (2021, accepted). Social influence of spectators. In J. Schüler, M. Wegner, H. Plessner, & R. Eklund (Eds.), *Sport Psychology.* https://psyarxiv.com/uet7f/.

Tilp, M., & Thaller, S. (2020, 05. November). Covid-19 has turned home advantage into home disadvantage in the German Soccer Bundesliga. *Frontiers in Sports and Active Living.* https://doi.org/10.3389/fspor.2020.593499.

Wunderlich, F., Weigelt, M., Rein, R., & Memmert, D. (2021). How does spectator presence affect football? Home advantage remains in European top-class football matches played without spectators during the COVID-19 pandemic. *Plos one, 16*(3), e0248590.

„The home is my castle": *(aus* https://universal_lexikon.deacademic.com/276035/). Accessed: 3 Dec 2023.

UEFA (2021, 27. Juni). Abolition of the away goals rule in all UEFA club competitions. *UEFA.com.* https://www.uefa.com/insideuefa/mediaservices/mediareleases/news/026a-1298aeb73a7a-5b64cb68d920-1000--abolition-of-the-away-goals-rule-in-all-uefa-club-competitions/.

1.2 Self-confidence

Bandura, A. (1997). *Self-efficacy: The exercise of control.* Freeman.

Carron, A. V., Hausenblas, H. A., & Eys, M. A. (2005). *Group Dynamics in Sport.* Fitness.

Feltz, D., Short, S. E., & Sullivan, P.J. (2007). *Self-Efficacy in Sport.* Human Kinetics.

Heuer, A. (2012). *Der perfekte Tipp Statistik des Fußballspiels.* Wiley.

Kane, T. D., Marks, M. A., Zaccaro, S. J., & Blair, V. (1996). Self-efficacy, personal goals, and wrestlers` self-regulation. *Journal of Sport and Exercise Psychology, 18*(1), 36–48.

Neave, N., & Wolfson, S. (2003). Testosterone, territoriality, and the 'home advantage'. *Physiology and Behavior, 78*(2), 269–275.

1.3 First match away? No matter!

Eugster, M. J. A., Gertheiss, J., & Kaiser, S. (2011). Having the second leg at home—advantage in the UEFA champions league knockout phase? *Journal of Quantitative Analysis in Sports, 7,* 1–11.

1.4 Voodoo, sorcerers, urinals

Calin-Jageman, R. J., & Caldwell, T. L. (2014). Replication of the superstition and performance study by Damisch, Stoberock, and Mussweiler (2010). *Social Psychology, 45,* 239–245.

Damisch, L., Stoberock, B., & Mussweiler, T. (2010). Keep your fingers crossed! How superstition improves performance. *Psychological Science, 21,* 1014–1020.

Köster, P. (2015, 07. Februar). Sternzeichen, Spiderman und Kondome. *11 Freunde.* https://11freunde.de/artikel/sternzeichen-spiderman-und-kondome/489160. Zugegriffen: 6. Mai 2022.

Schaar, T. (2012, 13 Februar). „Ein Gefühl der Leere". Interview mit Anthony Baffoe. https://11freunde.de/artikel/ein-gef%C3%BChl-der-leere/578214. Zugegriffen: 6. Mai 2022.

2 Art and intelligence

2.1 Reading the game

Aksum, K. M., Pokolm, M., Bjørndal, C. T., Rein., R., Memmert, D., & Jordet, G. (2021) Scanning activity in elite youth football players. *Journal of Sports Sciences, 39,* 2401–2410.

Hagemann, N., Lotz, S., & Cañal-Bruland, R. (2008). Wahrnehmungs-Handlungs-Kopplung beim taktischen Entscheidungstraining – eine exploratorische Studie. *E-Journal Bewegung und Training, 2,* 17–27.

Pulling, C., Kearney, P., Eldridge, D., & Dicks, M. (2018). Football coaches' perceptions of the introduction, delivery and evaluation of visual exploratory activity. *Psychology of Sport and Exercise, 39,* 81–89.

Schultz, F., Daniel, J., & Höner, O. (2018). Antizipation von Fußballtorhütern. Konzeption und Evaluation einer kognitiven Leistungsdiagnostik. *Leistungssport, 48*(1), 50–55.

Williams, A. M., Davids, K., & Williams, J. G. (1999). *Visual perception and action in sport.* E. & F. N. Spon.

2.2 Head thing

Harris, D., Wilson, M. R., & Vine, S. J. (2018). A systematic review of commercial cognitive training devices: Implications for use in sport. *Frontiers in Psychology, 9,* 709.

Memmert, D. (2019). *Fußballspiele werden im Kopf entschieden: Kognitives Training, Kreativität und Spielintelligenz im Amateur- und Leistungsbereich.* Meyer & Meyer.

Scharfen, H. E., & Memmert, D. (2019). Measurement of cognitive functions in experts and elite athletes: A meta-analytic review. *Applied Cognitive Psychology, 33*(5), 843–860.

Vestberg, T., Gustafson, R., Maurex, L., Ingvar, M., & Petrovic, P. (2012). Executive functions predict the success of top-soccer players. *PLoS ONE, 7*(4), e34731.

Vestberg, T., Reinebo, G., Maurex, L., Ingvar, M., & Petrovic, P. (2017). Core executive functions are associated with success in young elite soccer players. *PloS ONE, 12*(2), e170845.

2.3 From street soccer to creativity

Biermann, Ch. (2009). *Die Fußball-Matrix.* Kiepenheuer & Witsch.

Kempe, M., & Memmert, D. (2018). "Good, better, creative": The influence of creativity on goal scoring in elite soccer. *Journal of Sports Sciences, 36,* 2419–2423.

Memmert, D. (2010). Creativity, Expertise, and Attention: Exploring their Development and their Relationships. *Journal of Sport Science, 29,* 93–104.

Memmert, D., Hüttermann, S., & Orliczek, J. (2013). Decide like Lionel Messi! The impact of regulatory focus on divergent thinking in sports. *Journal of Applied Social Psychology, 43*(10), 2163–2167.

Vallett, D., Lamb, R., & Annetta, L. (2013). The gorilla in the room: The impacts of video-game play on visual Attention. *Computers in Human Behavior, 29,* 2183–2187.

2.4 Doers and thinkers

Beckmann, J., & Trux, J. (1991). Wen lasse ich wo spielen? Persönlichkeitseigenschaften und die Eignung für bestimmte Positionen in Sportspielmannschaften. *Sportpsychologie, 5*(3), 18–21.

Effenberg, S. (2012). *Ich hab`s allen gezeigt*. Bastei.

2.5 "mentality monsters": A mystery

Bem, S. L. (1981). Gender schema theory: A cognitive account of sex typing source. *Psychological Review, 88,* 354.

Dugandzic, D. (2019). Bälle erobern, Tore verhindern mit MENTALITÄT. https://misc.fussballtraining.com/blaetterfunktion/info33_tn/files/assets/common/downloads/dfb_talente_fordern_und_foerdern.pdf. Zugegriffen: 6. Mai 2022.

Evans, T. (2021, 02. März). Liverpool approach critical period as Jurgen Klopp's 'mentality monsters' face toughest test yet. *INDEPENDENT.* https://www.independent.co.uk/sport/football/premier-league/liverpool/jurgen-klopp-chelsea-fixture-b1809600.html. Zugegriffen: 6. Mai 2022.

Strauss, B., Köller, O., & Möller, J. (1996). Geschlechtsrollentypologien – die empirische Überprüfung des balancierten und des additiven Modells. *Zeitschrift für Differentielle und Diagnostische Psychologie, 17,* 67–83.

2.6 The clueless experts

Andersson, P., Edman, J., & Ekman, M. (2005). Predicting the World Cup 2002 in Soccer: performance and confidence of experts and non-experts. *International Journal of Forecasting, 21,* 565–576.

Andersson, P., Memmert, D., & Popowic, E. (2009). Forecasting Outcomes of the World Cup 2006 in Football: Performance and Confidence of Bettors and Naïve Laypeople. *Psychology of Sport & Exercise, 10,* 116–123.

Biermann, C. (2013). Der beste Profiwetter der Welt. *11Freunde #137,* 78–83.

Forrest, D., Goddard, J., & Simmons, R. (2005). Odds-setters as forecasters: the case of English football. *International Journal of Forecasting, 21,* 551–564.

Heuer, A. (2020, 19. März). From identification of random contributions to determination of the optimum forecast of a soccer match. *Arxiv.* https://arxiv.org/abs/2003.09352

Wunderlich, F., & Memmert, D. (2018). The betting odds rating system: Using soccer forecasts to forecast soccer. *PloS one, 13*(6), e0198668.

2.7 Computers decrypting the game

Memmert, D., & Rein, R. (2018). Match analysis, Big Data and tactics: current trends in elite soccer. *Deutsche Zeitschrift für Sportmedizin, 69,* 65–72.

Perl, J. (2004). A Neural Network approach to movement pattern analysis. *Human Movement Science, 23,* 605–620.

Perl, J., Grunz, A., & Memmert, D. (2013). Tactics in soccer: an advanced approach. *International Journal of Computer Science in Sport, 12,* 33–44.

Perl, J., & Memmert, D. (2011). Net-Based Game Analysis by Means of the Software Tool SOCCER. *International Journal of Computer Science in Sport, 10,* 77–84.

Rein, R., Raabe, D., & Memmert, D. (2017). "Which pass is better?" Novel approaches to assess passing effectiveness in elite soccer. *Human Movement Science, 55,* 172–181.

Rein, R., & Memmert, D. (2016). Big data and tactical analysis in elite soccer: future challenges and opportunities for sports science. *SpringerPlus, 5*(1), 1410.

3   Friends and enemies

3.1 The myth of the 11 friends
Carron, A. V., Colman, M. M., Wheeler, J., & Stevens, D. (2002). Cohesion and performance in sport: A meta analysis. *Journal of Sport and Exercise Psychology, 24*(2), 168–188.
Carron, A. V., Hausenblas, H. A., & Eys, M. A. (2005). *Group Dynamics in Sport*. Fitness.
Leinemann, J. (1997). *Ein Leben, eine Legende*. Rowohlt.
McLaren, C. D., & Spink, K. S. (2020). Do members of a winning soccer team engage in more communication than a losing team? A single-game study of two competing teams. *International Journal of Sport Communication, 13*(2), 145–156.
Raue, C., Dreiskämper, D., & Strauss, B. (2020). Do we agree on who is playing the ball? developing a video-based measurement for shared mental models in tennis doubles. *PLoS ONE, 15*(12). e0242783.
Schlicht, W., & Strauss, B. (2003). *Sozialpsychologie des Sports*. Hogrefe.
Wilhelm, A. (2001). *Im Team zum Erfolg*. Pabst.

3.2 Free speech, control and communication
Andersen, T. L., Moldenæs, T., & Ronglan, L. T. (2022). When different logics meet: the crisis communication of a national head coach in elite football. *Soccer & Society, 23*(2), 159–172.
Benoit, W. L. (1997). Image repair discourse and crisis communication. *Public relations review, 23*(2), 177–186.
Glantz, M. (2010). The Floyd Landis doping scandal: Implications for image repair discourse. *Public Relations Review, 36*(2), 157–163.
Tippenhauer, H.-D. (2012). *Der Einfluss von Führungsspielern in der Fußball-Bundesliga*. Lit-Verlag.

3.3 Fans, hate, violence
Bliesener, T. (2006). Sport und Hooligans. In H. Haag & B. Strauss (Eds.), *Themenfelder der Sportwissenschaft* (pp. 319–336). Hofmann.
Kerr, J. H. (1994). *Understanding Soccer Hooliganism*. Open University Press.
Pilz, G.A. (2012). Zuschauergewalt im Fußball – Vorurteile und Diskriminierung: Hooligans, Ultras und Hooltras. In B. Strauss (Eds.), *Sportzuschauer* (pp. 215–239). Hogrefe.
Statista (2022, 21. Januar). Anzahl der verletzten Personen bei Spielen der 1. Bundesliga und 2. Fußball-Bundesliga in der Spielzeit 2020/2021. https://de.statista.com/statistik/daten/studie/205791/umfrage/verletzte-personen-bei-bundesligaspielen/.

3.4 When citizens freak out

Le Bon, G. (1895). *Die Psychologie der Massen.* Alfred Körner. (Zitat von pp. 16 in der 38. Ed., 1931)

Haslam, S. A., Reicher, S. D., & Van Bavel, J. J. (2019). Rethinking the nature of cruelty: The role of identity leadership in the Stanford Prison Experiment. *American Psychologist, 74*(7), 809–822.

Le Texier, T. (2019). Debunking the Stanford Prison Experiment. *American Psychologist, 74*(7), 823–839.

Rabbie, J. M., & Horowitz, M. (1969). Arousal of ingroup-outgroup bias by a chance win or loss. *Journal of Personality and Social Psychology, 13,* 269–277.

Schlicht, W., & Strauss, B. (2003). *Sozialpsychologie des Sports.* Hogrefe.

Tajfel, H. (1982). Social psychology of intergroup relations. *Annual Review of Psychology, 33,* 1–39.

Zimbardo, P. G. (1969). The human choice. Individuation, reason, and order versus deindividuation, impulse, and chaos. In W.J. Arnold & D. Devine (Eds.), *Nebraska Symposium on Motivation* (Vol. 17, pp. 237–307). University of Nebraska Press.

4 Power and powerlessness

4.1 Cold love—pressure, exhaustion and depression

Jensen, S. N., Ivarsson, A., Fallby, J., Dankers, S., & Elbe, A. M. (2018). Depression in Danish and Swedish elite football players and its relation to perfectionism and anxiety. *Psychology of Sport and Exercise, 36,* 147–155.

Omalu, B. I., DeKosky, S. T., Minster, R. L., Kamboh, M. I., Hamilton, R. L., & Wecht, C. H. (2005). Chronic traumatic encephalopathy in a National Football League player. *Neurosurgery, 57*(1), 128–134.

Omalu, B. I., & Tabb, M.A. (2017). *Truth doesn't have a side: My alarming discovery about the danger of contact sports.* Zondervan.

Rice, S. M., Purcell, R., De Silva, S., Mawren, D., McGorry, P. D., & Parker, A. G. (2016). The mental health of elite athletes: A narrative systematic review. *Sports medicine, 46*(9), 1333–1353.

Schinke, R. J., Stambulova, N. B., Si, G., & Moore, Z. (2018). International society of sport psychology position stand: Athletes' mental health, performance, and development. *International Journal of Sport and Exercise Psychology, 16*(6), 622–639.

Windmann, A. (2020, 18. Juni). „Ich brauche keinen Beifall mehr". *Der Spiegel.* https://www.spiegel.de/sport/andre-schuerrle-beendet-ueberraschend-karriere-ich-brauche-keinen-beifall-meh r-a-00000000-0002-0001-0000-000172071849.

Windmann, A. (2018, 10. März): „Mensch im Trikot" in: *Der Spiegel,* Nr. 11/2018, 94–97

4.2 From the Turnvater Jahn principle to a flat hierarchy

References

Alfermann, D., & Würth, S. (2009). Gruppenprozesse und Intergruppenbeziehungen. In W. Schlicht & B. Strauss (Eds.), *Grundlagen der Sportpsychologie* (Vol. 1 , pp. 719–778). Hogrefe.

Carron, A. V., Bray, S. R., & Eys, M. (2007). Gruppen und Expertise im Sport. In N. Hagemann, M. Tietjens & B. Strauss (Eds.), *Psychologie der sportlichen Höchstleistung* (pp. 175–191). Hogrefe.

Kramer, J. (2012, 8. Oktober). „Bum Bum" Interview mit Uli Hoeneß, In *Der Spiegel* 41/2012 (pp. 158–161)

Mc, A. (2019). The Jurgen Klopp Masterclass – His Top 5 Leadership Approaches. *Conducting Consulting*. https://www.conduit.consulting/the-jurgen-klopp-masterclass-his-top-5-leadership-approaches/. Zugegriffen: 6. Mai 2021.

Schlicht, W., & Strauss, B. (2003). *Sozialpsychologie des Sports*. Hogrefe.

4.3 Who kicks the penalty?

Plessner, H., Unkelbach, C., Memmert, D., Baltes, A., & Kolb, A. (2009). Regulatory fit as a determinant of sport performance. *Psychology of Sport & Exercise, 10*, 108–115.

Memmert, D., Plessner, H., Hüttermann, S., Froese, G., Peterhänsel, C., & Unkelbach, C. (2015). Collective fit increases team performances: Extending regulatory fit from individuals to dyadic teams. *Journal of Applied Social Psychology, 45*, 274–281.

4.5 Lord over time

Apitzsch, T. (2011). *Kompetenzprofile von Trainern und Sportmanagern im Leistungssport*. (Dissertationsschrift, Deutsche Sporthochschule Köln).

König, S. (2008). Die Strukturen der Sieger – Überlegungen zu einer Theorie der Mannschaftsführung in Sportspielen. In A. Woll, W. Klöckner, M. Reichmann, & M. Schlag (Eds.), *Sportspielkulturen erfolgreich gestalten. Von der Trainerbank bis in die Schulklasse* (pp. 25–38). Czwalina.

4.4 The trainer, the multi-talent4.4 The trainer, the multi-talent

Dohmen, T. J. (2008). The influence of social forces: Evidence from the behavior of football referees. *Economic Inquiry, 46*(3), 411–424.

Dönmez, G., Torgutalp, Ş. Ş., Özkan, Ö., İlicepınar, Ö. F., Korkusuz, F., & Kudaş, S. (2021). Evaluation of stoppage time due to field injuries in professional football games: Do players really need medical help so often? *Research in Sports Medicine, online first*, 1–10.

Lago-Peñas, C., Gómez, M. A., & Pollard, R. (2021). The effect of the video assistant referee on referee's decisions in the spanish LaLiga. *International Journal of Sports Science and Coaching, 16*(3), 824–829.

Riedl, D., Strauss, B., Heuer, A., & Rubner, O. (2015). Finale furioso: Referee-biased injury times and their effects on home advantage in football. *Journal of Sports Sciences, 33*(4), 327–336.

Sutter, M., & Kocher, M. G. (2004). Favoritism of agents – the case of referees' home bias. *Journal of Economic Psychology, 25*, 461–469.

5 Illusion and reality

5.1 Is the fouled player allowed to shoot?
Bornkamp, B., Fritsch, A., Kuss, O., & Ickstadt, K. (2008). Penalty specialists among goalkeepers: A nonparametric bayesian analysis of 44 years of german bundesliga. In B. Schipp & W. Krämer (Eds.), *Statistical inference, econometric analysis and matrix algebra* (pp. 63–67). Springer.

Kuss, O., Kluttig, A., & Stoll, O. (2007). "The fouled player should not take the penalty himself": An empirical investigation of an old German football myth. *Journal of Sports Sciences, 25,* 963–967.

5.2 The run that does not exist
Avugos, S., Köppen, J., Czienskowski, U., Raab, M., & Bar-Eli, M. (2013). The "hot hand" reconsidered: A meta-analytic approach. *Psychology of Sport and Exercise, 14,* 21–27.

Ayton, P., & Braennberg, A. (2008). Footballer's fallacies. In P. Andersson, P. Ayton, & C. Schmidt (Eds.), *Myths and facts about football* (pp. 23–38). Cambridge Publishers.

Gilovich, F., Vallone, R., & Tversky, A. (1985). The hot hand in basketball: On the misperception of random sequences. *Cognitive Psychology, 17,* 295–314.

Heuer, A. (2012). *Der perfekte Tipp.* Wiley.

Heuer, A., & Rubner, O. (2009). Fitness, chance, and myths: An objective view on soccer results. *European Physical Journal B, 67*(3), 445–458.

Hughes, M., James, N., Hughes, M. T., Dancs, H., & Murray, S. (2019). Momentum and "hot hands". In M. Hughes, & I. Franks (Eds.), *Essentials of performance analysis in sport* (pp. 215–235). Taylor & Francis.

Raab, M., Gula, B., & Gigerenzer, G. (2012). The hot hand exists in volleyball and is used for allocation decisions. *Journal of Experimental Psychology, 18*(1), 81–94.

5.3 Chance, fate, luck and bad luck
Heuer, A. (2012). *Der perfekte Tipp.* Wiley.

Lames, M. (1999). Fußball – Ein Chaosspiel? In J.-P. Janssen, A. Wilhelm & M. Wegner (Eds.), *Empirische Forschung im Sportspiel – Methodologie, Fakten und Reflektionen* (pp. 141–156). Christian-Albrechts-Universität zu Kiel.

Loy, R. (2012). Zufall im Fußball – Eine empirische Untersuchung zur Art und Auftretenshäufigkeit zufälliger Ereignisse im Verlauf von Fußballspielen. In C. T. Jansen, C. Baumgart, M. W. Hoppe, & J. Freiwald (Eds.), *Trainingswissenschaftliche, geschlechtsspezifische und medizinische Aspekte des Hochleistungsfußballs. Beiträge und Analysen zum Fußballsport XVIII* (pp. 28–38). Czwalina.

Wunderlich, F., Seck, A., & Memmert, D. (2021). The influence of randomness on goals in football decreases over time. an empirical analysis of randomness involved in goal scoring in the english premier league. *Journal of Sports Sciences, 39*(20), 2322–2337.

5.4 New coach, new luck?

Besters, L. M., van Ours, J. C., & van Tuijl, M. A. (2016). Effectiveness of in-season manager changes in English Premier League Football. *De Economist, 164*(3), 335–356.

Breuer, C., & Singer, R. (1996). Trainerwechsel im Laufe der Spielsaison und ihr Einfluss auf den Mannschaftserfolg. *Leistungssport, 26,* 41–46.

Heuer A., Müller C., Rubner O., Hagemann N., & B. Strauss (2011). Usefulness of dismissing and changing the coach in professional soccer. *PLoS ONE, 6,* e17664.

Van Ours, J. C., & van Tuijl, M. A. (2016). In-season head-coach dismissals and the performance of professional football teams. *Economic Inquiry, 54,* 591–604.

Zart, S., & Güllich, A. (2022). In-season head-coach changes have positive short- and long-term effects on team performance in men's soccer—evidence from the premier league, bundesliga, and la liga. *Journal of Sports Sciences, 40*(6), 696–703.

5.5 Does money score goals?

Frick, B. (2005). ...Und Geld schießt doch eben Tore. *Sportwissenschaft, 35,* 250–270.

Heuer, A. (2012). *Der perfekte Tipp.* Wiley.

Lepschy, H., Wäsche, H., & Woll, A. (2020). Success factors in football: an analysis of the German Bundesliga. *International Journal of Performance Analysis in Sport, 20*(2), 150–164.

Peeters, T., & van Ours, J. C. (2021). Seasonal home advantage in English professional football; 1974–2018. *De Economist, 169*(1), 107–126.

5.6 Basking in reflecting in the glory of others

Cialdini, R. B., Borden, R. J., Thorne, A., Walker, M. R., Freeman, S., & Sloan, L. R. (1976). Basking in reflecting glory: Three (football) field studies. *Journal of Personality and Social Psychology, 34,* 366–375.

Cialdini, R. B., & Richardson, K. D. (1980). Two indirect tactics of image management: Basking and blasting. *Journal of Personality and Social Psychology, 39,* 406–415.

Snyder, C. R., Lassegard, M. A., & Ford, C. E. (1986). Distancing after group success and failure: Basking in reflecting glory and cutting of reflecting failure. *Journal of Personality and Social Psychology, 51,* 382–388.

Strauss, B. (Ed.). (2012). Die Welt der Zuschauer. In B. Strauss (Hrsg), *Sportzuschauer* (pp. 7–18). Hogrefe.

Tedeshi, J. T., Madi, N., & Lyakhovitzky, D. (1998). Die Selbstdarstellung von Zuschauern. In B. Strauss (Eds.), *Zuschauer* (pp. 93–109). Hogrefe.

Vollmer, A., (2021, 19. Januar). Schach ist das neue Klopapier. *Frankfurter Allgemeine.* https://www.faz.net/aktuell/stil/trends-nischen/queen-s-gambit-hat-einen-schachboom-ausgeloest-17148020.html.

Zeh, R., & Hagen, L. (2006). Fußball als Wahlentscheider?: Wie die deutsche Nationalmannschaft politische Popularität beeinflusst. In C. Holtz-Bacha (Eds.), *Fußball – Fernsehen – Politik* (pp. 193–213). VS Verl. für Sozialwiss.

5.7 Winning is not everything

Kahneman, D., & Tversky, A. (1979). Prospect theory: An analysis of decision under risk. *Econometrica, 47,* 263–291.

Moschini, G. (2010). Incentives and outcomes in a strategic setting: The 3-points-for-a-win system in soccer. *Economic Inquiry, 48,* 65–79.

Riedl, D., Heuer, A., & Strauss, B. (2015). Why the three-point rule failed to sufficiently reduce the number of draws in soccer: An application of prospect theory. *Journal of Sport & Exercise Psychology, 37,* 316–326.

Strauss, B., Hagemann, N., & Loffing, F. (2009). Die Drei-Punkte Regel in der deutschen 1. Fußballbundesliga und der Anteil unentschiedener Spiele. *Sportwissenschaft, 39,* 16–22.

5.8 Need for explanation, evasion, self-deception

Lau, R. R., & Russell, D. (1980). Attributions in the sports pages. *Journal of Personality and Social Psychology, 39,* 29–38.

Strauss, B., Senske, S., & Tietjens, M. (2009). Attributionen in Sportkommentaren. In H. Schramm & M. Marr (Eds.), *Die Sozialpsychologie des Sports in den Medien* (pp. 74–92). Herbert von Halem Verlag.

Weiner, B. (1974). *Achievement motivation and attribution theory.* General Learning Press.

6 Red light and yellow fever

6.1 The audience shows yellow

Nevill, A. M., Balmer, N. J., & Williams, A. M. (2002). The influence of crowd noise and experience upon refereeing decisions in football. *Psychology of Sport and Exercise, 3,* 261–272.

Unkelbach, C., & Memmert, D., (2010). Crowd noise as a cue in referee decisions contributes to the home advantage. *Journal of Sport and Exercise Psychology, 32,* 483–498.

6.2 When the referee gives yellow

Memmert, D., Unkelbach, C., Ertmer, J., & Rechner, M. (2008). Gelb oder kein Gelb? Persönliche Verwarnungen im Fußball als Kalibrierungsproblem. *Zeitschrift für Sportpsychologie, 15,* 1–11.

Unkelbach, C., & Memmert, D. (2008). Game-Management, Context-Effects and Calibration: The case of yellow cards in soccer. *Journal of Sport & Exercise Psychology, 30,* 95–109.

6.3 Sex training session

Boone, T., & Gilmore, S. (1995). Effects of sexual intercourse on maximal aerobic power, oxygen pulse, and double product in male sedentary subjects. *The Journal of sports medicine and physical fitness, 35*(3), 214–217.

Gebauer, G (2006). *Die Poetik des Fußballs.* Campus.

Johnson, W. (1968). Muscular performance following coitus. *Journal of Sex Research, 4,* 247–248.

Jokela, M., & Hanin, Y. L. (1999). Does the individual zones of optimal functioning model discriminate between successful and less successful athletes? A meta-analysis. *Journal of Sports Sciences, 17*(11), 873–887.

McGlone, S., & Shrier, I. (2000). Does sex the night before competition decrease performance? *Clinical Journal of Sport Medicine: Official Journal of the Canadian Academy of Sport Medicine, 10,* 233–234.

Schumacher, T. (1987). *Anpfiff.* Droemersche Verlagsanstalt.

Sztajzel, J., Périat, M., Marti, V., & Rutishauser, P. K. W. (2000). Effect of sexual activity on cycle ergometer stress test parameter, on plasmatic testosterone levels and on concentration capacity. *Journal of Sports Medicine and Physical Fitness, 40*(3), 233.

Zavorsky, G. S., & Newton, W. L. (2019). Effects of sexual activity on several measures of physical performance in young adult males. *The Journal of sports medicine and physical fitness, 59*(7), 1102–1109.

6.4 The winner wears red?

Apollaro, G., & Falcó, C. (2021). When taekwondo referees see red, but it is an electronic system that gives the points. *Frontiers in psychology, 12,* online first.

Attrill, M. J., Gresty, K. A., Hill, R. A., & Barton, R. A. (2008). Red shirt color is associated with long-term team success in English football. *Journal of Sport Sciences, 26,* 577–582.

Frank, C. (2009). *Trikotfarbe und Spielergebnisse in der Fußball-Bundesliga* (Unveröffentlichte Staatsexamensarbeit). AB Sportpsychologie.

Furley, P., Dicks, M., & Memmert, D. (2012). Nonverbal Behavior in Soccer: The Influence of Dominant and Submissive Body Language on the Impression Formation and Expectancy of Success of Soccer Players. *Journal of Sport & Exercise Psychology, 34,* 61–82.

Goldschmied, N., Furley, P., Trejo, S., Haddad, A., & Böning, A. (2022). Red shirt color has no effect on winning in European Soccer: Reanalysis of Attrill et al.(2008) of the English premier league and six additional European leagues. *Psychology of Sport and Exercise, 58,* 102064.

Hagemann, N., Strauss, B., & Leißing, J. (2008). When the referee sees red… *Psychological Science, 19,* 769–771.

Hill, R. A., & Barton, R. A. (2005). Red enhances human performances in contests. *Nature, 435,* 293.

Perception and deception

7.1 How to make the goalkeeper a penalty killer?
Memmert, D., Hüttermann, S., Hagemann, N., Loffing, F., & Strauss, B. (2013). Dueling in the penalty box: Evidence-Based recommendations on how shooters and goalkeepers can win penalty shootouts in soccer. *International Review of Sport and Exercise Psychology, 6*(1), 209–229.

Weigelt, M., Memmert, D., & Schack, T. (2012). Kick it like Ballack: The effects of goalkeeping gestures on goal-side selection in experienced soccer players and soccer novices. *Journal of Cognitive Psychology, 24*, 942–956.

7.2 The blind spot
Simons, D. J., & Chabris, C. F. (1999). Gorillas in our midst: Sustained inattentional blindness for dynamic events. *perception, 28*, 1059–1074.

Memmert, D. (2011). Creativity, expertise, and attention: Exploring their development and their relationships. *Journal of Sports Sciences, 29*(1), 93–102.

Memmert, D. (2005). Ich sehe was, was du nicht siehst!" – Das Phänomen Inattentional Blindness im Sport. *Leistungssport, 5*, 11–15.

Memmert, D., & Furley, P. (2007). "I spy with my little eye!" – Breadth of attention, inattentional blindness, and tactical decision making in team sports. *Journal of Sport & Exercise Psychology, 29*, 365–347.

7.3 Referee offside
Hüttermann, S., Noël, B., & Memmert, D. (2017). Evaluating erroneous offside calls in soccer. *PloS one, 12*(3), e0174358

Oudejans, R. R. D., Verheijen, R., Bakker, F. C., Gerrits, J. C., Steinbrueckner, M., & Beek, P. J. (2000). Errors in judging "offside" in football. *Nature, 404*, 33.

Ryall, E. (2012). Are there any Good Arguments Against Goal-Line Technology? *Sport, Ethics and Philosophy, 6*, 439–450.

Fasold, F., Wühr, P., & Memmert, D. (2017). Response requirements affect offside judgments in football (soccer). *Psychological Research, 83*, 924–934

Wühr, P., Fasold, F., & Memmert, D. (2020). The impact of team preferences on soccer offside judgments in laypersons: a quasi-experimental study. *Cognitive Research: Principles and Implications, 5*(1), 1–24.

Wühr, P., Fasold, F., & Memmert, D. (2015). Soccer offside judgments in laypersons with different types of static displays. *PLoS One, 10*(8), e0133687. https://doi.org/10.1371/journal.pone.0133687.

Wühr, P., & Memmert, D. (under revision). More offside decisions against Schalke 04 than against Borussia Dortmund in the German Bundesliga: A matter of shirt-background contrast?

7.4 The VAR - Cursed be justice
Spitz, J., Wagemans, J., Memmert, D., Williams, A. M., & Helsen, W. F. (2021). Video assistant referees (VAR): The impact of technology on decision making in association football referees. *Journal of Sports Sciences, 39*(2), 147–153.

7.5 The big disadvantage
McCarrick D., Brewer G., Lyons M., Pollet T.V., Neave N. (2020).Referee height influences decision making in British football leagues. *BMC psychology, 8*(1), 1–10.

Van Quaquebeke, N., & Giessner, S. R. (2010). How Embodied Cognitions Affect Judgments: Height-Related Attribution Bias in Football Foul Calls. *Journal of Sport and Exercise Psychology, 32,* 3–22.

Pressure and failure

8.1 Penalty shootout is not a lottery game
Memmert, D., Hüttermann, S., Hagemann, N., Loffing, F., & Strauss, B. (2013). Dueling in the penalty box: evidence-based recommendations on how shooters and goalkeepers can win penalty shootouts in soccer. *International Review of Sport and Exercise Psychology, 6*(1), 209–229.

Wunderlich, F., Berge, F., Memmert, D., & Rein, R. (2020). Almost a lottery: The influence of team strength on success in penalty shootouts. *International Journal of Performance Analysis in Sport, 20*(5), 857–869.

8.2 The fear of the Englishman at the penalty kick
Brinkschulte, M., Furley, P., & Memmert, D. (2020). English football players are not as bad at kicking penalties as commonly assumed. *Scientific Reports, 10,* 1–5.

Jordet, G. (2009). Why do English players fail in soccer penalty shootouts? A study of team status, self-regulation, and choking under pressure. *Journal of Sports Sciences, 27,* 97–106.

8.4 The Zinédine Zidane enigma
Burkert, A. (2012, 26.Mai). Blick auf die Haarwurzeln. *Süddeutsche Zeitung, 41.*

Englert, C., & Bertrams, A. (2012). Anxiety, ego depletion, and sports performance. *Journal of Sport and Exercise Psychology, 34,* 580–599.

Toussaint, J.-P. (2007). *Zidanes Melancholie.* Frankfurter Verlagsanstalt.

8.5 When the nerves fail
Baumeister, R. F., & Showers, C. J. (1986). A review of paradoxical performance effects: Choking under pressure in sports and mental tests. *European Journal of Social Psychology, 16,* 361–383.

Beilock, S. (2011). *Choke: What the secrets of the brain reveal about getting it right when you have to.* Atria Books.

Csikszentmihalyi, M. (2002). *Flow: The psychology of optimal experience* (2nd ed.). Harper & Row.

Dohmen, T. J. (2008). Do professionals choke under pressure? *Journal of economic behavior & organization, 65*(3–4), 636–653.

Gröpel, P., & Mesagno, C. (2019). Choking interventions in sports: A systematic review. *International Review of sport and exercise psychology, 12*(1), 176–201.

Otten, M. (2009). Choking vs. clutch performance: A study of sport performance under pressure. *Journal of Sport and Exercise Psychology, 31*(5), 583–601.

Otten, M. P. (2013). Clutch performance in sport: A positive psychology perspective. *International Journal of Sport Psychology, 44*(4), 285–287.

Schweickle, M. J., Swann, C., Jackman, P. C., & Vella, S. A. (2021). Clutch performance in sport and exercise: a systematic review. *International Review of Sport and Exercise Psychology, 14*(1), 102–129.

8.6 Social loafing

Høigaard, R., & Ommundsen, Y. (2007). Perceived social loafing and anticipated effort reduction among young football (soccer) players: An achievement goal perspective. *Psychological Reports, 100*, 857–875.

Kravitz, D. A., & Martin, B. (1986). Ringelmann rediscovered: The original article. *Journal of Personality and Social Psychology, 50*, 936–941.

Ohlert, J. (2009). *Teamleistung. Social Loafing in der Vorbereitung auf eine Gruppenaufgabe.* Dr. Kovac.

Ringelmann, M. (1913). Recherches sur les moteurs animés: Travail de l'homme. *Annales de l'Institut National Agronomique, 7*, 1–40.

Müller, J.-C. (2012, 22. Dezember) „Manchmal ist es gut, wenn es wehtut". *Frankfurter Rundschau* https://www.genios.de/presse-archiv/artikel/FR/20121222/-manchmal-ist-es-gut-wenn-es-wehtut/125F5A86-5E3B-46B4-B529-E162A9A52950.html.

8.7 Tired bodies, tired minds

Brink, M. S., Visscher, C., Coutts, A. J., & Lemmink, K. A. P. M. (2012). Changes in perceived stress and recovery in overreached young elite soccer players. *Scandinavian Journal of Medicine and Science in Sports, 22*, 285–292.

Kellmann, M., & Beckmann, J. (Eds.). (2021). *Recovery and well-being in sport and exercise: Interdisciplinary insights.* Routledge.

Naessens, G., Chandler T. J, Kibler W. B., & Driessens M. (2000). Clinical usefulness of nocturnal urinary noradrenaline excretion patterns in the follow-up of training process in high-level soccer players. *Journal of Strength and Conditioning Research, 14*, 125–131.

Kneer, C. (2010, 8. Oktober). "So kaputt war ich noch nie". *Süddeutsche Zeitung.* https://www.sueddeutsche.de/sport/philipp-lahm-im-gespraech-so-kaputt-war-ich-noch-nie-1.1009533.

Ndlec, M., McCall, A., Carling, C., Legall, F., Berthoin, S., & Dupont, G. (2012). Recovery in soccer: Part I-post-match fatigue and time course of recovery. *Sports Medicine, 42*, 997–1015.

Wicker, P., Weimar, D., & Orlowski, J. (2021). The 'real' birthday effect: post-birthday running performance of Football Bundesliga players. *Applied Economics Letters, online first*, 1–5.

8.8 Clap your own team to defeat

Baumeister, R. F., & Steinhilber, A. (1984). Paradoxical effects of supportive audiences on performance under pressure: The home field disadvantage in sports championships. *Journal of Personality and Social Psychology, 47,* 85–93.

Dohmen, T.J. (2008). Do professionals choke under pressure? *Journal of Economic Behavior & Organization, 65,* 636–653.

Filho, E. (2021). Total team collapse in the 2014 FIFA World Cup semi-final (Brazil 1 – Germany 7): Implications for coaching and sport psychology practice. *International Journal of Sport Psychology, 52,* online first.

Galeano, E. (1995). *Der Ball ist rund und Tore lauern überall.* Unionsverlag.

Staufenbiel, K., Lobinger, B., & Strauss, B. (2015). Home advantage in soccer – A matter of expectations, goal setting and tactical decisions of coaches? *Journal of Sports Sciences, 33*(18), 1932–1941.

Tauer, J. M., Guenther, C. L., & Rozek, C. (2009). Is there a home choke in decisive playoff basketball games? *Journal of Applied Sport Psychology, 21*(2), 148–162.

Van de Ven, N. (2011). Supporters are not necessary for the home advantage: Evidence from same-stadium derbies and games without an audience. *Journal of Applied Social Psychology, 41,* 7785–7792.

Harmony and drama

9.1 The pleasure of conflict

Bryant, J., Raney, A. A., & Zillmann, D. (1981). Sports television. In B. Strauss, M. Kolb, & M. Lames (Eds.), *sport-goes-media.de. Zur Medialisierung des Sports* (pp. 51–74). Hofmann.

9.2 The magic of the wave

Farkas, I., Helbing, D., & Vicsek, T. (2002). Mexican waves in an excitable medium. *Nature, 419,* 131–132.

Heuer, A. (2012). Der Zuschauer aus physikalischer Sicht. In B. Strauss (Eds.), *Sportzuschauer* (pp. 95–112). Hogrefe.

Zürcher, C. (2013). SRF macht aus Stille Fan-Gesang. *Tagesanzeiger.* https://www.tagesanzeiger.ch/zuerich/stadt/srf-macht-aus-stille-fangesang/story/23605854. Zugegriffen: 5. Mai 2022.

9.3 You'll Never Walk Alone

Effenberg, A., & Müller, A. (2013). SoundSoccer. http://sonification-online.com/forschung/sound-soccer/Zugriff. Zugegriffen: 3. Mai 2022.

Kopiez, R., & Brink, G. (1998). *Fußball-Fangesänge. Eine FANomenologie.* Königshausen & Neumann.

Kuhlhoff, B. (2012). „Die Queen sang leise mit". Interview mit Gerry Marsden. *11 Freunde.* https://11freunde.de/artikel/gerry-marsden-interview/594170. Zugegriffen: 6. Mai 2022.

Marra, P. S., & Trotta, F. (2019). Sound, music and magic in football stadiums. *Popular Music, 38*(1), 73–89.

Marsh, P. (1978). *Aggro: the illusion of violence.* Dent.

Morris, D. (1981). *The soccer tribe.* Cape.

Sänger, J., Müller, V., & Lindenberger, U. (2012). Intra- and interbrain synchronization and network properties when playing guitar in duets. *Frontiers in Human Neuroscience, 6,* 312.

Schaffert, N., Mattes, K., & Effenberg, A. O. (2010). A sound design for acoustic feedback in elite sports Lecture Notes in Computer *Sciences, 594,* 143–16.

9.4 Trapped in the history of the game

Plessner, H., & Betsch, T. (2001). Sequential Effects in important Referee Decisions. *Journal of Sport & Exercise Psychology, 23,* 254–339.

9.5 Goals with handwriting

Kranjec, A., Lehet, M., Bromberger, B., & Chatterjee, A. (2010). A sinister bias for calling fouls in soccer. *PLoS ONE, 5*(7), e11667.

Maass, A., Pagani, D., & Berta, E. (2007). How beautiful is the goal and how violent is the fistfight? spatial bias in the interpretation of human behavior. *Social Cognition, 25,* 833–852.

Risk and side effects

10.1 Capricorn and Aquarius prevail

Augste, C., & Lames, M. (2011). The relative age effect and success in german elite U-17 soccer teams. *Journal of Sports Sciences, 29,* 983–987.

Cobley, S. P., Schorer, J., & Baker, J. (2008). Relative age effects in professional german soccer: A historical analysis. *Journal of Sports Sciences, 26,* 1531–1538.

Deutscher Fußball-Bund. (2009). *Talente fordern und fördern. Konzepte und Strukturen vom Kinder- bis zum Spitzenfußball.* Philippka-Sportverlag.

Furley, P., & Memmert, D. (2016). Coaches' implicit associations between size and giftedness: implications for the relative age effect. *Journal of sports sciences, 34*(5), 459–466.

Furley, P., Memmert, D., & Weigelt, M. (2016). "How much is that player in the window? The one with the early birthday?" Relative age influences the value of the best soccer players, but not the best businesspeople. *Frontiers in Psychology, 7,* 84.

Mann, D. L., & van Ginneken, P. J. (2017). Age-ordered shirt numbering reduces the selection bias associated with the relative age effect. *Journal of sports sciences, 35*(8), 784–790.

10.2 First play, then practice

Côté, J., Baker, J., & Abernethy, B. (2007). Practice and play in the development of sport expertise. In G. Tenenbaum & R. C. Eklund (Eds.), *Handbook of Sport Psychology* (Vol. 3, pp. 184–202). John Wiley & Sons.

Ericsson, A., Krampe, R., & Tesch-Römer, C. (1993). The role of deliberate practice in the acquisition of expert performance. *Psychological Review, 100*, 363–406.

Memmert, D., Baker, J., & Bertsch, C. (2010). Play and practice in the development of sport-specific creativity in team ball sports. *High Ability Studies, 21*, 3–18.

Memmert, D., & Roth, K. (2007). The effects of non-specific and specific concepts on tactical creativity in team ball sports. *Journal of Sport Science, 25*, 1423–1432.

10.3 Loyal, more loyal, Die Hard

Flesch, M. (2021) "Wie Silvia Krüger die Corona-Zeit ohne Stadionbesuche erlebt." https://www.ksta.de/sport/1-fc-koeln/fc-fan-im-interview-wie-silvia-krueger-die-corona-zeit-ohne-stadionbesuche-erlebt-38146770. Zugegriffen: 6. Mai 2022.

Hornby, N. (1992). *Fever Pitch*. Gollancz.

Hirt, E. R., Zillmann, D., Erickson, G. A., & Kennedy, C. (1992). Costs and benefits of allegiance: Changes in fans` self-ascribed competencies after team victory versus defeat. *Journal of Personality and Social Psychology, 63*, 724–738.

Levental, O., Carmi, U., & Lev, A. (2021). Jinx, control, and the necessity of adjustment: Superstitions among football fans. *Frontiers in Psychology*, 4583.

Meier, H. E., Strauss, B., & Riedl, D. (2017). Feminization of sport audiences and fans? Evidence from the German men's national soccer team. *International Review for the Sociology of Sport, 52*(6), 712–733.

Schlicht, W., & Strauss, B. (2003). *Sozialpsychologie des Sports* (1. Ed.). Hogrefe.

Schwarz, N., Strack, F., Kammer, D., & Wagner, D. (1987). Soccer, rooms, and the quality of your life: Mood effects on judgements of satisfaction with life in general and with specific domains. *European Journal of Social Psychology, 17*, 69–79.

Schweitzer, K., Zillmann, D., Weaver, J.B., & Luttrell, E.S. (1992). Perception of threatening events in the emotional aftermath of a televised college football game. *Journal of Broadcasting and Electronic Media, 36*, 75–82.

Spannagel, L. (2012, 27. Januar). Wer sind die echten Fans? *Zeit Online.* https://www.zeit.de/sport/2012-01/fankultur-institut-ultras-fussball?utm_referrer=https%3A%2F%2Fwww.google.com%2F.

Vergeld, V., Krüßmann, D., & Strauss, B. (2021). Identification with a National Soccer Team and expectancies regarding success: two experiments on manipulated team salience. *International Journal of Sport and Exercise Psychology, online first*, 1–20.

Wann, D. L., & Branscombe, N. R. (1990). Die-hard and fair-weather fans: Effects of identification on BIRGing and CORFing tendencies. *Journal of Sport and Social Issues, 14*, 103–117.

Werner, L. (2020. 22. Mai). Wegen Corona-Krise Silvia Krüger verpasst erstmals in 34 Jahren Spiel des 1. FC Köln. *Kölner Stadt-Anzeiger.* https://www.ksta.de/koeln/wegen-corona-krise-silvia-krueger-verpasst-erstmals-in-34-jahren-spiel-des-1--fc-koeln-36735638.

10.4 Palpitations

Cornil, Y., & Chandon, P. (2013). From fan to fat? Vicarious losing increases unhealthy eating, but self-affirmation is an effective remedy. *Psychological science, 24*(10), 1936–1946.

Dickhuth, H.-H., Schumacher, Y. O., Röcker, K., König, D., & Korsten-Reck U. (2012). Sportzuschauer aus medizinischer Sicht: physische und psychische Gesundheit. In B. Strauss (Eds.), *Sportzuschauer* (pp. 109–122). Hogrefe.

Van der Meij, L., Almela, M., Hidalgo, V., Villada, C., IJzerman, H., van Lange, P. A. M., & Salvador, A. (2012). Testosterone and cortisol release among spanish soccer fans watching the 2010 world cup final. *PLoS ONE, 7*(4), e34814.

Wilpert-Lampen, U., Leistner, D., Greven, S., Pohl, T., Sper, S., Völker, C., Güthlin, D., Plasse, A., Knez, A., Küchenhoff, H., & Steinbeck, G. (2008). Cardiovascular events during world cup soccer. *New England Journal Medicine, 358,* 475–483.

GPSR Compliance

The European Union's (EU) General Product Safety Regulation (GPSR) is a set of rules that requires consumer products to be safe and our obligations to ensure this.

If you have any concerns about our products, you can contact us on

ProductSafety@springernature.com

In case Publisher is established outside the EU, the EU authorized representative is:

Springer Nature Customer Service Center GmbH
Europaplatz 3
69115 Heidelberg, Germany